BRING THEM UP

Biblical Principles for Family Relationships

by Ellen C. Smith

Copyright © 1999
by
Ellen C. Smith

All rights reserved.
No part of this book may be reproduced in any form,
except for the inclusion of brief quotations in a review,
without permission in writing from the author or publisher.

Scripture quotations are from the King James Version of the Bible.

ISBN: 0-7392-0407-6

Printed in the USA by

MP
MORRIS PUBLISHING

3212 East Highway 30 • Kearney, NE 68847 • 1-800-650-7888

Table of Contents

Introduction 1

Part One: Our Relationship with God 3
  Chapter 1: Putting God First 4
    In the Beginning 4
    Salvation through Jesus Christ 5
    Empowered by the Holy Spirit 7
    Growing by the Word of God 10
    Love God above All Else 11

Part Two: Marriage Relationship 13
  Chapter 2: Two Shall Be One 14
    Marriage Is God's Plan 14
    Blood Covenant 17
  Chapter 3: Roles of Husband and Wife 21
  Chapter 4: Separation and Divorce 27
  Chapter 5: Fornication and Adultery 31

Part Three: Relationships with Generations 39
  Chapter 6: Influence of Traditions and Patterns 40
  Chapter 7: Inheritance 45
    Labor of the People 45
    Riches 46
    Promises of God 47
    Blessings of Obedience 47
    Teaching and Training 48
    Prayer and Preparation 49
    Spoken Blessings 50
  Chapter 8: Family and Household 51
  Chapter 9: Widows and Fatherless 54

Part Four: Choices Affect Relationships 59
  Chapter 10: Choose Life 60
    Speak Life 61
    Names and Nicknames 63
    Sowing and Reaping 64
    Vision 66

Part Five: Partner Relationship with Our Creator 69
  Chapter 11: Fruit of the Womb 70
    Be Fruitful and Multiply 70
    Freed from Barrenness 71
    God Made Us 74
    Parents as Stewards 75

- Chapter 12: Childbearing 77
  - Freed from the Curse 77
  - Inquire of the Lord 77
  - Season of Gentle Care 78
  - Jesus and Little Ones 80
- Chapter 13: Faith Builders during Pregnancy 81

Part Six: Parent and Child Relationships **87**
- Chapter 14: Protecting Children 88
  - Good, Not Evil 88
  - Separate from the World 89
  - Keep Abominations Out 92
  - Do Not Sacrifice Your Children 95
- Chapter 15: Training Children 99
  - Parents' Responsibility 99
  - Authority 103
- Chapter 16: God's Word as Foundation 107
  - Wisdom and Understanding 107
  - Teaching 108
- Chapter 17: Obedience and Disobedience 112
  - Instruction and Correction 112
  - Honor and Obey Parents 113
  - Dealing with Disobedience 114
- Chapter 18: Preparing Youth for Adulthood 120

Part Seven: Father God's Relationship with His Children **125**
- Chapter 19: Father God as Example of Parent 126
  - God's Heart and Care for His Children 126
  - God's Correction and Mercy 132

Part Eight: Improving Family Relationships **135**
- Chapter 20: Overcoming Division 136
  - Strife 136
  - Pride 139
  - Selfishness 141
- Chapter 21: Love One Another 143
- Chapter 22: Forgiveness 148

Part Nine: Family and Church Relationships **153**
- Chapter 23: Congregation or Segregation? 154
  - Worldly Influence 154
  - Biblical Examples 156
- Chapter 24: Family and Church Ministry 162
  - Families in Ministry 162
  - Ministry to Families 168

Conclusion **173**

Introduction

God has placed in my heart a desire for families to live according to His design and plan. Some families already are living God's way, but there are many that are still struggling in their family life. I am sure that all of us have room for improvement in our family relationships.

Many people who are seeking help for their families are looking in the wrong places. Much of the advice available today adds to the problems instead of solving them. It is futile to sacrifice our time, our energy, or our families by following ungodly advice. It has no guarantee of success.

Family problems are spiritual problems. Satan is out to destroy families. Only God can bring true victory. God designed families, and He has the plan for how they should function. He has given us the plan in His Word, the Bible. There are principles in the Bible that cover every aspect of life. When we follow those principles, God promises success.

> "This book of the law shall not depart out of thy mouth; but thou shalt meditate therein day and night, that thou mayest observe to do according to all that is written therein: for then thou shalt make thy way prosperous, and **then thou shalt have good success**." (Joshua 1:8)

I believe God is turning the hearts of parents toward their children and the hearts of children toward their parents during this time before Jesus comes back for His church. It is time for us to seek God's Word to set our families in **His** order.

Some years ago, I felt God was leading me to share with others what He says about families. More recently, He has reminded me of this mission. As I was praying for opportunities, I began to see the possibility of sharing the message in book form. A book could go to more places than I could, and it would minister God's Word to other families even while I continued to minister to my own family. God began impressing on me the following Scripture:

> "And the LORD answered me, and said, Write the vision, and make *it* plain upon tables, that he may run that readeth it." (Habakkuk 2:2)

God has led me over and over again to search His Word for His instructions in family life. This has been for the benefit of our own family. It has also prepared me to write this book, which is an overview of my study. I have touched on many aspects of family relationships, but it is not within the scope of this book to elaborate on all of these aspects.

I have not included all of the Scriptures pertaining to or applicable to family life; that would include more of the Bible than I could fit on these pages. In some instances, I have selected one passage from a number of verses I had gathered. In other places, I have given several examples of Scripture to provide "two or more witnesses" to what the Bible says about a certain issue. Sometimes the Scriptures are included within the text of this book, but usually they are footnoted at the bottom of the page as the foundation for my text. (Footnotes are usually separated from the text by a short line. When a footnote has been continued from the previous page, it should be indicated by a long separation line.) Some passages, especially long ones, are referenced only. Scripture quotations are from the King James Version of the Bible. The italicized words are those that were added by the translators. I have added bold type to emphasize certain parts.

How to Use This Book

There are several ways to read this book. One is to read through the text above the footnote line. I have paraphrased some of the Scriptures so that readers can get the general idea of the footnoted verses. This could be the quickest way to get an overview of the book. Another way to go through the book is by reading each footnoted Scripture as you come to its notation in the text. I would also suggest that you go through the book reading only the Scriptures themselves. There is power in God's Word! As you read and meditate on the verses, the Holy Spirit can give you special instructions for your own specific situation. For more in-depth study, you can look up the Scriptures in the Bible and study them in context.

This book can be used as a reference to look up what the Bible says about a particular aspect of family life. It can be a resource for those who teach or counsel others on family matters.

Part One

Our Relationship with God

Chapter 1

Putting God First

The first thing we must do to set our families in order is to get our priorities right. God must have first place in our lives.[1] When He is our priority, all other things can be lined up in order also. He is our Creator, and we must be in right relationship with Him before the other areas of our lives will flow according to His design. The foundation must be laid before we can build upon it.[2]

In the Beginning

We can look back to the beginning to see God's design for families. On the sixth day of creation, God made man (male and female) in His own image and likeness. God blessed them and told them to bear fruit and multiply. He set them in authority over the earth and the creatures in it. God saw that what He had made was very good.[3] God created us for His pleasure, and He is worthy for us to please Him.[4]

God designed and established a perfect environment for Adam and Eve in the garden of Eden. Everything necessary for life was provided. They enjoyed the presence of God as He visited them in the cool of the day. But Satan was out to steal, kill, and destroy.[5] He started by casting doubts on what God had said.[6] The woman was deceived by his lies and ate the fruit that God had forbidden them to eat. She also gave some to her husband who was with her.[7] After eating of the tree of the knowledge of good and evil, their eyes were opened. Until then, they had only knowledge of good. Now evil was opened up to them. They felt shame and hid themselves from God.[8]

---

[1] Matt. 6:33 But **seek ye first the kingdom of God**, and his righteousness; and all these things shall be added unto you.

[2] 1 Cor. 3:11 For other **foundation** can no man lay than that is laid, which **is Jesus Christ**.

[3] Gen. 1:26 And God said, Let us **make man in our image, after our likeness**: and let them have dominion over the fish of the sea, and over the fowl of the air, and over the cattle, and over all the earth, and over every creeping thing that creepeth upon the earth. 27 So **God created man in his** *own* **image**, in the image of God created he him; **male and female** created he them. 28 And **God blessed them**, and God said unto them, **Be fruitful, and multiply**, and replenish the earth, and subdue it: **and have dominion** over the fish of the sea, and over the fowl of the air, and over every living thing that moveth upon the earth.... 31 And **God saw everything that he had made, and, behold,** *it was* **very good**. And the evening and the morning were the sixth day.

[4] Rev. 4:11 Thou art worthy, O Lord, to receive glory and honour and power: for thou hast created all things, and for thy pleasure they are and were created.

[5] John 10:10a The thief cometh not, but for to steal, and to kill, and to destroy....

[6] Gen. 3:1 Now the serpent was more subtil than any beast of the field which the LORD God had made. And he said unto the woman, Yea, **hath God said**, Ye shall not eat of every tree of the garden?

[7] Gen. 3:6 And when the woman saw that the tree *was* good for food, and that it *was* pleasant to the eyes, and a tree to be desired to make *one* wise, **she** took of the fruit thereof, and **did eat**, and gave also unto **her husband with her**; and **he did eat**.

[8] Gen. 3:7 And the **eyes of them both were opened**, and they knew that they *were* naked; and they sewed fig leaves together, and made themselves aprons. 8 And they heard the voice of the LORD God walking in the garden in the cool of the day:

Because of disobedience, a curse was loosed upon the earth.[9] Through the curse Satan has sought to bring evil into the lives of men, women, and children by trying to steal, kill, and destroy what God had designed for them to enjoy. God designed love, joy, peace, health, provision, fellowship, righteousness, faith, and victory for His children. Satan has brought in hatred, despair, confusion, sickness, poverty, strife, sin, fear, and defeat. I used to think that these negative things were all "just a part of life," but I discovered from God's Word that they are **not** a part of **life**; they **are** a part of **death**.[10] They are not God's plan for His children, but Satan's design to steal from God's children.

Salvation through Jesus Christ

Salvation includes both spiritual and physical deliverance. Spiritually, a person can be saved from the bondage of sin and from its judgment of eternal separation from God. Physically, salvation is deliverance from disease, poverty, danger, and other forms of destruction. In other words, salvation includes all the blessings of God that Jesus bought back for us when he died on the cross to pay the penalty for our sin.[11] Jesus came to destroy the works of the devil[12] and to restore to us abundant life![13]

When Adam and Eve chose to obey Satan instead of God, they gave their authority over to Satan. Thus sin and death were passed upon all people.[14] God could not contradict His own word by taking back the authority He had given to man, so He had to work through a man to bring mankind back into a right relationship with Him. Even though there was no righteous person in the earth to pay the price for man's sin, God already had a plan and He pronounced Satan's defeat by Jesus.[15] God prophesied that Jesus would be

---

and **Adam and his wife hid themselves from the presence of the LORD God** amongst the trees of the garden. 9 And the LORD God called unto Adam, and said unto him, Where *art* thou? 10 And he said, I heard thy voice in the garden, and I was afraid, because I *was* naked; and I hid myself.

[9] Gen. 3:16 Unto the woman he said, I will greatly multiply thy sorrow and thy conception; in sorrow thou shalt bring forth children; and thy desire *shall be* to thy husband, and he shall rule over thee. 17 And unto Adam he said, Because thou hast hearkened unto the voice of thy wife, and hast eaten of the tree, of which I commanded thee, saying, Thou shalt not eat of it: cursed *is* the ground for thy sake; in sorrow shalt thou eat *of* it all the days of thy life; 18 Thorns also and thistles shall it bring forth to thee; and thou shalt eat the herb of the field; 19 In the sweat of thy face shalt thou eat bread, till thou return unto the ground; for out of it wast thou taken: for dust thou *art*, and unto dust shalt thou return.

[10] Rom. 6:20 For when ye were the servants of sin, ye were free from righteousness. 21 What fruit had ye then in those things whereof ye are now ashamed? for the end of those things *is* death. 22 But now being made free from sin, and become servants to God, ye have your fruit unto holiness, and the end everlasting life. 23 For the wages of sin *is* death; but the gift of God *is* eternal life through Jesus Christ our Lord.

[11] Gal. 3:13 **Christ hath redeemed us from the curse** of the law, being made a curse for us: for it is written, Cursed *is* every one that hangeth on a tree:

[12] 1 John 3:8 He that committeth sin is of the devil; for the devil sinneth from the beginning. For this purpose the Son of God was manifested, that he might **destroy the works of the devil**.

[13] John 10:10b ... I am come that they might have life, and that they might have *it* more abundantly.

[14] Rom. 5:12 Wherefore, as by one man sin entered into the world, and death by sin; and so death passed upon all men, for that all have sinned:
Rom. 3:23 For all have sinned, and come short of the glory of God;

[15] Gen. 3:15 And I will put enmity between thee and the woman, and between thy seed and her seed; it shall bruise thy head, and thou shalt bruise his heel.

born of a virgin (the seed of a woman, not of a man); and although Satan would come against Him, Jesus would crush his head. When the time was right, God sent His own Son into the earth in the form of a man, born of a virgin by the Holy Spirit. Jesus was not corrupted by man's bloodline; so He was qualified to redeem mankind. That is why Jesus Christ is the **only** way to a right relationship with God.[16]

If Jesus Christ is not the foundation of your life, you can change that **right now**. You must make the choice to accept what He has done for you. Otherwise, you are automatically condemned.[17] The Holy Spirit convicts the world of **one** sin: not believing on Jesus.[18] All other sins have been judged, and Jesus has paid the punishment for them. However, if you do not believe what Jesus has done for you, it will do you no good. You will stay bound in sin with all its destruction.

God has already done **His part** by sending Jesus to pay the penalty for your sin by dying in your place.[19] Just as sin and death were brought into the world by one man (Adam), so righteousness and life were brought in by one man (Jesus Christ).[20] The Bible says that salvation comes by believing in your heart that God raised Jesus from the dead and by confessing with your mouth the Lord Jesus.[21] This is **your part**. You are promised forgiveness and cleansing of sin.[22] When you receive Jesus, you become a child of God.[23] This is called being born again.[24] You are then adopted into the family of God and are eligible for all the rights and privileges of being His child. You are made a new creation in Christ; old things are passed

---

[16] John 14:6 Jesus saith unto him, I am the way, the truth, and the life: **no man cometh unto the Father, but by me**.

[17] John 3:18 He that believeth on him is not condemned: but **he that believeth not is condemned already**, because he hath not believed in the name of the only begotten Son of God.

[18] John 16:8 And when he {Holy Spirit} is come, he will reprove the world of sin, and of righteousness, and of judgment: 9 Of sin, because they believe not on me;

[19] John 3:16 For God so loved the world, that he gave his only begotten Son, that whosoever believeth in him should not perish, but have everlasting life. 17 For God sent not his Son into the world to condemn the world; but that the world through him might be saved.
Rom. 5:8 But God commendeth his love toward us, in that, **while we were yet sinners**, Christ died for us.

[20] Rom. 5:19 For as by one man's disobedience many were made sinners, so by the obedience of one shall many be **made righteous**.
1 Cor. 15:22 For as in Adam all die, even so in Christ shall all be made alive.

[21] Rom. 10:9 That if thou shalt confess with thy mouth the Lord Jesus, and shalt believe in thine heart that God hath raised him from the dead, thou shalt be saved. 10 For with the heart man believeth unto righteousness; and with the mouth confession is made unto salvation.... 13 For whosoever shall call upon the name of the Lord shall be saved.

[22] 1 John 1:9 If we confess our sins, he is faithful and just to forgive us *our* sins, and to cleanse us from all unrighteousness.

[23] John 1:12 But as many as received him, to them gave he power to become the **sons of God**, *even* to them that believe on his name:

[24] John 3:3 Jesus answered and said unto him, Verily, verily, I say unto thee, Except a man be **born again**, he cannot see the kingdom of God.

away.[25] Through Jesus, you enter into covenant with God. You give your life over to Him, and He puts His life in you.

If you would like to become God's child and receive the gift of salvation, you can do that now. You may use the following prayer or your own words, as long as you are praying from your heart.

"God, I have been living life my own way. Now I choose to live it your way. I receive your Son, Jesus Christ, as my Lord and Savior. I believe He died for me and is risen from the dead. I surrender to Him as Lord. Come into my life, Jesus. Forgive me and make me the kind of person you would have me to be."

Empowered by the Holy Spirit

Perhaps you know that you have already been born again, but you have experienced failure in living up to the Christian standard. That was my experience. I received Jesus as my Savior when I was a child, but I was not walking in the fullness of what God had for me. It seemed that there must be more to the Christian life than I was experiencing. Twenty years after I had become a Christian, I finally learned about being baptized and empowered with the Holy Spirit.

Of course, the Holy Spirit is definitely involved when we are born again. He leads us and bears witness with us that we are the children of God.[26] He is sent into our hearts.[27] We become the temple of God, and His Spirit dwells in us.[28]

When we are **baptized** with the Holy Spirit, He is not only **in** us, but also **upon** us. Baptism means immersion, not just a filling. After Jesus arose from the dead, He told His followers that He would send the promise of His Father **upon** them and to wait in Jerusalem until they be **endued** with power from on high.[29] "Endued" as used here speaks of being clothed with something like a garment. Jesus explained that the "promise of His Father" was that they would be baptized with the Holy Spirit.[30] This promise was fulfilled on the Day of Pentecost. The house they were in was filled with a sound from heaven as of a mighty wind,

---

[25] 2 Cor. 5:17 Therefore if any man *be* in Christ, *he is* a new creature: old things are passed away; behold, all things are become new.

[26] Rom. 8:14 For as many as are **led by** the Spirit of God, they are the **sons of God**. 15 For ye have not received the spirit of bondage again to fear; but ye have received the Spirit of **adoption**, whereby we cry, **Abba, Father.** 16 The Spirit itself **beareth witness with** our spirit, that we are the children of God:

[27] Gal. 4:6 And **because ye are sons**, God hath sent forth the **Spirit of his Son into your hearts**, crying, **Abba, Father.**

[28] 1 Cor. 3:16 Know ye not that ye are the temple of God, and *that* the Spirit of God **dwelleth in** you?

[29] Luke 24:49 And, behold, I send the promise of my Father **upon** you: but tarry ye in the city of Jerusalem, until ye be **endued** with power from on high.

[30] Acts 1:4 And, being assembled together with *them*, commanded them that they should not depart from Jerusalem, but wait for the promise of the Father, which, *saith he*, ye have heard of me. 5 For John truly baptized with water; but ye shall be **baptized with the Holy Ghost** not many days hence.

tongues as of fire sat **upon** each of them, and they were **filled** with the Holy Spirit.[31] They were saturated inside and out with the Holy Spirit.

The baptism of the Holy Spirit was not a one-time historical event only for those who had followed Jesus **while** He was on the earth. The Day of Pentecost spoken of in Acts 2 is the day the Holy Spirit was poured out. We do not have to wait for Him to be sent to the earth; now He is available to every believer.

Following are two examples from the Bible showing the baptism of the Holy Spirit as a separate experience from the new birth. Acts 8 tells that people in Samaria believed the Gospel and were baptized in response to Philip's preaching. When the apostles at Jerusalem heard that they had received God's Word, they sent Peter and John to Samaria. Peter and John prayed for the new believers **that** they might receive the Holy Spirit because He had **not yet** fallen **upon** any of them. They had been baptized (in water) in the name of Jesus, but not yet baptized in the Holy Spirit. When Peter and John laid their hands on them, they received the Holy Spirit.[32]

The second example is in Acts 19. Paul came to Ephesus and asked some disciples there if they had received the Holy Spirit **since** they became believers. They said they had not even heard of the Holy Spirit. Paul laid his hands on them, and the Holy Spirit came on them.[33]

Receiving the Holy Spirit into our lives is a great advantage. First of all, He is promised by Jesus, and we should receive all the promises and gifts given through Jesus. The Holy Spirit will comfort us, teach us, and help us remember what Jesus said.[34] He will guide us and show us things to come. He will show us the things of God.[35] He will give us power to live a victorious Christian life and will make our lives a witness unto Jesus.[36] He makes intercession for us according to God's will and enriches our prayer life.[37] The Holy Spirit can provide the help necessary for a godly family life.

---

[31] Acts 2:1 And when the day of Pentecost was fully come, they were all with one accord in one place. 2 And suddenly there came a sound from heaven as of a rushing mighty wind, and it filled all the house where they were sitting. 3 And there appeared unto them cloven tongues like as of fire, and it sat **upon** each of them. 4 And they were all **filled with** the Holy Ghost, and began to speak with other tongues, as the **Spirit gave them utterance**.

[32] Acts 8:12 But when they believed Philip preaching the things concerning the kingdom of God, and the name of Jesus Christ, they were baptized, both men and women.... 14 Now when the apostles which were at Jerusalem heard that Samaria had received the word of God, they sent unto them Peter and John: 15 Who, when they were come down, prayed for them, that they might **receive** the Holy Ghost: 16 (For as yet he was **fallen upon** none of them: only they were baptized in the name of the Lord Jesus.) 17 Then laid they *their* hands on them, and they **received** the Holy Ghost.

[33] Acts 19:1 And it came to pass, that, while Apollos was at Corinth, Paul having passed through the upper coasts came to Ephesus: and finding certain **disciples**, 2 He said unto them, Have ye **received** the Holy Ghost **since ye believed**? And they said unto him, We have not so much as heard whether there be any Holy Ghost.... 6 And when Paul had laid *his* hands upon them, the Holy Ghost **came on** them; and they spake with tongues, and prophesied.

[34] John 14:26 But the **Comforter**, *which is* the **Holy Ghost**, whom the Father will send in my name, he shall **teach you all things, and bring all things to your remembrance**, whatsoever I have said unto you.

[35] John 16:13 Howbeit when he, the Spirit of truth, is come, he will **guide you into all truth**: for he shall not speak of himself; but whatsoever he shall hear, *that* shall he speak: and he **will shew you things to come**. 14 He shall glorify me: for he shall **receive of mine, and shall shew** *it* **unto you**.

[36] Acts 1:8 But ye shall **receive power**, after that the Holy Ghost is **come upon** you: and **ye shall be witnesses unto me** both in Jerusalem, and in all Judaea, and in Samaria, and unto the uttermost part of the earth.

Many people do not realize that even Jesus operated in the power of the Holy Spirit while He was on earth. He did not operate in His own power as God on earth, but as a man full of the Holy Spirit.[38] He set an example for us that we can follow, but only by the power of the Holy Spirit. Jesus "Christ" means Jesus, "the anointed One." He was anointed with the Holy Spirit and with power.[39] "**Christ**ians" are "anointed ones" (empowered by the Holy Spirit) to do the works of Jesus.[40]

Perhaps you feel like a powerless Christian as I did for many years. It could be that you, too, have not yet received the Holy Spirit and given Him control of your life. Jesus said that the Holy Spirit is given to those who **ask**.[41] That is **your part**. You must believe the promise, ask, and receive by faith (as with all of God's promises). As soon as I asked to be baptized with the Holy Spirit, my life changed dramatically. I believe you also will notice a wonderful difference in your life!

If you would like to receive the Holy Spirit, you can do that now. The prerequisite is that you must be born again. Jesus said that "the world" (unbelievers) cannot receive the Holy Spirit.[42] If you are not sure if you are born again, go back to the previous section and make sure. When you are born again, you are eligible to receive the Holy Spirit. You can ask Jesus to baptize you with the Holy Spirit.[43] Following is a sample prayer you may use or pray in your own words as God leads you.

---

[37] Rom. 8:26 Likewise the Spirit also helpeth our infirmities: for we know not what we should pray for as we ought: but the Spirit itself **maketh intercession** for us with groanings which cannot be uttered. 27 And he that searcheth the hearts knoweth what *is* the mind of the Spirit, because he **maketh intercession for the saints** according to *the will of* God.
Jude 20 But ye, beloved, building up yourselves on your most holy faith, **praying in the Holy Ghost**,

[38] Phil. 2:5 Let this mind be in you, which was also in **Christ Jesus**: 6 Who, being in the form of God, thought it not robbery to be equal with God: 7 But **made himself of no reputation**, and took upon him the form of a servant, and **was made in the likeness of men**:
Luke 3:21 Now when all the people were baptized, it came to pass, that **Jesus also being baptized**, and praying, the heaven was opened, 22 And the **Holy Ghost descended** in a bodily shape like a dove **upon him**, and a voice came from heaven, which said, Thou art my beloved Son; in thee I am well pleased.... 4:1 And Jesus being **full of the Holy Ghost** returned from Jordan, and was led by the Spirit into the wilderness,

[39] Luke 4:18 The **Spirit of the Lord** *is* **upon me** {Jesus}, because **he hath anointed me** to preach the gospel to the poor; he hath sent me to heal the brokenhearted, to preach deliverance to the captives, and recovering of sight to the blind, to set at liberty them that are bruised, 19 To preach the acceptable year of the Lord.... 21 And he {Jesus} began to say unto them, This day is this scripture fulfilled in your ears.
Acts 10:38 How God **anointed Jesus** of Nazareth **with the Holy Ghost and with power**: who went about doing good, and healing all that were oppressed of the devil; for God was with him.

[40] John 14:12 Verily, verily, I say unto you, **He that believeth on me**, the works that I do shall he do also; and **greater works** than these shall he do; because I go unto my Father.

[41] Luke 11:13 If ye then, being evil, know how to give good gifts unto your children: how much more shall *your* heavenly Father **give the Holy Spirit** to them that **ask** him?

[42] John 14:16 And I {Jesus} will pray the Father, and he shall give you another Comforter, that he may abide with you for ever; 17 *Even* the Spirit of truth; **whom the world cannot receive**, because it seeth him not, neither knoweth him: but ye know him; for he dwelleth with you, and shall be in you.

[43] Matt. 3:11 I {John the Baptist} indeed baptize you with water unto repentance: but he that cometh after me is mightier than I, whose shoes I am not worthy to bear: **he** {Jesus} **shall baptize you with the Holy Ghost**, and *with* fire:

"Heavenly Father, I thank You for Your promise of the Holy Spirit. Lord Jesus, I ask You to baptize me with the Holy Spirit. Holy Spirit, I receive You, and I willingly yield to Your control of my life."

Now that you have asked, believe that you receive, and you shall have.[44] Begin to thank God for answering your prayer, and the Holy Spirit will enable you to praise and worship God in a greater way than you have done before.

Growing by the Word of God

When you become born again, you are a "baby" Christian. Just as a newborn physical baby must have physical milk to grow, so a spiritual baby must have the milk of God's Word to grow.[45]

Even if you have been a Christian for a long time, you could still be a "baby" spiritually if you have not fed daily on God's Word. As a child, I developed the habit of reading my Bible, but I could not put into practice the parts I did not understand. I spent more time on the familiar parts and avoided the others. I was like a child that was nourished in some ways and starving in others. I needed a balanced diet of God's Word. When I received the Holy Spirit, God's Word "came alive" for me. He gave me a hunger for all of His Word. He also increased my understanding of it, so that I could be both a hearer **and a doer** of His Word.[46]

Hearing and doing God's Word provides a sure foundation upon which to build your house (family).[47] Many families are being destroyed because of a lack of knowledge of God's Word.[48] His Word is an instruction manual and will equip us for every good work[49] (including getting and keeping our families in order). The purpose of this book is to bring to your attention what God says about families, so that your family can be strong enough to weather the storms of life and to be a beacon of light for others.

---

[44] Mark 11:24 Therefore I say unto you, what things soever ye desire, when ye pray, believe that ye receive *them*, and ye shall have *them*.

[45] 1 Peter 2:2 As newborn babes, desire the sincere **milk of the word**, that ye may **grow** thereby:

[46] James 1:22 But be ye doers of the word, and not hearers only, deceiving your own selves.

[47] Matt. 7:24 Therefore whosoever **heareth** these sayings of mine, **and doeth them**, I will liken him unto a **wise man**, which **built his house upon a rock**: 25 And the rain descended, and the floods came, and the winds blew, and beat upon that house; and **it fell not: for it was founded upon a rock**. 26 And every one that heareth these sayings of mine, and doeth them not, shall be likened unto a foolish man, which built his house upon the sand: 27 And the rain descended, and the floods came, and the winds blew, and beat upon that house; and it fell: and great was the fall of it.
(See also Luke 6:47-49.)

[48] Hosea 4:6 **My people are destroyed for lack of knowledge**: because thou hast rejected knowledge, I will also reject thee, that thou shalt be no priest to me: seeing thou hast forgotten the law of thy God, I will also forget thy children.

[49] 2 Tim. 3:16 All scripture *is* given by inspiration of God, and *is* profitable for doctrine, for reproof, for correction, for instruction in righteousness: 17 That the man of God may be perfect, throughly furnished unto all good works.

Love God above All Else

Jesus said that the **first** commandment is to love the Lord our God with all our heart, soul, mind, and strength.[50] He quoted from Deuteronomy 6 where it not only tells us to love the Lord, but also commands us to diligently teach our children to do the same.[51] Teaching our children to love and obey God shows that **we** love and obey Him.

Jesus tells us not to love our family members more than we love Him.[52] We are not to put our family above Him. We are not to disobey God in order to please our families. To put our family before God would push the priorities out of order.

Jesus considers us as His family if we hear and do God's Word.[53] Even if our earthly family forsakes us because of our commitment to the Lord, we still have a family in Jesus. There is also hope that as our own families see our commitment to the Lord, they may also turn to Him. Even Jesus was rejected by some of His own family members.[54] Yet after His resurrection, they were among those waiting for the outpouring of the Holy Spirit.[55] So do not give up on family members who may not be following the Lord right now, but neither should you compromise your commitment to the Lord because of them.

We must honor God and show Him reverence. When we put Him first and commit everything to Him, He is free to move in our lives and bring about His plan for our families. We show our love for Him by hearing and obeying His Word [56] (including what He says about our family relationships).

---

[50] Mark 12:28 And one of the scribes came, and having heard them reasoning together, and perceiving that he had answered them well, asked him, Which is the **first commandment** of all? 29 And Jesus answered him, The first of all the commandments *is*, Hear, O Israel; The Lord our God is one Lord: 30 And thou shalt love the Lord thy God with all thy heart, and with all thy soul, and with all thy mind, and with all thy strength: this *is* the first commandment.
(See also Matt. 22:35-40 and Luke 10:25-28.)

[51] Deut. 6:4 Hear, O Israel: The LORD our God *is* one LORD: 5 And thou shalt love the LORD thy God with all thine heart, and with all thy soul, and with all thy might. 6 And these words, which I command thee this day, shall be in thine heart: 7 And thou shalt **teach them diligently unto thy children**, and shalt talk of them when thou sittest in thine house, and when thou walkest by the way, and when thou liest down, and when thou risest up. 8 And thou shalt bind them for a sign upon thine hand, and they shall be as frontlets between thine eyes. 9 And thou shalt write them upon the posts of thy house, and on thy gates.

[52] Matt. 10:37 He that loveth father or mother more than me is not worthy of me: and he that loveth son or daughter more than me is not worthy of me.

[53] Luke 8:21 And he answered and said unto them, **My mother and my brethren are these which hear the word of God, and do it**.
(See also Matt. 12:48-50 and Mark 3:33-35).

[54] John 7:5 For neither did his brethren believe in him.

[55] Acts 1:14 These all continued with one accord in prayer and supplication, with the women, and Mary the **mother** of Jesus, and with his **brethren**.

[56] John 14:15 If ye love me, keep my commandments.

Part Two

Marriage Relationship

Chapter 2

Two Shall Be One

Marriage Is God's Plan

Setting the marriage in order helps get the rest of the family relationships in order. Finding God's perfect plan for marriage is not only beneficial for us, but also for our children. We can begin imparting to our children God's perfect plan for them. We can encourage them to strive for His best right from the start so they can avoid the mistakes made by former generations.

The world's view of marriage has become so generally accepted in this present time that even many Christians have lost sight of God's original plan. It is time for us to look back at His plan and conform our lives to it, rather than trying to justify our own lifestyles. God's plan is simple: marry for life.[1] If couples accept His plan, they will never have to worry about adultery or divorce. If you have ever had to deal with either of these in the past, now is a good time to leave those failures behind and begin to reach toward God's plan for you where you are at the present time. Repent of missing God's best for you, ask for His forgiveness, and forgive yourself and whoever else was involved in the failure. Then start afresh by searching His Word to find out how to enter into His plan for you.

Genesis 1 tells us that God created mankind, male and female, in His own image. God saw that what He had made was very good.[2] Genesis 2 gives a more detailed account of God's creation of man and woman. Like a potter fashions and squeezes a vessel into shape, God formed man of the dust of the ground. Then He blew breath into him, and he came alive. God put him in the Garden of Eden to dress and keep it.[3] God said that it was not good for man to be alone, and He would make a helper for him. First, He brought the animals to Adam to name them, but there was still not found a helper suitable for him. God took a rib from Adam's side, and with it He built a woman.[4] This "building" of the woman included giving her the ability to bear children.

---

[1] Mark 10:6 But from the beginning of the creation God made them male and female. 7 For this cause shall a man leave his father and mother, and cleave to his wife; 8 And they twain shall be one flesh: so then they are no more twain, but one flesh. 9 What therefore God hath joined together, let not man put asunder.

[2] Gen. 1:27 So God created man in his *own* image, in the image of God created he him; **male and female** created he them.... 31 And God saw everything that he had made, and, behold, *it was* **very good**. And the evening and the morning were the sixth day.

[3] Gen. 2:4 These *are* the generations of the heavens and of the earth when they were created, in the day that the LORD God made the earth and the heavens,... 7 And the **LORD God formed man** *of* **the dust of the ground, and breathed into his nostrils the breath of life**; and man became a living soul. 8 And the LORD God planted a garden eastward in Eden; and there he put the man whom he had formed.... 15 And the LORD God took the man, and **put him into the garden of Eden to dress it and to keep it**.

[4] Gen. 2:18 And the **LORD God said,** *It is* **not good that the man should be alone; I will make him an help meet for him.** 19 And out of the ground the LORD God formed every beast of the field, and every fowl of the air; and brought *them* unto Adam to see what he would call them: and whatsoever Adam called every living creature, that *was* the name thereof. 20 And Adam gave names to all cattle, and to the fowl of the air, and to every beast of the field; but for Adam there was not found an help meet for him. 21 And the LORD God caused a deep sleep to fall upon Adam, and he slept: and he took one of his ribs, and closed

God set up the covenant of marriage for Adam and Eve and for all future generations. Man is to leave his parents and cleave to his wife. Adam and Eve were naked and were not ashamed.[5] The word translated ashamed also means confused or disappointed. Imagine having a marriage where there is no shame, no confusion, and no disappointments. That is God's plan for your marriage.

In Genesis 5 God gives the generations of Adam. When God created man and woman, He called **their** name Adam.[6] He recognized the two as one.

God designed marriage, and it is good.[7] Ecclesiastes lists some advantages of marriage: two have a good reward for their labor; if one falls the other will lift him up; two can keep each other warm; if someone comes against one of them, they both together will withstand the adversary. Best of all, a threefold cord is not quickly broken.[8] The threefold cord represents covenant relationship involving husband, wife, and God.

The Bible says that marriage is honorable in all.[9] Forbidding to marry is listed as a doctrine of devils.[10] In answering a question about marriage, Jesus gave two basic reasons for not getting married. One is physical limitation that would inhibit the marriage relationship. The other is the choice to forego marriage for the sake of God's kingdom.[11]

Paul's ministry call was accompanied by God's grace for him to be single. Paul encouraged the unmarried and widows to remain single also. However, he realized that God enables people for what He has

---

up the flesh instead thereof; 22 And **the rib, which the LORD God had taken from man, made he a woman, and brought her unto the man.** 23 And Adam said, This *is* now bone of my bones, and flesh of my flesh: she shall be called Woman, because she was taken out of Man.

[5] Gen. 2:24 Therefore shall a **man leave his father and his mother**, and shall **cleave unto his wife**: and they shall **be one flesh.** 25 And they were both naked, the man and his wife, and were **not ashamed**.

[6] Gen. 5:1 This *is* the book of the generations of Adam. In the day that God created man, in the likeness of God made he him; 2 Male and female created he them; and blessed them, and called **their** name Adam, in the day when they were created.

[7] Prov. 18:22 *Whoso* findeth a wife findeth a good *thing*, and obtaineth **favour of the LORD**.

[8] Eccl. 4:9 Two *are* better than one; because they have a good reward for their labour. 10 For if they fall, the one will lift up his fellow: but woe to him *that is* alone when he falleth; for *he hath* not another to help him up. 11 Again, if two lie together, then they have heat: but how can one be warm *alone*? 12 And if one prevail against him, two shall withstand him; and a **threefold cord is not quickly broken**.

[9] Heb. 13:4 Marriage *is* honourable in **all**....

[10] 1 Tim. 4:1 Now the Spirit speaketh expressly, that in the latter times some shall depart from the faith, giving heed to seducing spirits, and **doctrines of devils**; 2 Speaking lies in hypocrisy; having their conscience seared with a hot iron; 3 **Forbidding to marry**, *and commanding* to abstain from meats, which God hath created to be received with thanksgiving of them which believe and know the truth.

[11] Matt. 19:10 His disciples say unto him, If the case of the man be so with *his* wife, it is not good to marry. 11 But he said unto them, All *men* cannot receive this saying, save *they* to whom it is given. 12 For there are some eunuchs, which were so born from *their* mother's womb: and there are some eunuchs, which were made eunuchs of men: and there be eunuchs, which have made themselves eunuchs for the kingdom of heaven's sake. He that is able to receive *it*, let him receive *it*.

called them to be.[12] God accepts us in the state in which we were called by him,[13] whether married or single. It is not necessary to change our marital status to be more acceptable to God.

Paul wrote about marriage in 1 Corinthians 7. I have footnoted passages from this chapter in various places as they apply to the different areas of marriage. However, I encourage you to read and study the entire chapter, as well as 1 Corinthians 5 and 6 to see how they all relate to marriage.

In 1 Corinthians 7:25-38, Paul is writing concerning virgins. The word "virgin" can mean a marriageable maiden, a chaste woman, or a chaste man. In this passage, Paul seems to be speaking directly to unmarried men. The passage speaks of being bound to or loosed from a wife. If the couple were already married, they would not be virgins. Since this passage is addressed to virgins, I believe that it includes betrothed couples. In Bible times, betrothal was considered a binding commitment. The word translated "wife" can refer to a woman already married or to a betrothed woman.

Concerning virgins, Paul gave his judgment as one faithful to the Lord. I am giving my judgment of how to interpret what he is saying. I believe he is saying that due to the distress at the time he wrote Corinthians, it would be better for virgins to remain unmarried. If a man were bound (betrothed) unto a wife, he should not seek to be loosed; if a man were not betrothed or were loosed from a betrothal, he should not seek to be married. However, if a virgin man did marry, he has not sinned. Neither has a virgin woman sinned if she marries. Paul believed it would be less trouble to remain unmarried. A married person is concerned with how to please his (or her) spouse. An unmarried person can give full attention to serving the Lord. Paul is not trying to cast a snare upon anyone, but showing how to serve the Lord without distraction.

Verses 36-38 have been interpreted in various ways. I believe these verses are referring to betrothed couples. Sometimes betrothals were arranged by parents before the couple was of age to marry. When the couple becomes of age, they can marry; it is no sin. Paul said in verse 2 that to avoid fornication, let every man have his own wife and every woman her own husband. He said in verse 9 that if a couple cannot contain, let them marry. I believe this is what he is referring to in verse 36 when he says, "But if any man think that he behaveth himself uncomely toward his virgin, ... let them marry." However, if the betrothed man stands steadfast in his heart, having self-control, it is not necessary to marry. In verse 38, "her" is added by the translators. If I were the translator, I would have written, "So then he that gives [himself] in marriage does well; but he that does not give [himself] in marriage does better." [14]

---

[12] 1 Cor. 7:1 Now concerning the things whereof ye wrote unto me: *It is* good for a man not to touch a woman. 2 Nevertheless, *to avoid* fornication, let every man have his own wife, and let every woman have her own husband.... 6 But I speak this by permission, *and* not of commandment. 7 For I would that all men were even as I myself. But every man hath his proper gift of God, one after this manner, and another after that. 8 I say therefore to the unmarried and widows, It is good for them if they abide even as I. 9 But if they cannot contain, let them marry: for it is better to marry than to burn.... 39 The wife is bound by the law as long as her husband liveth; but if her husband be dead, she is at liberty to be married to whom she will; only in the Lord. 40 But she is happier if she so abide, after my judgment: and I think also that I have the Spirit of God.

[13] 1 Cor. 7:17 But as God hath distributed to every man, as the Lord hath called every one, so let him walk. And so ordain I in all churches.... 24 Brethren, let every man, wherein he is called, therein abide with God.

[14] 1 Cor. 7:25 Now **concerning virgins** I have no commandment of the Lord: yet I give my judgment, as one that hath obtained mercy of the Lord to be faithful. 26 I suppose therefore that this is good for the present distress, *I say*, that *it is* good for a man so to be. 27 Art thou bound unto a wife? seek not to be loosed. Art thou loosed from a wife? seek not a wife. 28 But and if thou marry, thou hast not sinned; and if a virgin marry, she hath not sinned. Nevertheless such shall have trouble in the flesh: but I spare you. 29 But this I say, brethren, the time *is* short: it remaineth, that both they that have wives be as though they had none; 30 And they that weep, as though they wept not; and they that rejoice, as though they rejoiced not; and they that buy, as though they possessed not; 31 And they that use this world, as not abusing *it*: for the fashion of this world passeth away. 32 But I would have you without carefulness. He that is unmarried careth for the things that belong to the Lord, how he may please the Lord: 33

These Scriptures imply that marriage is God's design for most people. However, if God has called someone to forego marriage for the sake of His kingdom, He will give special grace for that person to live a chaste life. God accepts us regardless of our marital status.

In the Old Testament, instructions were given for special treatment of betrothed couples and newlyweds. When the men were going out to battle against their enemies; the officers were to allow betrothed men to return home.[15] A newly married man was not to go out to war nor be charged with any business, but be free at home one year to cheer up his new wife.[16] The first year of marriage can be a major adjustment period. All too often there are too many other pressures that are put on the new couple, making this first adjustment period even more difficult. We should be more considerate of newlyweds in our families, churches, and communities and be sensitive not to put undue pressure and extra responsibilities upon them. Allow them time to get their marriages established on a solid foundation and to mesh their lives together as covenant partners.[17]

Blood Covenant

God's relationship with man is based on blood covenants: the Old Testament (or covenant) included the shedding of the blood of animals; the New Covenant is based on the shed blood of Jesus Christ. God designed marriage also to be a blood covenant relationship.

In studying about covenants, I found that blood covenants have been practiced around the world from very early in the history of man. There were certain steps taken to enter into a blood covenant. Two people desiring to enter into covenant with one another would come together with friends and a "priest." The two would exchange gifts, which represented that all they owned belonged to each other. Blood was shed. Sometimes this was done by the cutting of wrists. The two people would rub their wrists together to mingle their blood, signifying oneness. Curses and blessings would be pronounced: curses for breaking the covenant and blessings for keeping the covenant. Once a covenant was made, the covenant partners were recognized by others to be in covenant with one another. The covenant was considered so sacred that it must never be broken. If it was, it brought the death penalty.

Learning about covenant helps us to understand the Bible better. Genesis 15 tells about God "cutting covenant" with Abraham. Genesis 17 shows that circumcision was the token of that covenant. Deuteronomy

---

But he that is married careth for the things that are of the world, how he may please *his* wife. 34 There is difference *also* between a wife and a virgin. The unmarried woman careth for the things of the Lord, that she may be holy both in body and in spirit: but she that is married careth for the things of the world, how she may please *her* husband. 35 And this I speak for your own profit; not that I may cast a snare upon you, but for that which is comely, and that ye may attend upon the Lord without distraction. 36 But if any man think that he behaveth himself uncomely toward his virgin, if she pass the flower of *her* age, and need so require, let him do what he will, he sinneth not: let them marry. 37 Nevertheless he that standeth stedfast in his heart, having no necessity, but hath power over his own will, and hath so decreed in his heart that he will keep his virgin, doeth well. 38 So then he that giveth *her* in marriage doeth well; but he that giveth *her* not in marriage doeth better.

[15] Deut. 20:7 And what man *is there* that hath betrothed a wife, and hath not taken her? let him go and return unto his house, lest he die in the battle, and another man take her.

[16] Deut. 24:5 When a man hath taken a new wife, he shall not go out to war, neither shall he be charged with any business: *but* he shall be free at home one year, and shall cheer up his wife which he hath taken.

[17] Amos 3:3 Can two walk together, except they be agreed?

11, 27, and 28 list blessings for keeping God's covenant and curses for not keeping the covenant. Today, when Christians partake of the Lord's Supper (Communion), they are remembering the New Covenant. The bread and grape juice represent Jesus' giving of His flesh and blood so we could be in covenant with Him.

This study of covenants also helped me to understand why certain things are done at wedding ceremonies and receptions. We followed traditions at our wedding without knowing the significance of them because, at that time, we knew very little about covenants. Now we realize that the giving of wedding rings, the bride's taking of her husband's last name, and the spoken vows are all connected with covenant rituals. The reception is symbolic of a covenant meal. The bride and groom drink from the same cup and feed cake to each other to symbolize their entering into covenant with one another.

God designed that the consummation of the marriage would seal the covenant in blood. We should teach our children the importance of remaining virgins until marriage.

God calls marriage a covenant.[18] In the Old Testament God compares His relationship to Jerusalem with the covenant relationship between a husband and wife.[19] In the New Testament (Ephesians 5) God compares the relationship of husband and wife to that of Christ and the church. In Revelation the new Jerusalem is compared to a bride.[20]

David and Jonathan in the Old Testament had a covenant of friendship. We can learn from them some of the covenant principles that also apply to marriage. Jonathan gave David gifts. His robe and garments symbolized wealth and possessions; his sword, bow, and belt represented strength and protection.[21]

God told the children of Israel not to enter into covenant relationships with the ungodly.[22] However, the Israelites failed to ask His counsel and were deceived into making a covenant with the very ones God had

---

[18] Mal. 2:14 Yet ye say, Wherefore? Because the LORD hath been witness between thee and the wife of thy youth, against whom thou hast dealt treacherously: yet *is* she thy companion, and the wife of thy **covenant**.

[19] Ezek. 16:3 And say, Thus saith the Lord GOD unto Jerusalem.... 8 Now when I passed by thee, and looked upon thee, behold, thy time *was* the time of love; and I spread my skirt over thee, and covered thy nakedness: yea, I sware unto thee, and entered into a **covenant** with thee, saith the Lord GOD, and thou becamest mine.
Isa. 62:5 ... and *as* the bridegroom rejoiceth over the bride, *so* shall thy God rejoice over thee.

[20] Rev. 19:7 Let us be glad and rejoice, and give honour to him: for the marriage of the Lamb is come, and his wife hath made herself ready. 8 And to her was granted that she should be arrayed in fine linen, clean and white: for the fine linen is the righteousness of saints. 9 And he saith unto me, Write, Blessed *are* they which are called unto the marriage supper of the Lamb. And he saith unto me, These are the true sayings of God.
Rev. 21:2 And I John saw the holy city, new Jerusalem, coming down from God out of heaven, prepared as a bride adorned for her husband.

[21] 1 Sam. 18:3 Then **Jonathan and David made a covenant**, because he loved him as his own soul. 4 And Jonathan stripped himself of the robe that *was* upon him, and gave it to David, and his garments, even to his sword, and to his bow, and to his girdle.

[22] Deut. 7:1 When the LORD thy God shall bring thee into the land whither thou goest to possess it, and hath cast out many nations before thee, the Hittites, and the Girgashites, and the Amorites, and the Canaanites, and the Perizzites, and the Hivites, and the Jebusites, seven nations greater and mightier than thou; 2 And when the LORD thy God shall deliver them before thee; thou shalt smite them, *and* utterly destroy them; thou shalt **make no covenant with them**, nor shew mercy unto them: 3 **Neither shalt thou make marriages with them**; thy daughter thou shalt not give unto his son, nor his daughter shalt thou take unto thy son. 4 For they will turn away thy son from following me, that they may serve other gods: so will the anger of the LORD be kindled against you, and destroy thee suddenly.

warned them about. When the people of Gibeon heard about Joshua's victory in battles with Jericho and Ai, they disguised themselves to look like travelers from a far country. They wore old clothes and shoes and took old, patched wine bottles and dry, moldy bread. They came to Joshua and the men of Israel and asked them to make a league with them. They did, and three days later, Joshua found out they were neighbors.[23]

Even though the Israelites had disobeyed God, He still expected them to honor the covenant they had made.[24] Because of their covenant, the Israelites were called on to defend the Gibeonites in battle.[25] God got involved and backed up their commitment to defend the Gibeonites. He intervened in supernatural ways to insure a victory for the Israelites. He sent great hailstones and even made the sun stand still until their enemies were defeated.[26] After all, God had made a covenant with the Israelites; and He, too, was bound by covenant to defend them.

From this example of the covenant between the Israelites and the Gibeonites, we can see how God looks at covenant relationships. Even if we entered into a marriage covenant with someone not of God's choosing, He still expects us to honor that covenant. When we are born again, we enter into covenant with God. When we are in covenant with Him, He is obligated to involve Himself with us. We can trust Him to enable us to keep **our** covenants as He helped Israel keep theirs.

---

[23] Josh. 9:3 And when the inhabitants of Gibeon heard what Joshua had done unto Jericho and to Ai, 4 They did work wilily, and went and made as if they had been ambassadors, and took old sacks upon their asses, and wine bottles, old, and rent, and bound up; 5 And old shoes and clouted upon their feet, and old garments upon them; and all the bread of their provision was dry *and* mouldy. 6 And they went to Joshua unto the camp at Gilgal, and said unto him, and to the men of Israel, We be come from a far country: now therefore make ye a league with us.... 14 And the men took of their victuals, and **asked not** *counsel* **at the mouth of the LORD**. 15 And Joshua made peace with them, and made a league with them, to let them live: and the princes of the congregation sware unto them. 16 And it came to pass at the end of three days after they had made a league with them, that they heard that they *were* their neighbours, and *that* they dwelt among them.

[24] Josh. 9:18 And the **children of Israel smote them not, because the princes** of the congregation **had sworn unto them by the LORD God** of Israel. And all the congregation murmured against the princes. 19 But all the princes said unto all the congregation, **We have sworn unto them by the LORD God of Israel: now therefore we may not touch them.** 20 This we will do to them; **we will even let them live**, lest wrath be upon us, **because of the oath** which we sware unto them.

[25] Josh. 10:6 And the **men of Gibeon sent unto Joshua** to the camp to Gilgal, saying, Slack not thy hand from thy servants; **come up to us quickly, and save us, and help us**: for all the kings of the Amorites that dwell in the mountains are gathered together against us. 7 So Joshua ascended from Gilgal, he, and all the people of war with him, and all the mighty men of valour.

[26] Josh. 10:8 And the LORD said unto Joshua, Fear them not: for I have delivered them into thine hand; there shall not a man of them stand before thee. 9 Joshua therefore came unto them suddenly, *and* went up from Gilgal all night. 10 And the LORD discomfited them before Israel, and slew them with a great slaughter at Gibeon, and chased them along the way that goeth up to Bethhoron, and smote them to Azekah, and unto Makkedah. 11 And it came to pass, as they fled from before Israel, *and* were in the going down to Bethhoron, that the LORD cast down great stones from heaven upon them unto Azekah, and they died: *they were* more which died with hailstones than *they* whom the children of Israel slew with the sword. 12 Then spake Joshua to the LORD in the day when the LORD delivered up the Amorites before the children of Israel, and he said in the sight of Israel, Sun, stand thou still upon Gibeon; and thou, Moon, in the valley of Ajalon. 13 And the sun stood still, and the moon stayed, until the people had avenged themselves upon their enemies. *Is* not this written in the book of Jasher? So the sun stood still in the midst of heaven, and hasted not to go down about a whole day. 14 And there was no day like that before it or after it, that the LORD hearkened unto the voice of a man: for the **LORD fought for Israel**.

The New Testament also tells us not to be yoked with unbelievers.[27] Christians who marry non-Christians are either not aware of this warning, or they simply choose to disobey. We should train our children so that they will not even consider marrying an unbeliever.

Some couples were both unbelievers when they got married, but since the wedding, one of them got saved. Then they experienced this unequal yoke. If you are a Christian and your spouse is not, you are in a position to be a channel for God to reach your mate. God has access to work in your marriage through your covenant with Him. I believe that God can and will save a marriage and save the unbelieving spouse **if** the Christian spouse will make the commitment that is necessary. Sometimes it is easy to let the "channel" get clogged with strife, unforgiveness, criticism, pride, and such things. But you have to allow God to clean all that out of your life, so His love can flow freely **through you** to your mate.

Even a husband who is not obeying God's Word can be won over by the good example of his wife. Wives should be subject to their own husbands and set a good example in conduct and manner of life, as well as in what they say. A wife should not just look good on the outside, but should also develop a meek and quiet spirit.[28] This will go a long way toward winning her husband to the Lord.

If a spouse that is an unbeliever is willing to stay with the spouse that is a believer, they should stay together. This gives opportunity for the Christian spouse to be a blessing and a good influence for the unsaved mate and a channel of God's love. When one spouse is in covenant with God, the children and the unbelieving spouse will benefit from that covenant.[29]

Years ago, when we set up a "not-for-profit" corporation for our Christian education ministry, we were required to agree to donate our assets to another "not-for-profit" organization upon dissolution of our corporation. This was not a covenant, but a contract. Recently, I have heard of marriages that include "pre-nuptial agreements" indicating how the assets will be distributed upon dissolution of the marriages. Couples who enter into marriage this way are not realizing that marriage is a covenant, not a contract. No engaged couple should make provision for the dissolution of their marriage. The marriage covenant is binding until the death of one of the covenant partners.[30] The Bible includes "covenantbreakers" in its list of the unrighteous.[31] God does not take covenants lightly, and neither should we.

---

[27] 2 Cor. 6:14 Be ye not unequally yoked together with unbelievers: for what fellowship hath righteousness with unrighteousness? and what communion hath light with darkness?

[28] 1 Pet. 3:1 Likewise, ye **wives,** *be* **in subjection to your own husbands**; that, if any obey not the word, they also may **without the word be won** by the **conversation** of the wives; 2 **While they behold** your chaste **conversation** *coupled* with fear. 3 Whose adorning let it not be that outward *adorning* of plaiting the hair, and of wearing of gold, or of putting on of apparel; 4 But *let it be* the hidden man of the heart, in that which is not corruptible, *even the ornament* of a **meek and quiet spirit,** which is in the sight of God of great price.

[29] 1 Cor. 7:12 But to the rest speak I, not the Lord: If any brother hath a wife that believeth not, and she be pleased to dwell with him, let him not put her away. 13 And the woman which hath an husband that believeth not, and if he be pleased to dwell with her, let her not leave him. 14 **For the unbelieving husband is sanctified by the wife, and the unbelieving wife is sanctified by the husband: else were your children unclean; but now are they holy.** 15 But if the unbelieving depart, let him depart. A brother or a sister is not under bondage in such *cases*: but God hath called us to peace. 16 **For what knowest thou, O wife, whether thou shalt save** *thy* **husband? or how knowest thou, O man, whether thou shalt save** *thy* **wife?**

[30] 1 Cor. 7:39 The wife is bound by the law as long as her husband liveth; but if her husband be dead, she is at liberty to be married to whom she will; only in the Lord.

[31] Rom. 1:31 Without understanding, **covenantbreakers**, without natural affection, implacable, unmerciful:

Chapter 3

Roles of Husband and Wife

The roles of Jesus and His Church compare with the roles of husband and wife.[1] Jesus Christ is the head of the Church; the Church is the body of Christ. In a physical body, the head receives impulses from parts of the body. The head interprets these impulses and gives direction to the body parts. The body responds in obedience to the head's direction. This interaction provides for protection, movement, and necessary functions of the body. This is God's design for Jesus and the Church and for husband and wife. What wonderful churches and marriages we would have if we would follow this design!

Husbands should pattern their treatment of their wives after the way Jesus treats His Church. Wives should be to their husbands as the Church should be to Jesus. In addition to the examples of Jesus and His Church, the Bible gives specific instructions for the husband-wife relationship.

When God instituted marriage, He said that a man shall leave his parents and cleave to his wife.[2] Couples must leave their parents in order to cleave to each other. Realize that when you get married, your relationship with your spouse becomes your primary relationship (next to your personal relationship with God). All other relationships (including those with parents, children, friends, employers, and church leaders) become secondary.

In the one-flesh relationship of marriage, the bodies of husband and wife belong to each other.[3] This type of intimacy is God's wedding gift to married couples. The gift is not given until after the wedding, so it should not be "opened" early.

The Bible says that a husband should enjoy his wife.[4] A man must drink only from his own well.[5] I used to have difficulty understanding Proverbs 5:15-16 because after it said for a man to drink from his own

---

[1] Eph. 5:22 Wives, submit yourselves unto your own husbands, **as unto the Lord.** 23 For the husband is the head of the wife, even **as Christ is the head of the church:** and he is the saviour of the body. 24 Therefore **as the church is subject unto Christ,** so *let* the wives *be* to their own husbands in every thing. 25 Husbands, love your wives, **even as Christ also loved the church, and gave himself for it**; 26 That he might sanctify and cleanse it with the washing of water by the word, 27 That he might present it to himself a glorious church, not having spot, or wrinkle, or any such thing; but that it should be holy and without blemish. 28 So ought men to love their wives as their own bodies. He that loveth his wife loveth himself. 29 For no man ever yet hated his own flesh; but nourisheth and cherisheth it, **even as the Lord the church:** 30 For **we are members of his body,** of his flesh, and of his bones. 31 For this cause shall a man leave his father and mother, and shall be joined unto his wife, and they two shall be one flesh. 32 This is a great mystery: but **I speak concerning Christ and the church.** 33 Nevertheless let every one of you in particular so love his wife even as himself; and the wife *see* that she reverence *her* husband.

[2] Gen. 2:24 Therefore shall a man leave his father and his mother, and shall cleave unto his wife: and they shall be one flesh.

[3] 1 Cor. 7:1 Now concerning the things whereof ye wrote unto me: *It is* good for a man not to touch a woman. 2 Nevertheless, *to avoid* fornication, let every man have his own wife, and let every woman have her own husband. 3 Let the husband render unto the wife due benevolence: and likewise also the wife unto the husband. 4 The wife hath not power of her own body, but the husband: and likewise also the husband hath not power of his own body, but the wife. 5 Defraud ye not one the other, except *it be* with consent for a time, that ye may give yourselves to fasting and prayer; and come together again, that Satan tempt you not for your incontinency.

cistern and well, it went on to say he should let his fountains be dispersed abroad and rivers of waters in the streets. It seemed verse 16 was contrary to verse 15. If a man was to drink at his own well, why should his waters be dispersed abroad and in the streets? When I studied the words used, I recognized a progression. A cistern is a pit to hold water; a well has water that springs up into it; a fountain springs forth and overflows. "Rivers of waters in the streets" indicates being enlarged and broadened, taking up more room. In other words, a man's relationship with his wife should always be living and growing. It should never become stagnant.

How much a man enjoys his wife depends partly on his wife. Women, you can choose what kind of wife you will be. Proverbs gives some contrasts between the bad and the good.[6] You can choose to be hateful (odious), shameful, and foolish. On the other hand, you can make it easier for your husband to enjoy you by choosing to become prudent, wise, and virtuous. Proverbs 31 describes a virtuous woman in more detail.[7] If you will seek the Lord, He will help you to become a virtuous woman.

Concerning submission, the Bible says that Christians should submit to one another.[8] That includes Christian spouses. Each should recognize the other as part of the body of Christ.[9] Remember that husband and wife are heirs together in Christ.[10]

---

[4] Eccl. 9:9 **Live joyfully with the wife** whom thou lovest all the days of the life of thy vanity, which he hath given thee under the sun, all the days of thy vanity: for that *is* thy portion in *this* life, and in thy labour which thou takest under the sun.
Gen. 26:8 And it came to pass, when he had been there a long time, that Abimelech king of the Philistines looked out at a window, and saw, and, behold, **Isaac *was* sporting with Rebekah his wife**.

[5] Prov. 5:15 Drink waters out of thine own cistern, and running waters out of thine own well. 16 Let thy fountains be dispersed abroad, *and* rivers of waters in the streets. 17 Let them be only thine own, and not strangers' with thee. 18 Let thy fountain be blessed: and **rejoice with the wife of thy youth**. 19 *Let her be as* the loving hind and pleasant roe; let her breasts satisfy thee at all times; and be thou ravished always with her love.

[6] Prov. 12:4 A **virtuous** woman *is* a crown to her husband: but **she that maketh ashamed** *is* as rottenness in his bones.
Prov. 14:1 Every **wise** woman buildeth her house: but the **foolish** plucketh it down with her hands.
Prov. 16:21 The wise in heart shall be called **prudent**....
Prov. 19:14b ... a **prudent** wife *is* from the LORD.
Prov. 30:21 For three *things* the earth is disquieted, and for four *which* it cannot bear: 22 For a servant when he reigneth; and a fool when he is filled with meat; 23 For an **odious** *woman* when she is married; and an handmaid that is heir to her mistress.

[7] Prov. 31:10 Who can find a **virtuous** woman? for her price *is* far above rubies. 11 The heart of her **husband doth safely trust in her**, so that he shall have no need of spoil. 12 She will **do him good and not evil** all the days of her life. 13 She seeketh wool, and flax, and **worketh willingly** with her hands. 14 She is like the merchants' ships; she bringeth her food from afar. 15 She riseth also while it is yet night, and giveth meat to her household, and a portion to her maidens. 16 She considereth a field, and buyeth it: with the fruit of her hands she planteth a vineyard. 17 She girdeth her loins with strength, and strengtheneth her arms. 18 She perceiveth that her merchandise *is* good: her candle goeth not out by night. 19 She layeth her hands to the spindle, and her hands hold the distaff. 20 She stretcheth out her hand to the poor; yea, she reacheth forth her hands to the needy. 21 She is not afraid of the snow for her household: for all her household *are* clothed with scarlet. 22 She maketh herself coverings of tapestry; her clothing *is* silk and purple. 23 Her husband is known in the gates, when he sitteth among the elders of the land. 24 She maketh fine linen, and selleth *it*; and delivereth girdles unto the merchant. 25 **Strength and honour** *are* her clothing; and she shall **rejoice** in time to come. 26 She openeth her mouth with **wisdom**; and in her tongue *is* the law of **kindness**. 27 She **looketh well to the ways of her household**, and eateth not the bread of idleness. 28 Her **children arise up, and call her blessed**; her **husband *also*, and he praiseth her**. 29 Many daughters have done virtuously, but thou excellest them all. 30 Favour *is* deceitful, and beauty *is* vain: *but* a woman *that* feareth the LORD, she shall be praised. 31 Give her of the fruit of her hands; and let her own works praise her in the gates.

[8] Eph. 5:21 **Submitting yourselves one to another** in the fear of God.

However, there are specific instructions in a marriage relationship for a husband to be the head of his wife and the wife to submit (be subject) to her own husband.[11] Realize that spouses do not choose these roles. Husbands did not choose to be born male, and wives did not choose to be born female. The anointing and appointing are given by God, and your role was determined before you were born.

There would be no conflict if we would just obey God. If husbands were heads over their wives **as** Christ is over the church, no **Christian** wife should have any trouble with that. The husband would be submitting to his head, which is Christ, **as** Christ is submitting to God.[12] When we look at how Jesus acted as Head of the church, we find that He served and ministered.[13]

If wives were subject unto their own husbands **as** unto the Lord, no Christian husband should have any trouble with that. Instructions are given to the church to obey those who have the rule over it and to submit to them.[14] When a wife follows this example, her husband can be her head **with joy** and not with grief. When a wife is fully submitted to God, she should have no trouble submitting to her own husband because her submission to him is her obedience to God.[15]

The trouble comes if we rebel against our own role or try to make our spouse take on his (or her) role. God did not tell wives to make sure that their husbands take the role of headship. It is not her responsibility to do that. If she tries to push her husband to take the headship position, she is acting as his head. Likewise, a husband should not try to force his wife to submit to him. Submission is an attitude. The Biblical instruction to submit is given **to the wife**. It is not an instruction for the husband to try to enforce. That is not his responsibility. Even though a husband could probably force his wife to **obey** him, it would be possible for her to obey without submission. In other words, she could obey on the outside (in action), but rebel on the inside (have the wrong attitude). Elders in the church are to lead by example, not by lording it over those under their authority.[16] I believe this same principle applies to husbands.

---

[9] Gal. 3:28 There is neither Jew nor Greek, there is neither bond nor free, there is **neither male nor female**: for ye are **all one in Christ Jesus**.

[10] 1 Pet. 3:7 Likewise, ye husbands, dwell with *them* according to knowledge, giving honour unto the wife, as unto the weaker vessel, and **as being heirs together of the grace of life**; that your prayers be not hindered.

[11] Eph. 5:22 **Wives, submit** yourselves unto your own husbands, **as unto the Lord**. 23 For the **husband is the head of the wife**, even **as Christ is the head of the church**: and he is the saviour of the body. 24 Therefore **as the church is subject unto Christ**, so *let* the **wives be to their own husbands** in every thing.
Col. 3:18 **Wives, submit** yourselves unto your own husbands, as it is fit in the Lord.

[12] 1 Cor. 11:3 But I would have you know, that the head of every man is Christ; and the head of the woman *is* the man; and the head of Christ *is* God.

[13] Matt. 20:27 And whosoever will be chief among you, let him be your servant: 28 Even as the Son of man came not to be ministered unto, but to minister, and to give his life a ransom for many.

[14] Heb. 13:17 Obey them that have the rule over you, and submit yourselves: for they watch for your souls, as they that must give account, that they may do it with joy, and not with grief: for that *is* unprofitable for you.

[15] Col. 3:23 And whatsoever ye do, do *it* heartily, **as to the Lord**, and not unto men; 24 Knowing that of the Lord ye shall receive the reward of the inheritance: for ye serve the Lord Christ.

[16] 1 Pet. 5:3 **Neither** as being **lords over** *God's* heritage, **but being ensamples** to the flock.

Wives should be obedient to their own husbands. In the New Testament the older women were instructed to teach the younger women to love their husbands and to be obedient to them.[17]

Queen Vashti disobeyed her husband and refused to come at his commandment. He had sent for her to come to his party to show off her beauty to his guests. Her refusal caused quite a stir in the kingdom. It was feared that the queen's example would cause the other women in the kingdom to despise their husbands. It was decided that Queen Vashti would be replaced. When other wives saw what happened to her, they would give honor to their own husbands. Letters were sent throughout the kingdom to make sure that every man would bear rule in his own house.[18]

Sara is given as an example of a wife who was subject to her husband and obeyed him.[19] Even so, the Bible is not saying that wives have no say-so. God told Abraham to do what Sara said in a particular matter even though it grieved him to do it.[20]

It is important not to let worldly ideas dictate to you what headship and submission roles are. For example, a wife may complain that her husband expects her to write the checks for all the bills, but she thinks that job belongs to her husband. The Bible does not say whose job it is. Some roles are different in

---

[17] Titus 2:3 The aged women likewise, that *they be* in behaviour as becometh holiness, not false accusers, not given to much wine, teachers of good things; 4 That they may teach the young women to be sober, to love their husbands, to love their children, 5 *To be* discreet, chaste, keepers at home, good, **obedient to their own husbands**, that the word of God be not blasphemed.

[18] Esther 1:10 On the seventh day, when the heart of the **king** was merry with wine, he **commanded** Mehuman, Biztha, Harbona, Bigtha, and Abagtha, Zethar, and Carcas, the seven chamberlains that served in the presence of Ahasuerus the king, 11 **To bring Vashti the queen before the king** with the crown royal, to shew the people and the princes her beauty: for she *was* fair to look on. 12 But the **queen Vashti refused to come** at the king's commandment by *his* chamberlains: therefore was the king very wroth, and his anger burned in him. 13 Then the king said to the wise men, which knew the times, (for so *was* the king's manner toward all that knew law and judgment: 14 And the next unto him *was* Carshena, Shethar, Admatha, Tarshish, Meres, Marsena, *and* Memucan, the seven princes of Persia and Media, which saw the king's face, *and* which sat the first in the kingdom;) 15 **What shall we do unto the queen Vashti** according to law, because **she hath not performed the commandment of the king Ahasuerus** by the chamberlains? 16 And Memucan answered before the king and the princes, Vashti the queen hath not done wrong to the king only, but also to all the princes, and to all the people that *are* in all the provinces of the king Ahasuerus. 17 For *this* deed of the queen shall come abroad unto all women, so that they shall despise their husbands in their eyes, when it shall be reported, The **king Ahasuerus commanded Vashti the queen to be brought in before him, but she came not.** 18 *Likewise* shall the ladies of Persia and Media say this day unto all the king's princes, which have heard of the deed of the queen. Thus *shall there arise* too much contempt and wrath. 19 If it please the king, let there go a royal commandment from him, and let it be written among the laws of the Persians and the Medes, that it be not altered, That Vashti come no more before king Ahasuerus; and **let the king give her royal estate unto another** that is better than she. 20 And when the king's decree which he shall make shall be published throughout all his empire, (for it is great,) **all the wives shall give to their husbands honour**, both to great and small. 21 And the saying pleased the king and the princes; and the king did according to the word of Memucan: 22 For he sent letters into all the king's provinces, into every province according to the writing thereof, and to every people after their language, **that every man should bear rule in his own house**, and that *it* should be published according to the language of every people.

[19] 1 Pet. 3:5 For after this manner in the old time the holy women also, who trusted in God, adorned themselves, **being in subjection unto their own husbands**: 6 Even **as Sara obeyed Abraham, calling him lord**: whose daughters ye are, as long as ye do well, and are not afraid with any amazement.

[20] Gen. 21:9 And Sarah saw the son of Hagar the Egyptian, which she had born unto Abraham, mocking. 10 Wherefore she said unto Abraham, Cast out this bondwoman and her son: for the son of this bondwoman shall not be heir with my son, *even* with Isaac. 11 And the **thing was very grievous in Abraham's sight** because of his son. 12 And **God said** unto Abraham, **Let it not be grievous** in thy sight because of the lad, and because of thy bondwoman; **in all that Sarah hath said unto thee, hearken unto her voice**; for in Isaac shall thy seed be called.

different cultures. In some cultures, nobody writes checks. So do not get locked in to doing things a certain way because it is "proper" in a certain culture or because that is the way it was done in your parents' home. Go with what the Bible says. And the Bible says a wife is to be a help meet (suitable) for **her** husband.[21] If he needs you to help him by writing the checks, then write the checks!

Wives, you should give thanks for and pray for your husbands as the one in authority over you.[22] If you think your husband is heading in a wrong direction, you can pray that the Lord will turn his heart the right way.[23] Just remember that your heart is also in the hand of the Lord, and you must allow Him to change your heart if necessary. If two mules are pulling in opposite directions, they will not make any progress. If one will yield to the other and both pull in the same direction, even if the direction seems wrong, they will **both** realize it sooner and can get going in the right direction quickly.

Sad to say, there are marriages where there is actually demonic oppression operating through one or both spouses. God tells wives to submit to their own husbands, but He never says to submit to the devil.[24] If your spouse is bound by the devil in any way, you must pray for him (or her). You must stand against the devil's attack. Remember that your spouse is not the enemy; the devil is. Continue to love your spouse and realize that your intercession can free him (or her) from this bondage. Be strong in the Lord, stand in faith, and minister to your spouse; but refuse to be oppressed by demonic words or actions operating through him (or her).

There is a principle in God's Word for disobeying an authority over you **if** their demands would cause you to disobey God.[25] He is the highest authority, and His Word overrules all those in authority under Him. Remember, though, you are not to disobey just because you did not like the demand, but **only if** it is contrary to God's Word. Realize that if you must disobey, you **can** do it respectfully.

Love for the wife and respect for the husband are foundational in a marriage.[26] One spouse should not wait on the other to get in line with God's Word. Wife, do not say you will submit to your husband only **when** he starts loving you as Christ loves the church. Husband, do not say you will love your wife only **when** she starts respecting you. Whoever is reading this should take the first step. You have to sow seeds before you reap a harvest.

---

[21] Gen. 2:18 And the LORD God said, *It is* not good that the man should be alone; I will make him an **help meet for him**.

[22] I Tim. 2:1 I exhort therefore, that, first of all, supplications, prayers, intercessions, *and* giving of thanks, be made for all men; 2 For kings, and *for* **all that are in authority**; that we may lead a quiet and peaceable life in all godliness and honesty.

[23] Prov. 21:1 The king's heart *is* in the hand of the LORD, *as* the rivers of water: he turneth it whithersoever he will.

[24] James 4:7 **Submit** yourselves therefore **to God. Resist the devil**, and he will flee from you.

[25] Acts 4:18 And they called them, and commanded them not to speak at all nor teach in the name of Jesus. 19 But Peter and John answered and said unto them, **Whether it be right in the sight of God to hearken unto you more than unto God, judge ye**.
Acts 5:28 Saying, Did not we straitly command you that ye should not teach in this name? and, behold, ye have filled Jerusalem with your doctrine, and intend to bring this man's blood upon us. 29 Then Peter and the *other* apostles answered and said, **We ought to obey God rather than men**.

[26] Eph. 5:33 Nevertheless let every one of you in particular so **love his wife** even as himself; and the wife *see* that she **reverence *her* husband**.
Col. 3:19 **Husbands, love *your* wives**, and be not bitter against them.

Do not do things for your spouse just to manipulate him (or her) to do what you desire. It is important to please your spouse, not just yourself. Observe your own spouse to see what pleases him (or her).[27] Then make it a practice to do those things that please. Do what God says out of obedience to Him. He will honor your obedience and bless you for it.

Do not compare your spouse or marriage to others.[28] Yours is special. Besides, you do not know the "whole picture" of others. They may not always be as they seem to you.

If you are experiencing failure in any area of your marriage, check up on your love. Love never fails! (See Chapter 21.)

---

[27] 1 Cor. 7:33 But he that is married careth for the things that are of the world, **how he may please *his* wife**. 34 ... but she that is married careth for the things of the world, **how she may please *her* husband**.

[28] 2 Cor. 10:12 For we dare not make ourselves of the number, or compare ourselves with some that commend themselves: but they measuring themselves by themselves, and **comparing** themselves among themselves, **are not wise**.

Chapter 4

Separation and Divorce

When conflict comes in a marriage, the tendency is to get away from it. We seem to think things will go easier if the conflicting partners go separate ways instead of staying together and solving the problems. Separation may provide immediate, temporary relief, but brings its own set of problems in addition to the ones that caused the separation in the first place. Separation or divorce does not end the conflict. If the hearts of the spouses are not changed, the conflict will follow them wherever they go (even into another marriage if they remarry). I know of divorced couples that have continued their conflict after their divorce. Sometimes one spouse will purposely harass the other, like repeatedly taking them to court over petty issues or turning the children against the other parent. Some divorced spouses have to deal with lack of finances and provision. Children are sometimes bounced back and forth between separated parents with no sense of security. Divorce does not release the couple from the bondage they were in when they were together. In other words, **divorce is not the answer**.

Taking your spouse (your covenant partner) to court will not solve your problems. The Bible says you should not take a conflict between brothers before unbelievers for them to judge the situation. It would be better to suffer the wrong than to do that.[1] It also says you should not walk in the counsel of the ungodly.[2] If the conflict in your marriage is so great that you think you should involve others, then go to Christians who will counsel you according to God's Word. If both spouses are going for counsel, I recommend seeking counsel from a couple whose marriage is stable and their commitment to their marriage covenant is strong. If only one spouse is going for counseling, then that one should go to a Christian of the same sex. In other words, a husband should not go to another woman, and a wife should not go to another man for personal marriage counseling. The devil is all too ready to move in on a situation like that and bring in more problems. I do not advise anyone having marriage conflicts to seek counsel from those who have been involved in a divorce of their own. Our tendency is to find someone to take our side in the conflict, but the best counsel is to go God's way, not our own.

The answer is to choose God's way no matter what the circumstances look like. The devil will try to deceive couples into thinking that their situation is impossible. He will try to make them think that there are only two choices: to put up with the situation as it is or to separate. But there is another choice: choose to stay committed to your marriage covenant and make your marriage work. That very decision will release God to work in your situation to turn it around. When God turns the situation around, your marriage will be better than ever, and there will be no reason to even consider divorce. If you do not choose God's way, then you are automatically choosing the devil's way.

---

[1] 1 Cor. 6:1 Dare any of you, having a matter against another, go to law before the unjust, and not before the saints?... 5 I speak to your shame. Is it so, that there is not a wise man among you? no, not one that shall be able to judge between his brethren? 6 But brother goeth to law with brother, and that before the unbelievers. 7 Now therefore there is utterly a fault among you, because ye go to law one with another. Why do ye not rather take wrong? why do ye not rather *suffer yourselves to* be defrauded? 8 Nay ye do wrong, and defraud, and that *your* brethren.

[2] Psalm 1:1a Blessed *is* the man that walketh not in the counsel of the ungodly....

When conflict comes in a marriage, it is vitally important to realize that your spouse is not your enemy, even if he (or she) acts like it. The devil is the enemy who tries to pit spouses against each other to divide and conquer them. Also, realize that if the devil was successful in bringing divorce to your parents (or someone else in your family), he may try to do the same with you. If divorce is a curse in your family, it must be broken so that it does not pass on to you or your descendants. Recognize that it is an attack of Satan and stand against it.

I believe that churches should become more involved in preventing divorce. This can be done by more teaching of God's plan for marriage. If a couple in your midst is having conflict in marriage, others in the church can intercede for them and help them to resist Satan's attack. All counseling should be based on God's Word, not man's evaluation of the situation.

We have said that you should choose God's way for marriage. What is God's way? We will look at some Scriptures about marriage and divorce in the rest of this chapter. Parts Four and Eight of this book ("Choices Affect Relationships" and "Improving Family Relationships") will also help in dealing with conflicts in marriage.

Some religious leaders asked Jesus if it was lawful for a man to put away his wife. Jesus asked them about the law of Moses. They answered that Moses had allowed ("suffered") a man to write a bill of divorcement and put away his wife.[3] Jesus said it was because of the hardness of their hearts that Moses wrote them this precept (rule of conduct), but it was not according to God's plan. His plan was that the man would leave his parents and cleave to his wife, and they were to become one flesh. This cleaving was to be like being glued or cemented together, and they were to stay with each other. Man was not to separate what God had joined together.[4] Some might argue that because they did not seek God's counsel in choosing their marriage partner, that God did not really join them together. Therefore, they feel justified in separating. However, marriage is God's design for joining couples in the marriage covenant; in that sense, all married couples are joined by God. This agrees with what we learned about covenants: God expects us to honor our covenant even if He did not choose our covenant partner.

---

[3] Mark 10:2 And the Pharisees came to him, and asked him, Is it lawful for a man to put away *his* wife? tempting him. 3 And he answered and said unto them, What did Moses command you? 4 And they said, Moses suffered to write a bill of divorcement, and to put *her* away.
Deut. 24:1 When a man hath taken a wife, and married her, and it come to pass that she find no favour in his eyes, because he hath found some uncleanness in her: then let him write her a bill of divorcement, and give *it* in her hand, and send her out of his house. 2 And when she is departed out of his house, she may go and be another man's *wife*.

[4] Mark 10:5 And Jesus answered and said unto them, **For the hardness of your heart** he wrote you this precept. 6 But **from the beginning** of the creation God made them male and female. 7 For this cause shall a man leave his father and mother, and **cleave** to his wife; 8 And they **twain shall be one flesh**: so then they are no more twain, but one flesh. 9 What therefore God hath joined together, **let not man put asunder**.
Matt. 19:3 The Pharisees also came unto him, tempting him, and saying unto him, Is it lawful for a man to put away his wife for every cause? 4 And he answered and said unto them, Have ye not read, that he which made *them* **at the beginning** made them male and female, 5 And said, For this cause shall a man leave father and mother, and shall cleave to his wife: and they **twain shall be one flesh**? 6 Wherefore they are no more twain, but one flesh. What therefore God hath joined together, **let not man put asunder**. 7 They say unto him, Why did Moses then command to give a writing of divorcement, and to put her away? 8 He saith unto them, Moses **because of the hardness of your hearts** suffered you to put away your wives: but **from the beginning** it was not so.

Jesus said that whoever puts away his wife and marries another, commits adultery against her; and if a woman puts away her husband and marries another, she commits adultery.[5] He said this because the covenant of marriage is designed to be in effect until the death of one of the covenant partners.[6]

Many Christians who are having trouble in their marriages would not be so quick to divorce if they knew they would never remarry. They would choose instead to seek the Lord diligently on how to save their present marriage. Jesus' words would be a deterrent to divorce if Christians would take seriously what He said. There are some Christians who actually search the Word for a loophole to justify getting out of their present marriage so they can marry someone else. One such loophole is the "exception clause" ("except it be for **fornication**") found twice in the book of Matthew.[7] These two verses say that whoever puts away his wife, except for the cause of fornication, and marries another, commits adultery and causes his wife to commit adultery. Also, whoever marries a woman that is divorced commits adultery.

While I was studying these passages, I noticed something I had never seen before. When I read these verses before, I was **thinking** "except for **adultery**." But it **says**, "except for **fornication**." Why did Jesus use the word "fornication" for the exception and later in the same sentence use the word "adultery" for those who divorced and married another? Adultery refers to a **married** person's having sex with someone other than his (or her) spouse. Fornication generally refers to having sex **before** marriage. I believe Jesus used the word "fornication" here to indicate sex before marriage to differentiate it from adultery. In Bible times, betrothal (engagement) was considered a binding commitment. To break an engagement was like divorce (or putting away). So if a man was engaged to a woman and found out she had been involved in fornication, he was allowed to put her away. In other words, if a man found out that the woman he was engaged to was no longer a virgin, he was allowed to break the engagement. Then if he married someone else, it would not be considered adultery. This is what **I believe** Jesus was saying. This may be difficult for us to comprehend if we are in a culture that does not consider an engagement as a binding commitment. I realize this is not the usual teaching on this passage, but I encourage you to seek the Lord concerning this and study it for yourself.

In any case, you have to admit that the verses do **not** say that a man must divorce his wife if she was involved in fornication. He can choose reconciliation. He can choose to forgive her and allow God to heal the marriage relationship. (The same applies to a wife whose husband was involved in fornication.)

---

[5] Mark 10:10 And in the house his disciples asked him again of the same *matter*. 11 And he saith unto them, Whosoever shall put away his wife, and marry another, committeth adultery against her. 12 And if a woman shall put away her husband, and be married to another, she committeth adultery.
Luke 16:18 Whosoever putteth away his wife, and **marrieth another, committeth adultery**: and whosoever marrieth her that is put away from *her* husband committeth adultery.

[6] Rom. 7:1 Know ye not, brethren, (for I speak to them that know the law,) how that the law hath dominion over a man as long as he liveth? 2 For the woman which hath an husband is bound by the law to *her* husband so long as he liveth; but if the husband be dead, she is loosed from the law of *her* husband. 3 So then if, while *her* husband liveth, she be married to another man, she shall be called an adulteress: but if her husband be dead, she is free from that law; so that she is no adulteress, though she be married to another man.

[7] Matt. 5:31 **It hath been said**, Whosoever shall put away his wife, let him give her a writing of divorcement: 32 **But I say unto you, That whosoever shall put away his wife, saving for the cause of fornication, causeth her to commit adultery: and whosoever shall marry her that is divorced committeth adultery.**
Matt. 19:9 And I say unto you, Whosoever shall put away his wife, **except** *it be* **for fornication**, and shall **marry another, committeth adultery**: and whoso marrieth her which is put away doth commit adultery.

Under the old covenant law, adultery was punishable by death.[8] Breaking the marriage covenant brought the death penalty. Instead of being divorced for unfaithfulness, the adulterer (or adulteress) was stoned. This automatically left the living spouse free to remarry. If every adulterer and adulteress of today were stoned, there would be many more widows and widowers! It is a good thing that Jesus took the death penalty in our place. He paid the price for our sin so that we can have life.

The Apostle Paul repeated the Lord's command for married people to stay together when he said for wives not to depart from their husbands, and husbands not to put away their wives. He also said that even if a wife did depart, she should remain unmarried or be reconciled to her husband.[9] She should keep the way open for reconciliation. The Lord hates divorce.[10] Divorce hurts His children: the grownup ones and the little ones.

There may be some who are reading this that have already experienced divorce and remarriage. You cannot go back and undo the past. You have to start right where you are **now**. You must be faithful to the covenant you are in **now**. The Bible says that if a woman was divorced and remarried and divorced again (or her second husband died), she was not to return to her first husband.[11] So **do not** get the idea that you can make things right by divorcing your present spouse and remarrying your first spouse. What you **can** do is to ask God to forgive you for breaking the marriage covenant in the past. Forgive yourself and anyone else involved and leave the past behind. You must repent (determine not make the same mistake again) and commit yourself to keeping your present marriage covenant.

There are many women who have been deserted by their husbands; some have children to bring up without the help of their fathers. These women must forgive those who hurt them and look to God to make up the difference. I believe that God's special grace that is on widows and the fatherless extends to cover the wife and children who are without husband and father in their home. (See Chapter 9.)

---

[8] Lev. 20:10 And the man that committeth adultery with *another* man's wife, *even he* that committeth adultery with his neighbour's wife, the adulterer and the adulteress shall surely be put to death.
Deut. 22:22 If a man be found lying with a woman married to an husband, then they shall both of them die, *both* the man that lay with the woman, and the woman: so shalt thou put away evil from Israel.

[9] 1 Cor. 7:10 And **unto the married** I command, *yet* not I, but the Lord, **Let not the wife depart from *her* husband**: 11 But and if she depart, let her remain unmarried, or be reconciled to *her* husband: and **let not the husband put away *his* wife**.

[10] Mal. 2:15b ... Therefore take heed to your spirit, and let none deal treacherously against the wife of his youth. 16 For the LORD, the God of Israel, saith that **he hateth putting away**: for *one* covereth violence with his garment, saith the LORD of hosts: therefore take heed to your spirit, that ye deal not treacherously.

[11] Deut. 24:3 And *if* the latter husband hate her, and write her a bill of divorcement, and giveth *it* in her hand, and sendeth her out of his house; or if the latter husband die, which took her *to be* his wife; 4 **Her former husband**, which sent her away, **may not take her again** to be his wife, after that she is defiled; for **that *is* abomination before the LORD**: and thou shalt not cause the land to sin, which the LORD thy God giveth thee *for* an inheritance.

Chapter 5

Fornication and Adultery

Fornication is voluntary sexual intercourse between unmarried persons. Adultery is voluntary sexual intercourse between a married person and someone other than his (or her) spouse. In either case, it is outside of God's plan and against His law. Sexual intimacy, as God designed it, is to be reserved exclusively for one's own spouse (during their marriage, not before).

Fornication includes incest, premarital sex, homosexuality, and other sexual perversions. In some cultures or families, incest and other perversions are considered "normal." If your background is from one of these, take note: these perversions are not normal in God's design. If you are involved in any of these perversions, stop! If you do not know how to get out of a situation you are in, get help. God will deliver you if you ask and trust Him to.

God warned the children of Israel that they were not to do like the heathen living around them.[1] Leviticus 18 lists incest, adultery, homosexuality, and other forms of sexual immorality. By these the heathen nations were defiled.[2] God forbids His children to commit any of these abominable customs.[3]

Leviticus 18:6-18 shows that God forbids incest.[4] He also forbids homosexuality, even though the word "homosexual" is not found in the King James Version of the Bible. Homosexuality is described in both the Old and New Testaments. Under Old Testament law, it was punishable by death.[5]

Premarital sex is also against God's law. If a man had sexual intercourse with a virgin that was not betrothed, he was required to make payment to her father and to marry her and never put her away.[6] If a man

---

[1] Lev. 18:1 And the LORD spake unto Moses, saying, 2 Speak unto the children of Israel, and say unto them, I am the LORD your God. 3 **After the doings of the land** of Egypt, wherein ye dwelt, **shall ye not do**: and after the doings of the land of Canaan, whither I bring you, shall ye not do: **neither shall ye walk in their ordinances**. 4 Ye shall do my judgments, and keep mine ordinances, to walk therein: I *am* the LORD your God. 5 Ye shall therefore keep my statutes, and my judgments: which if a man do, he shall live in them: I *am* the LORD.

[2] Lev. 18:24 Defile not ye yourselves in any of these things: for in all these the nations are defiled which I cast out before you: 25 And the land is defiled: therefore I do visit the iniquity thereof upon it, and the land itself vomiteth out her inhabitants.

[3] Lev. 18:30 Therefore shall ye keep mine ordinance, that *ye* commit not *any one* of these abominable customs, which were committed before you, and that ye defile not yourselves therein: I *am* the LORD your God.

[4] Lev. 18:6 None of you shall approach to any that is near of kin to him, to uncover *their* nakedness: I *am* the LORD.

[5] Lev. 18:22 Thou shalt not lie with mankind, as with womankind: it *is* abomination.
Lev. 20:13 If a man also lie with mankind, as he lieth with a woman, both of them have committed an abomination: they shall surely be put to death; their blood *shall be* upon them.
Rom. 1:26 For this cause God gave them up unto **vile affections**: for even their **women did change the natural use into that which is against nature**: 27 And likewise also the men, leaving the natural use of the woman, burned in their lust one toward another; **men with men working that which is unseemly**, and receiving in themselves that recompence of their error which was meet.

had sexual intercourse with a virgin that was betrothed, it was judged as adultery. If it happened in the city, they were both to be stoned to death because the man had humbled his neighbor's betrothed and because the woman had not cried out for help. (It was expected that if a woman cried out in the city, someone would have heard her and come to her rescue.) If it happened in the field, only the man would die because he forced her, and there was no one around to save her.[7]

The law also said that if a man took a wife, and he discovered she was not a virgin, she should be stoned to death. If a husband falsely accused his wife of not being a virgin when he married her, he was chastised and fined, and he was never allowed to divorce her. A woman was not to play the whore in her father's house.[8] Neither was a father to prostitute his daughter.[9]

Two of the Ten Commandments deal with adultery. The seventh one says not to commit adultery. The tenth one says not to covet your neighbor's wife (or anything else that is your neighbor's).[10] That would prevent adultery. In the Old Testament, adultery was punishable by death.[11] In the New Testament, the Ten Commandments are summed up in two commandments: love God and love your neighbor. If you love your neighbor, you will not commit adultery with his (or her) spouse.[12] The New Testament says God will judge adulterers.[13]

---

[6] Deut. 22:28 If a man find a damsel *that is* a virgin, which is not betrothed, and lay hold on her, and lie with her, and they be found; 29 Then the man that lay with her shall give unto the damsel's father fifty *shekels* of silver, and she shall be his wife; because he hath humbled her, he may not put her away all his days.

[7] Deut. 22:23 If a damsel *that is* a virgin be betrothed unto an husband, and a man find her in the city, and lie with her; 24 Then ye shall bring them both out unto the gate of that city, and ye shall stone them with stones that they die; the damsel, because she cried not, *being* in the city; and the man, because he hath humbled his neighbour's wife: so thou shalt put away evil from among you. 25 But if a man find a betrothed damsel in the field, and the man force her, and lie with her: then the man only that lay with her shall die: 26 But unto the damsel thou shalt do nothing; *there is* in the damsel no sin *worthy* of death: for as when a man riseth against his neighbour, and slayeth him, even so *is* this matter: 27 For he found her in the field, *and* the betrothed damsel cried, and *there was* none to save her.

[8] Deut 22:13 If any man take a wife, and go in unto her, and hate her, 14 And give occasions of speech against her, and bring up an evil name upon her, and say, I took this woman, and when I came to her, I found her not a maid: 15 Then shall the father of the damsel, and her mother, take and bring forth *the tokens of* the damsel's virginity unto the elders of the city in the gate: 16 And the damsel's father shall say unto the elders, I gave my daughter unto this man to wife, and he hateth her; 17 And, lo, he hath given occasions of speech *against her*, saying, I found not thy daughter a maid; and yet these *are the tokens of* my daughter's virginity. And they shall spread the cloth before the elders of the city. 18 And the elders of that city shall take that man and chastise him; 19 And they shall amerce him in an hundred *shekels* of silver, and give *them* unto the father of the damsel, because he hath brought up an evil name upon a virgin of Israel: and she shall be his wife; he may not put her away all his days. 20 But if this thing be true, *and the tokens of* virginity be not found for the damsel: 21 Then they shall bring out the damsel to the door of her father's house, and the men of her city shall stone her with stones that she die: because she hath wrought folly in Israel, to play the whore in her father's house: so shalt thou put evil away from among you.

[9] Lev. 19:29 Do not prostitute thy daughter, to cause her to be a whore; lest the land fall to whoredom, and the land become full of wickedness.

[10] Exod. 20:14 **Thou shalt not commit adultery**.... 17 Thou shalt not covet thy neighbour's house, **thou shalt not covet thy neighbour's wife**, nor his manservant, nor his maidservant, nor his ox, nor his ass, nor any thing that *is* thy neighbour's.
Deut. 5:18 **Neither shalt thou commit adultery**.... 21a **Neither shalt thou desire thy neighbour's wife**....

[11] Deut. 22:22 If a man be found lying with a woman married to an husband, then they shall both of them die, *both* the man that lay with the woman, and the woman: so shalt thou put away evil from Israel.

[12] Rom. 13:9 For this, **Thou shalt not commit adultery**, Thou shalt not kill, Thou shalt not steal, Thou shalt not bear false witness, Thou shalt not covet; and if *there be* any other commandment, it is briefly comprehended in this saying, namely, Thou shalt love thy neighbour as thyself. 10 Love worketh no ill to his neighbor: therefore love *is* the fulfilling of the law.

There are many other passages in the Bible about adultery. In the book of Job it is called "an heinous crime" and a fire that consumes to destruction and roots out all of a man's increase.[14] In the book of Malachi, God says He has been a witness between the man and his wife against whom he has dealt treacherously (unfaithfully). God does not regard that man's crying out to Him, nor does He receive his offering with good will. God says He will be a swift witness against adulterers.[15] In the New Testament, Paul says that the name of God is blasphemed among the Gentiles through those who boast of the law, yet dishonor God by breaking the law, such as in committing adultery.[16]

The Bible gives the example of adultery between King David and Bathsheba. It records how King David fell into adultery, how he was confronted with his sin, his repentance, and the tragic consequences of his sin. First of all, he was in the wrong place at the wrong time. It was the time for kings to go forth to battle, but David sent his men to the battle while he himself stayed in Jerusalem. While he was there, he got out of bed one evening and was walking upon the roof of his house. From there he saw a beautiful woman bathing. He found out she was already married, but he sent for her and committed adultery with her. She became pregnant and sent word to King David.[17] In order to cover up his sin, David tried to get Bathsheba's husband Uriah home from battle to be with her so it would look like she had gotten pregnant by her husband. However, Uriah would not go down to his house while his fellow soldiers were still on the battlefield.[18]

---

[13] Heb. 13:4 Marriage *is* honourable in all, and the bed undefiled: but **whoremongers and adulterers God will judge**.

[14] Job 31:9 If mine heart have been deceived by a woman, or *if* I have laid wait at my neighbour's door; 10 *Then* let my wife grind unto another, and let others bow down upon her. 11 For this *is* **an heinous crime**; yea, it *is* an iniquity *to be punished by* the judges. 12 For it *is* **a fire *that* consumeth to destruction**, and would root out all mine increase.

[15] Mal. 2:13 And this have ye done again, covering the altar of the LORD with tears, with weeping, and with crying out, insomuch that he regardeth not the offering any more, or receiveth *it* with good will at your hand. 14 Yet ye say, Wherefore? **Because the LORD hath been witness between thee and the wife of thy youth, against whom thou hast dealt treacherously**: yet *is* she thy companion, and the wife of thy covenant. 15 And did not he make one? Yet had he the residue of the spirit. And wherefore one? That he might seek a godly seed. Therefore take heed to your spirit, and **let none deal treacherously against the wife of his youth**. 16 For the LORD, the God of Israel, saith that he hateth putting away: for *one* covereth violence with his garment, saith the LORD of hosts: therefore take heed to your spirit, that ye **deal not treacherously**.
Mal. 3:5 And I will come near to you to judgment; and I will be a swift witness against the sorcerers, and **against the adulterers**, and against false swearers, and against those that oppress the hireling in *his* wages, the widow, and the fatherless, and that turn aside the stranger *from his right*, and fear not me, saith the LORD of hosts.

[16] Rom. 2:22 **Thou that sayest a man should not commit adultery, dost thou commit adultery?** thou that abhorrest idols, dost thou commit sacrilege? 23 Thou that makest thy boast of the law, through breaking the law dishonourest thou God? 24 For the name of God is blasphemed among the Gentiles through you, as it is written.

[17] 2 Sam. 11:1 And it came to pass, after the year was expired, at the time when kings go forth *to battle*, that David sent Joab, and his servants with him, and all Israel; and they destroyed the children of Ammon, and besieged Rabbah. **But David tarried still at Jerusalem.** 2 And it came to pass in an eveningtide, that David arose from off his bed, and walked upon the roof of the king's house: and from the roof **he saw a woman washing herself**; and **the woman *was* very beautiful to look upon**. 3 And David sent and enquired after the woman. And *one* said, *Is* not this Bathsheba, the daughter of Eliam, the wife of Uriah the Hittite? 4 And **David** sent messengers, and **took her**; and she came in unto him, **and he lay with her**; for she was purified from her uncleanness: and she returned unto her house. 5 And **the woman conceived**, and sent and told David, and said, I *am* with child.

[18] 2 Sam. 11:6 And David sent to Joab, *saying*, **Send me Uriah the Hittite**. And Joab sent Uriah to David. 7 And when Uriah was come unto him, David demanded *of him* how Joab did, and how the people did, and how the war prospered. 8 And David said to Uriah, **Go down to thy house**, and wash thy feet. And Uriah departed out of the king's house, and there followed him a mess *of meat* from the king. 9 But **Uriah slept at the door of the king's house** with all the servants of his lord, **and went not down to his house**. 10 And when they had told David, saying, Uriah went not down unto his house, David said unto Uriah, Camest thou not from *thy* journey? why *then* didst thou not go down unto thine house? 11 And Uriah said unto David, The ark,

When David's cover-up plan did not work, he arranged to have Uriah killed in battle. Then David took Bathsheba to be his wife. What David did displeased the Lord.[19]

God sent the prophet Nathan to confront David with his sin and to tell him the consequences. The sword would not depart from David's house, and someone out of his own house would have sexual intercourse with David's wives in public. David was quick to admit his sin and was forgiven. (His prayer is recorded in Psalm 51.) His life was spared, but the child to be born would die.[20]

The consequences spoken by Nathan came to pass. First, David's child by Bathsheba became sick and died. (However, God gave them another child, Solomon.)[21] Later David and his household fled from Jerusalem, but left ten concubines to keep the house. Absalom, his son who had risen up against him, spread a tent upon the top of the house and went in unto his father's concubines in the sight of all Israel.[22]

---

and Israel, and Judah, abide in tents; and my lord Joab, and the servants of my lord, are encamped in the open fields; **shall I then go into mine house, to eat and to drink, and to lie with my wife?** *as* thou livest, and *as* thy soul liveth, **I will not do this thing.** 12 And David said to Uriah, Tarry here to day also, and to morrow I will let thee depart. So Uriah abode in Jerusalem that day, and the morrow. 13 And when **David** had called him, he did eat and drink before him; and he **made him drunk**: and at even **he went out to lie on his bed with the servants of his lord, but went not down to his house.**

[19] 2 Sam. 11:14 And it came to pass in the morning, that **David wrote a letter to Joab, and sent** *it* **by the hand of Uriah.** 15 And he wrote in the letter, saying, **Set ye Uriah in the forefront of the hottest battle**, and retire ye from him, **that he may be smitten, and die.** 16 And it came to pass, when Joab observed the city, that he assigned Uriah unto a place where he knew that valiant men *were*. 17 And the men of the city went out, and fought with Joab: and there fell *some* of the people of the servants of David; and **Uriah the Hittite died** also. 18 Then Joab sent and told David all the things concerning the war;... 26 And when the wife of Uriah heard that Uriah her husband was dead, she mourned for her husband. 27 And when the mourning was past, **David sent and fetched her to his house, and she became his wife, and bare him a son. But the thing that David had done displeased the LORD.**

[20] 2 Sam. 12:1a And the **LORD sent Nathan unto David.** And he came unto him, and said unto him.... 9 Wherefore hast thou despised the commandment of the LORD, to do evil in his sight? **thou hast killed Uriah** the Hittite with the sword, **and hast taken his wife** *to be* thy wife, and hast slain him with the sword of the children of Ammon. 10 Now **therefore the sword shall never depart from thine house**; because thou hast despised me, and hast taken the wife of Uriah the Hittite to be thy wife. 11 Thus saith the LORD, Behold, I will **raise up evil against thee out of thine own house**, and I will take thy wives before thine eyes, and give *them* unto thy neighbour, and **he shall lie with thy wives in the sight of this sun.** 12 For thou didst *it* secretly: but I will do this thing before all Israel, and before the sun. 13 And David said unto Nathan, **I have sinned against the LORD.** And Nathan said unto David, **The LORD also hath put away thy sin; thou shalt not die.** 14 Howbeit, because by this deed thou hast given great occasion to the enemies of the LORD to blaspheme, **the child also** *that is* **born unto thee shall surely die.**

[21] 2 Sam. 12:15 And Nathan departed unto his house. And the LORD struck the child that Uriah's wife bare unto David, and it was very sick.... 18a And it came to pass on the seventh day, that the child died.... 24 And David comforted Bathsheba his wife, and went in unto her, and lay with her: and she bare a son, and he called his name Solomon: and the LORD loved him. 25 And he sent by the hand of Nathan the prophet; and he called his name Jedidiah, because of the LORD.

[22] 2 Sam. 15:16 And the king went forth, and all his household after him. And the king left ten women, *which were* concubines, to keep the house.
2 Sam. 16:21 And Ahithophel said unto Absalom, Go in unto thy father's concubines, which he hath left to keep the house; and all Israel shall hear that thou art abhorred of thy father: then shall the hands of all that *are* with thee be strong. 22 So they spread Absalom a tent upon the top of the house; and Absalom went in unto his father's concubines in the sight of all Israel.
2 Sam. 20:3 And David came to his house at Jerusalem; and the king took the ten women *his* concubines, whom he had left to keep the house, and put them in ward, and fed them, but went not in unto them. So they were shut up unto the day of their death, living in widowhood.

The Bible gives many warnings about the adulterer and the adulteress (including several found in Proverbs).[23] It says that to keep from being seduced, we must give attention to God's commandments and exercise godly wisdom. Adultery, as any other sin, is not a sudden act. It starts as a thought in the mind that comes from the devil through the world around us.[24] It is important to get rid of evil thoughts and not meditate on them.[25] If they are meditated on long enough, they get down into the heart. Jesus said that sin comes out of the heart.[26]

Pornography is a sure way to let sin into the heart. Lustful romance novels and soap operas also have destructive effects. These are designed by the devil to ensnare and addict.[27] Evil lust is never satisfied; there will always be a desire for more. If you continually seek to fulfill lust, you will be carried deeper and deeper into sin. The more you submit to a spirit of lust, the greater the hold it has on you, and the more you will be enslaved to it. You must resist it before it takes you down the pathway to death. There is a way to escape these temptations: keep your eyes from evil.[28]

Jesus said that whoever looks on a woman with the purpose of lusting after her has already committed adultery with her in his heart. He said if something is offending you (causing you to sin), cut it off and cast it from you. It is better to do without it than to be cast into hell because of it.[29] Things that offend (or cause to sin) that we should cut out of our lives today include certain magazines, books, movies, and TV programs. It is extremely important to guard your heart.[30] If you let evil into your mind and heart, it will grow and bring

---

[23] Job 24:15 The eye also of the **adulterer** waiteth for the twilight, saying, No eye shall see me: and disguiseth *his* face. 16 In the dark they dig through houses, *which* they had marked for themselves in the daytime: they know not the light. 17 For the morning *is* to them even as the shadow of death: if *one* know *them, they are in* the terrors of the shadow of death.
Eccl. 7:26 And I find more bitter than death the **woman, whose heart *is* snares and nets,** *and* her hands *as* bands: whoso pleaseth God shall escape from her; but the sinner shall be taken by her.
Prov. 2:10-11, 16-19; 5 (whole chapter); 6:23-35; 7 (whole chapter); 9:13-18; 22:14; 23:27-28; 31:3.

[24] James 4:4 Ye **adulterers and adulteresses**, know ye not that the **friendship of the world is enmity with God?** whosoever therefore will be a **friend of the world is the enemy of God.**

[25] 2 Cor. 10:3 For though we walk in the flesh, we do not war after the flesh: 4 (For the weapons of our warfare *are* not carnal, but mighty through God to the pulling down of strong holds;) 5 **Casting down imaginations**, and every high thing that exalteth itself against the knowledge of God, and **bringing into captivity every thought to the obedience of Christ;**

[26] Mark 7:20 And he said, That which cometh out of the man, that defileth the man. 21 For from within, **out of the heart** of men, **proceed** evil thoughts, **adulteries, fornications,** murders, 22 Thefts, covetousness, wickedness, deceit, lasciviousness, an evil eye, blasphemy, pride, foolishness: 23 All **these evil things come from within,** and defile the man.
Matt. 15:18 But those things which proceed out of the mouth **come forth from the heart**; and they defile the man. 19 **For out of the heart proceed** evil thoughts, murders, **adulteries, fornications,** thefts, false witness, blasphemies: 20 These are *the things* which defile a man: but to eat with unwashen hands defileth not a man.

[27] 2 Pet. 2:14 Having **eyes full of adultery,** and **that cannot cease from sin**; beguiling unstable souls: an heart they have exercised with covetous practices; cursed children:

[28] Job 31:1 I **made a covenant with mine eyes**; why then should I think upon a maid?

[29] Matt. 5:27 Ye have heard that **it was said** by them of old time, **Thou shalt not commit adultery:** 28 **But I say** unto you, That **whosoever looketh on a woman to lust after her hath committed adultery with her already in his heart.** 29 And if thy right eye offend thee, pluck it out, and cast *it* from thee: for it is profitable for thee that one of thy members should perish, and not *that* thy whole body should be cast into hell. 30 And if thy right hand offend thee, cut it off, and cast *it* from thee: for it is profitable for thee that one of thy members should perish, and not *that* thy whole body should be cast into hell.

[30] Prov. 4:23 Keep thy heart with all diligence; for out of it *are* the issues of life.

forth evil in your words and actions. If you allow only good in, then good is what will come forth from your heart. The example you set in your household is the example you are setting for your children.[31]

Fornication and adultery are sins against a person's own body. Those who are involved in these sins shall not inherit the kingdom of God. However, there is forgiveness and cleansing in Jesus for those who will turn to Him and turn away from the sin. When you become a Christian, your body becomes a member of Christ and the temple of the Holy Spirit. You should not take the members of Christ and join them to a harlot, which defiles the temple of the Holy Spirit. You are not your own; you are bought with a price, the precious blood of Jesus. Therefore, you must glorify God in your body and in your spirit, which are God's.[32] It is God's will for His people to know how to possess their bodies in holiness and honor to Him.[33]

If you have been involved in fornication or adultery, whether it was because of ignorance of God's Word or because of willful disobedience, it is time to repent. God calls to the backsliders to return to Him, and He will heal their backslidings.[34] When you have sinned, do not run from God, but run **to** Him.

The New Testament shows the mercy, love, and forgiveness of Jesus in dealing with those involved in adultery. One example is of the woman Jesus met at the well in Samaria. The woman came to draw water, and Jesus started a conversation with her. He offered her eternal life. He already knew that she had had five husbands and was living in an adulterous relationship. Yet he ministered to her in such a way that she was eager to tell others about Him. Through her witness, many came to believe on Him.[35] Another

---

[31] Psalm 101:2 I will behave myself wisely in a perfect way. O when wilt thou come unto me? **I will walk within my house with a perfect heart.** 3 **I will set no wicked thing before mine eyes**: I hate the work of them that turn aside; *it* shall not cleave to me.

[32] Eph. 5:3 But fornication, and all uncleanness, or covetousness, let it not be once named among you, as becometh saints;... 5 For this ye know, that no whoremonger, nor unclean person, nor covetous man, who is an idolater, hath any inheritance in the kingdom of Christ and of God.
1 Cor. 6:9 Know ye not that the **unrighteous shall not inherit the kingdom of God**? Be not deceived: neither **fornicators**, nor idolaters, nor **adulterers**, nor effeminate, nor abusers of themselves with mankind, 10 Nor thieves, nor covetous, nor drunkards, nor revilers, nor extortioners, shall inherit the kingdom of God. 11 And such were some of you: but ye are washed, but ye are sanctified, but ye are justified in the name of the Lord Jesus, and by the Spirit of our God.... 13b ... Now the **body** *is* **not for fornication, but for the Lord**; and the Lord for the body. 14 And God hath both raised up the Lord, and will also raise up us by his own power. 15 Know ye not that **your bodies are the members of Christ**? shall I then take the members of Christ, and make *them* the members of an harlot? God forbid. 16 What? know ye not that he which is joined to an harlot is one body? for two, saith he, shall be one flesh. 17 But he that is joined unto the Lord is one spirit. 18 **Flee fornication**. Every sin that a man doeth is without the body; but **he that committeth fornication sinneth against his own body**. 19 What? know ye not that **your body is the temple of the Holy Ghost** *which is* in you, which ye have of God, and ye are not your own? 20 For ye are bought with a price: therefore **glorify God in your body, and in your spirit, which are God's**.

[33] 1 Thess. 4:3 For this is the will of God, *even* your sanctification, that ye should abstain from fornication: 4 That every one of you should know how to possess his vessel in sanctification and honour;

[34] Jer. 3:1 They say, If a man put away his wife, and she go from him, and become another man's, shall he return unto her again? shall not that land be greatly polluted? but thou hast played the harlot with many lovers; yet return again to me, saith the LORD. 20 Surely *as* a wife treacherously departeth from her husband, so have ye dealt treacherously with me, O house of Israel, saith the LORD. 21 A voice was heard upon the high places, weeping *and* supplications of the children of Israel: for they have perverted their way, *and* they have forgotten the LORD their God. 22 **Return, ye backsliding children**, *and* **I will heal your backslidings**. Behold, we come unto thee; for thou *art* the LORD our God.

[35] John 4:14 But whosoever drinketh of the water that I shall give him shall never thirst; but the water that I shall give him shall be in him a well of water springing up into everlasting life.... 16 Jesus saith unto her, Go, call thy husband, and come hither. 17 The woman answered and said, I have no husband. Jesus said unto her, Thou hast well said, I have no husband: 18 For thou hast had five husbands; and **he whom thou now hast is not thy husband**: in that saidst thou truly. 19 The woman saith unto him,

example is that of the woman who was caught in the act of adultery. She was brought to Jesus to see what He would say about it. Jesus did not condemn her, but told her to stop sinning.[36]

God stands ready to forgive you and to cleanse you when you come to Him in repentance.[37] You, too, must forgive yourself and whoever else was involved. You can walk free of condemnation![38]

What if your spouse has committed adultery? Then you must forgive your spouse and anyone else involved. If you feel responsible in some way, then you must forgive yourself. You cannot afford to let hurt, unforgiveness, and bitterness ruin your life. It will follow you and bind you up if you are unwilling to forgive. Forgiveness will release both you and those involved in the adultery, and it will give God access to bring healing and restoration to your marriage. (See Chapter 22 for more on forgiveness.)

You must realize that the sin of adultery is a sin **against God**; He is the one who gave the law against adultery. Breaking His law is a sin against Him. I found three examples in Scripture that confirm this. One example was when King Abimelech had taken Sarah because he was told that she was Abraham's sister. After Abimelech had taken her, he had not come near her. When God confronted him about taking another man's wife, God said to him, "I also withheld you from sinning **against Me**."[39] The second example came from Joseph's experience in Potiphar's house. Potiphar's wife tried to get Joseph to commit adultery with her, but he refused and said, "How then can I do this great wickedness, and **sin against God**?"[40] The third

---

Sir, I perceive that thou art a prophet.... 28 The woman then left her waterpot, and went her way into the city, and saith to the men, 29 **Come, see a man**, which told me all things that ever I did: **is not this the Christ**? 30 Then they went out of the city, and came unto him.... 39 And **many of the Samaritans of that city believed on him for the saying of the woman, which testified**, He told me all that ever I did.

[36] John 8:3 And the scribes and Pharisees brought unto him a **woman taken in adultery**; and when they had set her in the midst, 4 They say unto him, Master, this woman was taken in adultery, in the very act. 5 Now Moses in the law commanded us, that **such should be stoned**: but what sayest thou? 6 This they said, tempting him, that they might have to accuse him. But Jesus stooped down, and with *his* finger wrote on the ground, *as though he heard them not.* 7 So when they continued asking him, he lifted up himself, and said unto them, He that is without sin among you, let him first cast a stone at her. 8 And again he stooped down, and wrote on the ground. 9 And they which heard *it*, being convicted by *their own* conscience, went out one by one, beginning at the eldest, *even* unto the last: and Jesus was left alone, and the woman standing in the midst. 10 When Jesus had lifted up himself, and saw none but the woman, he said unto her, Woman, where are those thine accusers? hath no man condemned thee? 11 She said, No man, Lord. **And Jesus said unto her, Neither do I condemn thee: go, and sin no more.**

[37] 1John 1:9 If we confess our sins, he is faithful and just to forgive us *our* sins, and to cleanse us from all unrighteousness.

[38] Rom. 8:1 *There is* therefore now no condemnation to them which are in Christ Jesus, who walk not after the flesh, but after the Spirit. 2 For the law of the Spirit of life in Christ Jesus hath made me free from the law of sin and death.

[39] Gen. 20:1 And Abraham journeyed from thence toward the south country, and dwelled between Kadesh and Shur, and sojourned in Gerar. 2 And Abraham said of Sarah his wife, She *is* my sister: and **Abimelech king of Gerar sent, and took Sarah.** 3 But **God** came to Abimelech in a dream by night, and **said** to him, Behold, **thou *art but* a dead man, for the woman which thou hast taken; for she *is* a man's wife.** 4 But Abimelech had not come near her: and he said, Lord, wilt thou slay also a righteous nation? 5 Said he not unto me, She *is* my sister? and she, even she herself said, He *is* my brother: in the integrity of my heart and innocency of my hands have I done this. 6 And **God said** unto him in a dream, Yea, I know that thou didst this in the integrity of thy heart; for **I also withheld thee from sinning against me**: therefore suffered I thee not to touch her. 7 Now therefore **restore the man *his* wife**; for he *is* a prophet, and **he shall pray for thee, and thou shalt live**: and **if thou restore *her* not, know thou that thou shalt surely die**, thou, and all that *are* thine.

[40] Gen. 39:7 And it came to pass after these things, that his master's wife cast her eyes upon Joseph; and she said, Lie with me. 8 But he refused, and said unto his master's wife, Behold, my master wotteth not what *is* with me in the house, and he has committed all that he hath to my hand; 9 *There is* none greater in this house than I; neither hath he kept back any thing from me but thee, because thou *art* his wife: how then can I do this great wickedness, and **sin against God**?

example was after David had been confronted about his adultery with Bathsheba. He said it was **against God** that he had sinned.[41]

Maybe you consider adultery committed by your spouse to be a sin against you because your spouse was unfaithful to your marriage covenant. In that situation, your spouse did break commitment to you. However, there is no benefit to you to take the offense unto yourself. Consider Moses' response when the children of Israel murmured against him.[42] He counted their murmurings as being **against the Lord**, not against him and Aaron.[43] Also, consider that when the elders of Israel came to Samuel to ask for a king, that displeased him. But God said that it was not Samuel that the people had rejected; **they had rejected God** from reigning over them.[44] It is to our advantage to roll offenses over on the Lord, and let Him handle them, rather than let them ruin our lives.

As I meditated on this, I began to realize the freedom that gives us. Since adultery (as well as all other sin) is a sin against God, then we do not have to be offended every time someone does wrong. We never have to take it personally because it is God that they sinned against, not us. We were not the ones who made the rules in the first place. We really have no right to be offended and no right to retaliate. It is between the sinner and God. We should forgive and intercede for the sinner, but we should not take the offense onto ourselves. The Bible says not to avenge ourselves; God will repay.[45] Let us leave it up to Him.

---

[41] 2 Sam. 12:13a And David said unto Nathan, **I have sinned against the LORD**....
Psalm 51: 4 **Against thee, thee only, have I sinned**, and done *this* evil in thy sight: that thou mightest be justified when thou speakest, *and* be clear when thou judgest.

[42] Exod. 16:2 And the whole congregation of the children of Israel murmured against Moses and Aaron in the wilderness:

[43] Exod. 16:7 And in the morning, then ye shall see the glory of the LORD; for that he heareth your murmurings against the LORD: and what *are* we, that ye murmur against us? 8 And Moses said, *This shall be,* when the LORD shall give you in the evening flesh to eat, and in the morning bread to the full; for that the LORD heareth your murmurings which ye murmur against him: and what *are* we? **your murmurings *are* not against us, but against the LORD**.

[44] 1 Sam. 8:6 But the thing displeased Samuel, when they said, Give us a king to judge us. And Samuel prayed unto the LORD. 7 And the **LORD said** unto Samuel, Hearken unto the voice of the people in all that they say unto thee: for **they have not rejected thee, but they have rejected me**, that I should not reign over them.

[45] Rom. 12:19 Dearly beloved, avenge not yourselves, but *rather* give place unto wrath: for it is written, Vengeance *is* mine; I will repay, saith the Lord.
Heb. 10:30 For we know him that hath said, Vengeance *belongeth* unto me, I will recompense, saith the Lord. And again, The Lord shall judge his people.

Part Three

Relationships with Generations

Chapter 6

Influence of Traditions and Patterns

One generation passes on and another comes,[1] but God's kingdom endures throughout all generations.[2] I believe God desires that we would have a broader view than just of our own generation or just of the generations living on the earth during our lifetime here. We should consider those who went before us. Some contributed to the problems that are in the world today; some contributed to the benefits we enjoy today. We should also consider future generations and how what we do and say will affect them. What are we passing on to them?

The Bible says that children are like arrows in the hand of a mighty man.[3] They will go forth to places their parents will not go; they will reach into future generations beyond their parents. What are we, as parents, depositing in our children that they will take beyond us? How will they influence those lives they touch in this generation and in future generations?

God is the God of all generations. His family includes people of all times. His covenant with His people continues beyond their death and unto future generations.[4] God made promises to His people that would take generations to fulfill. These people stood in faith knowing that they would not be on the earth to see the fulfillment, but trusting God to keep His Word and bring it to pass in future generations.[5] These who have gone on before are like a great cloud of witnesses surrounding us. They are like our cheerleaders encouraging us on in the race set before us.[6] They know the victory is ours!

Many times patterns set by a generation are followed in future generations. This can be good or bad depending on the patterns set and the usefulness of them to future generations.

The New Testament gives an example of good patterns set in the life of Timothy, who was a pastor and worker with the apostle Paul. His grandmother and mother were full of faith, and so was he.[7] From a child he had known the Scriptures.[8]

---

[1] Eccl. 1:4 *One* generation passeth away, and *another* generation cometh: but the earth abideth for ever.

[2] Psalm 145:13 Thy kingdom *is* an everlasting kingdom, and thy dominion *endureth* **throughout all generations.**

[3] Psalm 127:4 As arrows *are* in the hand of a mighty man; so *are* children of the youth.

[4] Deut. 7:9 Know therefore that the LORD thy God, he *is* God, the faithful God, which **keepeth covenant** and mercy with them that love him and keep his commandments to a **thousand generations;**

[5] Heb. 11:13 These all died in faith, **not having received the promises, but having seen them afar off**, and were persuaded of *them*, and embraced *them*, and confessed that they were strangers and pilgrims on the earth.

[6] Heb. 12:1 Wherefore seeing we also are compassed about with so great a **cloud of witnesses**, let us lay aside every weight, and the sin which doth so easily beset *us*, and let us run with patience the race that is set before us,

[7] 2 Tim. 1:2 To Timothy, *my* dearly beloved son: Grace, mercy, *and* peace, from God the Father and Christ Jesus our Lord.... 5 When I call to remembrance the unfeigned **faith that is in thee**, which **dwelt first in thy grandmother Lois, and thy mother Eunice;** and I am persuaded that in thee also.

My mother told me recently that her parents were always faithful to go to church meetings. She was brought up with this pattern, and she also attended church meetings regularly. Even when she had a house full of children, she was faithful to take them. I was brought up with that pattern, and our family has carried it on. This is a good pattern to set, and I pray our children will continue this throughout future generations.

If you are carrying on good traditions and patterns set by past generations, then keep them up. Do not try to change what is already right.[9] Just make sure that the patterns you set are good for this generation and for future generations. Seek the Lord to find out what He would have you to do.

On the other hand, many traditions and patterns should not be continued. Some traditions were set because of certain practices done long ago that are no longer done today. Some things were done a certain way because of what was available at the time, but are done differently today because different things are available. Worst of all is that many traditions have ungodly roots. People may continue the tradition without knowing what started it.

Here is an example of a pattern set because of a practice that was done long ago. I remember, as a child, I used to wonder why women sat on one side of our church building, and men sat on the other side. (There was also a middle section where men and women sat together.) It was years after I had left my childhood home before I found out the reason for the separate seating of men and women. I was reading that in early days in some church gatherings they had "foot-washings." The men washed the men's feet, and the women washed the women's feet. Of all the 18 years I had been a part of this particular church, I never saw or heard of a foot-washing service there, but the tradition of men and women sitting on opposite sides of the church building was still being carried on.

Another example is of habits established because of what was available at the time. Before I had an automatic clothes dryer, I used to put fabric softener in a tray in the clothes washer. The tray had to be removed to put in or take out the clothes. After I got a clothes dryer, I used fabric softener sheets in the dryer. I no longer used the fabric softener tray in the washer; however, I continued to take the tray in and out as I put in or took clothes out of the washer. I do not know how long I had been doing this before I realized it would be much more efficient to just take out the tray and leave it out. I felt rather foolish. How foolish we sometimes are to carry on with things that are no longer useful and serve only to complicate our lives.

An example of a tradition with ungodly roots is the celebration of Halloween. Many people, even Christians, continue to celebrate Halloween without realizing that it is a satanic holiday. There are actually real witches and other Satan worshippers who gather to celebrate on October 31. If people realized the roots of Halloween, they would have no trouble understanding why so much evil goes on at this time of the year.

There are also expressions people say without realizing what they are saying. They repeat things they hear others say. One example is superstitious sayings. Another example is that is of saying "good luck." I used to say that frequently. Then I discovered that luck, as well as fate and fortune, were actually names of Greek and Roman gods and goddesses. When I was saying good luck to someone, it was like saying, "May the god of luck favor you." This was certainly not in keeping with my Christian beliefs, and I made a decision to "weed" this out of my vocabulary. It took me a while, but now it is replaced with, "God bless you," which reflects my belief in the one true God.

---

[8] 2 Tim. 3:15a ... And that from a child thou hast known the holy scriptures....

[9] Prov. 22:28 Remove not the ancient landmark, which thy fathers have set.

So we see that it is not always wise to follow a tradition just because it was passed down to us from generations before. Neither is it wise to forsake God's command of obeying Him.[10] When people forsake the Lord, their future generations may become worse than they were.[11] When both fathers and sons sin, both will fall; both will be punished.[12]

Some people may think that their traditions are all right because they are religious ones. However, there are many religious traditions that are wrong. Before the apostle Paul became a Christian, he was called Saul. He was very religious. He believed he was doing a good thing by persecuting Christians,[13] but he found out when Jesus spoke to him on the road to Damascus that he was working against God instead of for Him.

Many religious people today, even Christians, still resist the Holy Spirit[14] and disobey God, holding their traditions above the Word of God. Jesus said that traditions can make the commandment of God of no effect. He illustrated this when the religious leaders came to Him and asked why His disciples did not obey the elders' tradition of washing their hands. Jesus asked them why they disobeyed God's commandment by their tradition. The elders had set up a tradition that allowed a person to take what should have been for his parents and give it elsewhere as a gift unto God. This bypassed God's commandment to honor parents.[15]

There are religious groups today that have been around for generations, yet they are not Christian. Because they do benevolent things and give an appearance of good, many Christians have been deceived into joining them. They may talk of God and even mention Jesus, but do they line up with the Word of God?

---

[10] 2 Kings 17:13 Yet the LORD testified against Israel, and against Judah, by all the prophets, *and by* all the seers, saying, Turn ye from your evil ways, and keep my commandments *and* my statutes, according to all the **law which I commanded your fathers**, and which I sent to you by my servants the prophets. 14 Notwithstanding **they would not hear, but hardened their necks, like to the neck of their fathers**, that did not believe in the LORD their God.

[11] Jer. 7:26 Yet they hearkened not unto me, nor inclined their ear, but hardened their neck: **they did worse than their fathers**.

[12] Jer. 6:16 Thus saith the LORD, Stand ye in the ways, and see, and ask for the old paths, where *is* the good way, and walk therein, and ye shall find rest for your souls. But they said, We will not walk *therein*. 17 Also I set watchmen over you, *saying*, Hearken to the sound of the trumpet. But they said, We will not hearken.... 21 Therefore thus saith the LORD, Behold, I will lay stumblingblocks before this people, and **the fathers and the sons together shall fall** upon them; the neighbour and his friend shall perish.

[13] Gal. 1:13 For ye have heard of my conversation in time past in the Jews' **religion**, how that beyond measure **I persecuted the church of God**, and wasted it: 14 And profited in the Jews' religion above many my equals in mine own nation, **being more exceedingly zealous of the traditions of my fathers**.

[14] Acts 7:51 Ye stiffnecked and uncircumcised in heart and ears, ye do always resist the Holy Ghost: **as your fathers *did*, so *do* ye**.

[15] Matt. 15:1 Then came to Jesus scribes and Pharisees, which were of Jerusalem, saying, 2 Why do thy disciples transgress the **tradition of the elders**? for they wash not their hands when they eat bread. 3 But he answered and said unto them, Why do ye also **transgress the commandment of God by your tradition**? 4 For God commanded, saying, Honour thy father and mother: and, He that curseth father or mother, let him die the death. 5 But ye say, Whosoever shall say to *his* father or *his* mother, *It is* a gift, by whatsoever thou mightest be profited by me; 6 And honour not his father or his mother, *he shall be free*. **Thus have ye made the commandment of God of none effect by your tradition.**

Who is their "God," and who do they believe Jesus to be? If a religious group does not believe Jesus to be who the Bible says He is, you should not join with them. Christians cannot be in unity with darkness.[16]

Some religious groups are associated with the occult. The word "occult" has to do with secret, hidden, and mysterious things. Some groups require secret initiation rites and oaths to join their religious "brotherhood." Even oaths are contrary to God's Word.[17]

One of the problems with joining erroneous religious groups is that demonic activity can be released in the lives and families of those affiliated with them. This demonic activity can result in patterns of sickness, divorce, financial bondage, and other problems. Do not associate yourself with any religious group that does not believe that Jesus is the Lord and Savior and the **only** way to God the Father.[18] If you have already affiliated yourself with any of them, you must ask God's forgiveness and renounce them (give them up and refuse further association with them). If your parents or other family members have been involved in such things, you should bind any associated curses from affecting you or your descendants.[19] "Close the door" to all demonic activity that has been released in your life or family through wrong affiliations.

When God gave the Ten Commandments, He said not to make any graven images and not to bow down to them nor serve them because He is a jealous God. He said he would visit the iniquity of the fathers upon the children unto the third and fourth generation **of those that hate Him**. Yet He would show mercy unto thousands **that love Him and keep His commandments**.[20] Later, He said that fathers would not be put to death for the children, and children would not be put to death for the fathers; but every one would be put to death for his own sin.[21] We do not have to continue in the traditions and patterns of our forefathers if they are contrary to obeying God's Word. We do not have to bear the iniquity of those who came before us.[22] The cycle can be broken now. We do not have to follow the pattern of evil generations. We have been bought back by the precious blood of Jesus from the vain way of life that we received by tradition from our

---

[16] 2 Cor. 6:14 Be ye not unequally yoked together with unbelievers: for what fellowship hath righteousness with unrighteousness? and what communion hath light with darkness? 15 And what concord hath Christ with Belial? or what part hath he that believeth with an infidel? 16 And what agreement hath the temple of God with idols? for ye are the temple of the living God; as God hath said, I will dwell in them, and walk in *them*; and I will be their God, and they shall be my people. 17 Wherefore come out from among them, and be ye separate, saith the Lord, and touch not the unclean *thing*; and I will receive you, 18 And will be a Father unto you, and ye shall be my sons and daughters, saith the Lord Almighty.

[17] James 5:12 But above all things, my brethren, swear not, neither by heaven, neither by the earth, neither by any other oath: but let your yea be yea; and *your* nay, nay; lest ye fall into condemnation.

[18] John 14:6 Jesus saith unto him, I am the way, the truth, and the life: no man cometh unto the Father, but by me.

[19] Matt. 16:19 And I will give unto thee the keys of the kingdom of heaven: and whatsoever thou shalt bind on earth shall be bound in heaven: and whatsoever thou shalt loose on earth shall be loosed in heaven.

[20] Exod. 20:4 Thou shalt not make unto thee any graven image, or any likeness *of any thing* that *is* in heaven above, or that *is* in the earth beneath, or that *is* in the water under the earth: 5 Thou shalt not bow down thyself to them, nor serve them: for I the LORD thy God *am* a jealous God, visiting the **iniquity of the fathers upon the children** unto the third and fourth *generation* **of them that hate me**; 6 And shewing **mercy unto thousands of them that love me**, and keep my commandments.

[21] Deut. 24:16 The fathers shall not be put to death for the children, neither shall the children be put to death for the fathers: every man shall be put to death for his own sin.

[22] Ezek. 18:20 The soul that sinneth, it shall die. The son shall not bear the iniquity of the father, neither shall the father bear the iniquity of the son: the righteousness of the righteous shall be upon him, and the wickedness of the wicked shall be upon him.

fathers.[23] Now is the time to lay the axe to the root and cut off all traditions and other things passed down from former generations that do not bring forth good fruit.[24]

God sometimes calls people to leave the land of their fathers or to leave the ways of their fathers. He called Abraham to leave his homeland and his kin.[25] Gideon was told to tear down his father's altar to Baal, to build an altar to God, and to sacrifice his father's bullock on it.[26] When God is displeased with your fathers, do not be like them. If you will turn to Him, He will turn to you, no matter what your fathers did before you.[27] Josiah, the son of an evil king, is a good example of this. He turned to the Lord and began repairing the house of the Lord after he became king. In the process, the book of the law was found. He realized when the Word was read, that his fathers had not obeyed it. He sought the Lord concerning this and was spared of the destruction to come because he had humbled himself before the Lord.[28]

Do not connect yourself with anything that is ungodly and bound for judgment, or you could be included in that judgment. Come out from among them.[29] You do not have to become a slave to man-made traditions. Jesus can set you free from this bondage. When Jesus makes you free, you are free indeed![30]

---

[23] 1 Pet. 1:18 Forasmuch as ye know that ye were not **redeemed** with corruptible things, *as* silver and gold, **from your vain conversation** *received* **by tradition from your fathers**; 19 But with the precious blood of Christ, as of a lamb without blemish and without spot:

[24] Luke 3:9 And now also the **axe is laid unto the root** of the trees: every tree therefore which bringeth not forth good fruit is hewn down, and cast into the fire.

[25] Gen. 12:1 Now the LORD had said unto **Abram, Get thee out of thy country**, and **from thy kindred**, and **from thy father's house**, unto a land that I will shew thee: 2 And I will make of thee a great nation, and I will bless thee, and make thy name great; and thou shalt be a blessing: 3 And I will bless them that bless thee, and curse him that curseth thee: and **in thee shall all families of the earth be blessed**.

[26] Judges 6:25 And it came to pass the same night, that the **LORD said** unto him, **Take thy father's young bullock**, even the second bullock of seven years old, and **throw down the altar of Baal that thy father hath**, and cut down the grove that *is* by it: 26 And **build an altar unto the LORD thy God** upon the top of this rock, in the ordered place, and **take the second bullock, and offer a burnt sacrifice** with the wood of the grove which thou shalt cut down.

[27] Zech. 1:2 **The LORD hath been sore displeased with your fathers**. 3 Therefore say thou unto them, Thus saith the LORD of hosts; **Turn ye unto me**, saith the LORD of hosts, **and I will turn unto you**, saith the LORD of hosts. 4 **Be ye not as your fathers**, unto whom the former prophets have cried, saying, Thus saith the LORD of hosts; Turn ye now from your evil ways, and *from* your evil doings: but they did not hear, nor hearken unto me, saith the LORD.

[28] 2 Kings 22:13 Go ye, **inquire of the LORD for me**, and for the people, and for all Judah, **concerning the words of this book** that is found: for great *is* the wrath of the LORD that is kindled against us, because **our fathers have not hearkened unto the words of this book**, to do according unto all that which is written concerning us.... 18 But to the king of Judah which sent you to enquire of the LORD, thus shall ye say to him, Thus saith the LORD God of Israel, *As touching* the words which thou hast heard; 19 **Because thine heart was tender, and thou hast humbled thyself before the LORD**, when thou heardest what I spake against this place, and against the inhabitants thereof, that they should become a desolation and a curse, and hast rent thy clothes, and wept before me; I also have heard *thee*, saith the LORD. 20 Behold therefore, I will gather thee unto thy fathers, and **thou shalt be gathered into thy grave in peace**; and thine eyes shall not see all the evil which I will bring upon this place. And they brought the king word again.

[29] Rev. 18:4 And I heard another voice from heaven, saying, Come out of her, my people, that ye be not partakers of her sins, and that ye receive not of her plagues.

[30] John 8:36 If the Son therefore shall make you free, ye shall be free indeed.

Chapter 7

Inheritance

This chapter will encourage us to consider what has been passed on to us by former generations and what we will pass on to future generations. We can receive an inheritance from the family in which we were born or adopted. We can receive inheritance rights as a child of God when we are born again into His family. We can receive a heritage just because of when and where we were born. I was born in the United States and have received a heritage of freedom. I had nothing to do with it; I was just born in the right place at the right time to receive the freedoms that were fought for by former generations.

We have received much from those who have gone before us and should not take it lightly. The Bible tells of Esau who took his birthright so lightly that he was willing to sell it for bread and a pot of lentils when he came in hungry from the field.[1] Another Bible character, Reuben (the son of Jacob), lost his birthright through sin.[2] On the other hand, Naboth was not willing to give up his inheritance to the evil king Ahab.[3] Neither should we allow the evil one to take our inheritance from us.

Labor of the People

When God brought the children of Israel into the Promised Land, they inherited the labor of the people.[4] The "labor of the people" included the development of the land, such as the planting of trees and the building of cities. When the Israelites came in, all this work had already been done. All they had to do was to take possession of it. God even helped them with that.

---

[1] Heb. 12:16 Lest there *be* any fornicator, or profane person, as **Esau, who for one morsel of meat sold his birthright**. (See also Gen. 25:29-34.)

[2] 1 Chron. 5:1 Now the sons of Reuben the firstborn of Israel, (for **he *was* the firstborn; but, forasmuch as he defiled his father's bed, his birthright was given unto the sons of Joseph** the son of Israel: and the genealogy is not to be reckoned after the birthright.
(See also Gen. 35:22.)

[3] 1 Kings 21:3 And Naboth said to Ahab, The LORD forbid it me, that I should give the inheritance of my fathers unto thee.

[4] Psalm 105:44 And gave them the lands of the heathen: and **they inherited the labour of the people**; 45 That they might observe his statutes, and keep his laws. Praise ye the LORD.
Deut. 6:10 And it shall be, when the LORD thy God shall have brought thee into the land which he sware unto thy fathers, to Abraham, to Isaac, and to Jacob, to give thee great and goodly cities, which thou buildedst not, 11 And houses full of all good *things*, which thou filledst not, and wells digged, which thou diggedst not, vineyards and olive trees, which thou plantedst not; when thou shalt have eaten and be full; 12 *Then* beware lest thou forget the LORD, which brought thee forth out of the land of Egypt, from the house of bondage.
Josh. 24:13 And I have given you a land **for which ye did not labour,** and cities which ye built not, and ye dwell in them; of the vineyards and oliveyards which ye planted not do ye eat.
Neh. 9:25 And they took strong cities, and a fat land, and possessed houses full of all goods, wells digged, vineyards, and oliveyards, and fruit trees in abundance: so they did eat, and were filled, and became fat, and delighted themselves in thy great goodness.

As I thought about this, I began to realize how much we have benefited from the labor of those who have gone before us. There are many inventions and conveniences that have been developed that make our lifestyles easier. When going on trips, I have thanked God for those who built the roads, railroad tracks, and other means of transportation that we are enjoying today. Even the computer and software I am using to write this book is my heritage of the "labor of the people" before me. I thought about what a task it would have been to have written this book with pencil and paper or even with a plain typewriter. We have so much today that those before us worked hard to develop. We have inherited the translations and printing of the Bible. We have books that have been authored by people who have spent time studying God's Word and seeking His revelation of it. The list could go on.

King Solomon, the king known for his wisdom, wondered who would receive his labor. Would they be wise stewards, or would they foolishly waste his work? [5] We should be wise stewards over what we have received. If we pour wisdom into our children and train them up in the Lord's way, we can help them to become wise stewards also. We can be more confident when we leave an inheritance to them, that our labor will not be in vain.

Riches

King Solomon called it "a sore evil" for owners to keep all their riches and give nothing to their children.[6] I believe this is one reason there is so much debt on people today. Young people who inherited no riches from their parents or grandparents had very little available to start their own households. They borrowed money to buy a house and spent most of their lives working off the debt. By the time their children were ready to leave home, there was nothing saved up to give them. Therefore, they began their households in debt, and the cycle repeated.

The Bible says that parents and grandparents should give an inheritance to their children and grandchildren.[7] I believe the best way to prepare to give an inheritance to your descendents is to give tithes and offerings to the Lord and to train your children to do so also. This allows God to be a partner in yours and your children's finances and gives Him a channel to bless and prosper you.[8]

---

[5] Eccl. 2:18 Yea, I hated all my labour which I had taken under the sun: because I should leave it unto the man that shall be after me. 19 And who knoweth whether he shall be a wise *man* or a fool? yet shall he have rule over all my labour wherein I have laboured, and wherein I have shewed myself wise under the sun. This *is* also vanity.

[6] Eccl. 5:13 There is **a sore evil** *which* I have seen under the sun, *namely*, **riches kept for the owners** thereof to their hurt. 14 But those riches perish by evil travail: and **he begetteth a son, and** *there is* **nothing in his hand**. 15 As he came forth of his mother's womb, naked shall he return to go as he came, and shall take nothing of his labour, which he may carry away in his hand.

[7] Prov. 19:14 **House and riches** *are* **the inheritance of fathers**: and a prudent wife *is* from the LORD.
Prov. 13:22 **A good** *man* **leaveth an inheritance to his children's children**: and the wealth of the sinner *is* laid up for the just.

[8] Mal. 3:7 Even **from the days of your fathers ye are gone away from mine ordinances**, and have not kept *them*. **Return unto me, and I will return unto you,** saith the LORD of hosts. But ye said, Wherein shall we return? 8 Will a man rob God? Yet ye have robbed me. But ye say, Wherein have we robbed thee? In **tithes and offerings**. 9 Ye *are* cursed with a curse: for ye have robbed me, *even* this whole nation. 10 **Bring ye all the tithes** into the storehouse, that there may be meat in mine house, and prove me now herewith, saith the LORD of hosts, if I will not **open you the windows of heaven, and pour you out a blessing,** that *there shall* not *be room* enough *to receive it*. 11 And **I will rebuke the devourer for your sakes**, and he shall not

Promises of God

There is more to inheritances than money and material possessions. God's promises can be an inheritance for future generations. God made promises to fathers that were inherited by their descendants. The **children** of the Israelites who came out of Egypt were the ones who got to go into the Promised Land.[9]

The "seed" was a chosen people because of an oath God had made with their fathers.[10] God called Abraham out from the land of his fathers, but it was his seed that inherited the promised land.[11] Best of all is that today we are still included in God's promise for salvation through Jesus Christ![12]

Blessings of Obedience

Now that we have seen how forefathers can affect their future generations, we should look beyond ourselves and consider what we can do for our descendants. One important thing is to set a good example. God promises many blessings to those that fear and obey Him. The blessings are also promised to their seed. Our seed can inherit the blessings of **our** obedience.

When we observe the Lord's commands and do what is right, it will go well with us and our descendants after us.[13] The Psalmist said he had never seen the righteous forsaken, nor his seed begging bread.[14] The man that fears the Lord and delights in his commandments shall have wealth and riches in his

---

destroy the fruits of your ground; neither shall your vine cast her fruit before the time in the field, saith the LORD of hosts. 12 And all nations **shall call you blessed**: for ye shall be a delightsome land, saith the LORD of hosts.

[9] Neh. 9:23 Their children also multipliedst thou as the stars of heaven, and broughtest them into the land, concerning which thou hadst promised to their fathers, that they should go in to possess *it*.

[10] Deut. 7:6 For thou *art* an holy people unto the LORD thy God: the LORD thy **God hath chosen thee to be a special people unto himself,** above all people that *are* upon the face of the earth. 7 The LORD did not set his love upon you, nor choose you, because ye were more in number than any people; for ye *were* the fewest of all people: 8 But **because the LORD loved you, and because he would keep the oath which he had sworn unto your fathers,** hath the LORD brought you out with a mighty hand, and redeemed you out of the house of bondmen, from the hand of Pharaoh king of Egypt. 9 Know therefore that the LORD thy God, he *is* God, the faithful God, which keepeth covenant and mercy with them that love him and keep his commandments to a thousand generations;
Deut. 10:15 Only the **LORD had a delight in thy fathers to love them**, and **he chose their seed after them,** *even* you above all people, as *it is* this day.

[11] Acts 7:4 Then came he out of the land of the Chaldaeans, and dwelt in Charran: and from thence, when his father was dead, he removed him into this land, wherein ye now dwell. 5 And he gave him none inheritance in it, no, not *so much as* to set his foot on: yet **he promised that he would give it to him for a possession, and to his seed after him,** when *as yet* he had no child.

[12] Acts 13:32 And we declare unto you **glad tidings**, how that **the promise which was made unto the fathers,** 33 **God hath fulfilled the same unto us their children,** in that **he hath raised up Jesus** again; as it is also written in the second psalm, Thou art my Son, this day have I begotten thee.

[13] Deut. 12:28 Observe and hear all these words which I command thee, **that it may go well with thee, and with thy children after thee for ever, when thou doest *that which is* good and right** in the sight of the LORD thy God.

[14] Psalm 37:25 I have been young, and *now* am old; yet have I **not seen the righteous forsaken, nor his seed begging bread.**

house, and his seed shall be mighty upon the earth.[15] The seed of the righteous shall be known among the people and acknowledged as the seed that the Lord has blessed.[16]

Teaching and Training

Godly teaching and training is another way to give a good inheritance to our children. What we teach them will go with them even when we are not with them ourselves.[17] It is important that we teach them about the Lord so that our generation will not pass away without their generation knowing the Lord and the works that He has done.[18]

In Psalm 78, we are told to teach our children God's law and His words. We must show to the generation to come the praises of the Lord and His strength and His wonderful works. We are to do this so that our children can pass it on to their children, and none will forget God. This is God's plan for future generations to set their hope in God and obey Him.[19]

Teaching our children to obey God's Word is not a vain thing, but it is life to them and us. Through obeying God's Word, we will prolong our days.[20] We are to make known God's truth[21] and declare His righteousness to our children.[22]

---

[15] Psalm 112:1 Praise ye the LORD. Blessed *is* the man *that* feareth the LORD, *that* delighteth greatly in his commandments. 2 His seed shall be mighty upon earth: the generation of the upright shall be blessed. 3 Wealth and riches *shall be* in his house: and his righteousness endureth for ever.

[16] Isa. 61:9 And **their seed shall be known among the Gentiles**, and their offspring among the people: all that see them shall acknowledge them, that **they** *are* **the seed** *which* **the LORD hath blessed**.

[17] Prov. 6:20 My son, keep thy **father's commandment**, and forsake not the **law of thy mother**: 21 Bind them continually upon thine heart, *and* tie them about thy neck. 22 **When thou goest, it shall lead thee; when thou sleepest, it shall keep thee; and** *when* **thou awakest, it shall talk with thee**. 23 For the commandment *is* a lamp; and the law *is* light; and reproofs of instruction *are* the way of life:

[18] Judges 2:10 And also all that generation were gathered unto their fathers: and there arose another generation after them, which knew not the LORD, nor yet the works which he had done for Israel.

[19] Psalm 78:1 Give ear, O my people, *to* my law: incline your ears to the words of my mouth. 2 I will open my mouth in a parable: I will utter dark sayings of old: 3 Which we have heard and known, and **our fathers have told us**. 4 We will **not hide them from their children**, shewing to the generation to come **the praises of the LORD, and his strength, and his wonderful works that he hath done**. 5 For he established a testimony in Jacob, and appointed a **law in Israel**, which he commanded our fathers, that they **should make them known to their children**: 6 **That the generation to come might know** *them*, *even* the children *which* should be born; *who* should arise **and declare** *them* **to their children**: 7 **That they might set their hope in God, and not forget the works of God, but keep his commandments**: 8 And might not be as their fathers, a stubborn and rebellious generation; a generation *that* set not their heart aright, and whose spirit was not stedfast with God.

[20] Deut. 32:46 And he said unto them, Set your hearts unto all the **words** which I testify among you this day, which **ye shall command your children to observe to do, all the words of this law**. 47 For it *is* not a vain thing for you; because it *is* your life: and through this thing ye shall prolong *your* days in the land, whither ye go over Jordan to possess it.

[21] Isa. 39:19 The living, the living, he shall praise thee, as I *do* this day: **the father to the children shall make known thy truth**.

[22] Psalm 22:31 They shall come, and **shall declare his righteousness unto a people that shall be born**, that he hath done *this*.

We are also to share with them our testimony of the great things the Lord has done for us.[23] In the Old Testament, the children of Israel celebrated the Passover as a means of declaring to their descendants the mighty works of the Lord in delivering them out of Egypt.[24] In the New Testament, Jesus gave His followers the memorial of the Lord's Supper as a reminder of our covenant with Him.[25]

Our sharing of God's Word and testifying of His wonderful works should last a lifetime.[26]

Prayer and Preparation

Another way to give a good inheritance to our children is to pray for their future and to prepare them to fulfill the call of God on their lives. Let us look at the example of David and Solomon. David had it in his heart to build a house for the Lord, but God said it would be his son Solomon who would build the temple.[27]

David began encouraging Solomon in the work the Lord had given him to do. He began making preparations for building the house of the Lord by gathering materials and laborers.[28] God had given David the pattern of the temple, and he gave it to Solomon.[29] David received offerings of the people for materials for the temple.[30] He prayed for his son that God would give him a perfect heart to keep His commands and

---

[23] Psalm 145:3 Great *is* the LORD, and greatly to be praised; and his greatness *is* unsearchable. 4 **One generation shall praise thy works to another, and shall declare thy mighty acts.**

[24] Exod. 12:26 And it shall come to pass, **when your children shall say unto you, What mean ye by this service?** 27 That **ye shall say,** It *is* the sacrifice of the LORD'S passover, who passed over the houses of the children of Israel in Egypt, when he smote the Egyptians, and delivered our houses. And the people bowed the head and worshipped.

[25] Luke 22:19 And he took bread, and gave thanks, and brake *it*, and gave unto them, saying, This is my body which is given for you: **this do in remembrance of me.** 20 Likewise also the cup after supper, saying, This cup *is* the new testament in my blood, which is shed for you.

[26] Psalm 71:6 By thee have I been holden up from the womb: thou art he that took me out of my mother's bowels: my praise *shall be* continually of thee.... 17 O God, thou hast taught me from my youth: and hitherto have I declared thy wondrous works. 18 Now also when I am old and grayheaded, O God, forsake me not; until I have shewed thy strength unto *this* generation, *and* thy power to every one *that* is to come.

[27] 1 Chron. 17:11 And it shall come to pass, when thy days be expired that thou must go *to be* with thy fathers, that I will raise up thy seed after thee, which shall be of thy sons; and I will establish his kingdom. 12 **He shall build me an house,** and I will stablish his throne for ever.

[28] 1 Chron. 22:5 And David said, Solomon my son *is* young and tender, and the house *that is* to be builded for the LORD must *be* exceeding magnifical, of fame and of glory throughout all countries: **I will *therefore* now make preparation for it. So David prepared abundantly before his death.** 6 Then he called for Solomon his son, and charged him to build an house for the LORD God of Israel.... 11 Now, my son, the LORD be with thee; and prosper thou, and build the house of the LORD thy God, as he hath said of thee. 12 Only **the LORD give thee wisdom and understanding**, and give thee charge concerning Israel, that thou mayest keep the law of the LORD thy God.

[29] 1 Chron. 28:11 Then David gave to Solomon his son the pattern of the porch, and of the houses thereof, and of the treasuries thereof, and of the upper chambers thereof, and of the inner parlours thereof, and of the place of the mercy seat, 12 And the pattern of all that he had **by the spirit**, of the courts of the house of the LORD, and of all the chambers round about, of the treasuries of the house of God, and of the treasuries of the dedicated things:

[30] 1 Chron. 29:1 Furthermore David the king said unto all the congregation, Solomon my son, whom alone God hath chosen, *is yet* young and tender, and the work *is* great: for the palace *is* not for man, but for the LORD God. 2 Now **I have prepared with all my might** for the house of my God the gold for *things to be made* of gold, and the silver for *things* of silver, and

to do all that he was to do, including the building of the temple.[31] After Solomon became king, he built the house of the Lord, using the things David had prepared.[32]

Spoken Blessings

The words we speak to and about our children can follow them throughout their days. We should make sure that we speak things that bless and edify them. When words of correction are needed, we should speak them in such a way that they will improve the child's behavior and his heart attitude without putting down the child. Praising our children will go a long way toward motivating them in the right direction. (See Chapter 10.)

In the Old Testament fathers and grandfathers, before their deaths, made it a point to speak a blessing over their sons and grandsons. Jacob was one of them. He called his sons together and spoke a blessing over each one of them. He did not leave the earth until he had blessed his sons.[33] He also blessed his grandsons.[34]

---

the brass for *things* of brass, the iron for *things* of iron, and wood for *things* of wood; onyx stones, and *stones* to be set, glistering stones, and of divers colours, and all manner of precious stones, and marble stones in abundance.... 9 Then the people rejoiced, for that they offered willingly, because with perfect heart they offered willingly to the LORD: and David the king also rejoiced with great joy.

[31] 1 Chron. 29:19 And give unto Solomon my son a perfect heart, to keep thy commandments, thy testimonies, and thy statutes, and to do all *these things*, and to build the palace, *for* the which I have made provision.

[32] 2 Chron. 5:1 Thus all the work that Solomon made for the house of the LORD was finished: and Solomon brought in *all* the things that David his father had dedicated; and the silver, and the gold, and all the instruments, put he among the treasures of the house of God.

[33] Gen. 49:1 And Jacob called unto his sons, and said, Gather yourselves together, that I may tell you *that* which shall befall you in the last days. 2 Gather yourselves together, and hear, ye sons of Jacob; and hearken unto Israel your father.... 28 All these *are* the twelve tribes of Israel: and this *is it* that their father spake unto them, and blessed them; every one according to his blessing he blessed them.... 33 And when Jacob had made an end of commanding his sons, he gathered up his feet into the bed, and yielded up the ghost, and was gathered unto his people.

[34] Heb. 11:21 By faith Jacob, when he was a dying, blessed both the sons of Joseph; and worshipped, *leaning* upon the top of his staff.

Chapter 8

Family and Household

It is time to get a family perspective instead of seeing things from only an individual point of view. What affects us also affects our families and others around us. We should take responsibility for our families and households.

Joshua challenged the Israelites to choose whom they would serve: the one true God or the false gods of the heathen. He made his choice, but he did not include only himself. He took a stand that **he and his house** would serve the Lord.[1] By making this commitment, he was taking the responsibility to see that his household also followed the Lord.

When Ezra came out of captivity in Babylon to go to Jerusalem, he proclaimed a fast along the way. The purpose of it was for him (and those who traveled with him) to seek the Lord for direction for them, for their little ones, and for all their substance.[2] Many of us often ask the Lord for direction for ourselves, but how often do we ask Him for direction for our families?

When Nehemiah and those with him were rebuilding the walls of Jerusalem, their enemies came against them. Despite the threats, they continued their work girded with their swords in case they would be needed. Nehemiah encouraged the people not to be afraid of the enemies, but to remember that the Lord is greater. He told them to fight for their families and houses.[3] When the enemy comes against our families, we must remember how great our Lord is and fight for our families. We must not allow the enemy to overcome any member.

Queen Esther risked her life to intercede for her kindred and people. Wicked Haman had plotted against the Jews to have them destroyed. Esther had been asked to make request of the king for her people. She knew about the law that said that anyone who came before the king without being called would be killed unless the king held out his golden scepter. She took that risk and was spared. The king also granted her request which saved her people from destruction.[4]

---

[1] Josh. 24:14 Now therefore fear the LORD, and serve him in sincerity and in truth: and put away the gods which your fathers served on the other side of the flood, and in Egypt; and serve ye the LORD. 15 And if it seem evil unto you to serve the LORD, **choose you this day whom ye will serve**; whether the gods which your fathers served that *were* on the other side of the flood, or the gods of the Amorites, in whose land ye dwell: **but as for me and my house, we will serve the LORD.**

[2] Ezra 8:21 Then I proclaimed a fast there, at the river of Ahava, that we might afflict ourselves before our God, to seek of him a right way for us, and for our little ones, and for all our substance.

[3] Neh. 4:14 And I looked, and rose up, and said unto the nobles, and to the rulers, and to the rest of the people, Be not ye afraid of them: remember the Lord, *which is* great and terrible, and **fight for your brethren, your sons, and your daughters, your wives, and your houses.**

[4] Esther 8:5 And said, If it please the king, and if I have found favour in his sight, and the thing *seem* right before the king, and I *be* pleasing in his eyes, let it be written to reverse the letters devised by Haman the son of Hammedatha the Agagite, which he wrote to destroy the Jews which *are* in all the king's provinces: 6 For **how can I endure to see the evil that shall come unto my people? or how can I endure to see the destruction of my kindred?**

The Bible gives a number of examples of families and households who were saved because of the faithfulness of one or more of their members. The Old Testament tells of Noah and his family being saved from the flood.[5] Lot and his daughters were delivered from Sodom and Gomorrah before it was destroyed for its wickedness. All his family had opportunity for escape, but his sons-in-law refused the deliverance. His wife also was included in the escape, but she looked back toward the city and ended up being destroyed with it.[6] Joseph sent for his father Jacob and all his family to come to Egypt where there was food to keep them through the famine.[7] Rahab showed kindness by hiding the spies that Joshua had sent to Jericho. Because of this, she and her family were brought out of the city before it was destroyed.[8]

In the New Testament we can read of Cornelius, who gathered his household to hear the words of Peter. They were all saved and received the Holy Spirit.[9] Lydia received the things Paul said; she and her household were saved and baptized.[10] When Paul and Silas were freed by an earthquake from the Philippian jail, they stopped the jailer from committing suicide. Paul and Silas ministered to him and the members of his household, and they were saved and baptized.[11]

---

[5] Gen. 6: 18 But with thee will I establish my covenant; and thou shalt **come into the ark, thou, and thy sons, and thy wife, and thy sons' wives with thee**.
(For more of the story, read Gen. 6:5-9:19.)

[6] Gen. 19:12 And the **men said unto Lot, Hast thou here any besides? son in law, and thy sons, and thy daughters, and whatsoever thou hast in the city, bring** *them* **out of this place:** 13 For we will destroy this place, because the cry of them is waxen great before the face of the LORD; and the LORD hath sent us to destroy it. 14 And Lot went out, and spake unto his sons in law, which married his daughters, and said, Up, get you out of this place; for the LORD will destroy this city. **But he seemed as one that mocked unto his sons in law.** 15 And when the morning arose, then the angels hastened Lot, saying, **Arise, take thy wife, and thy two daughters**, which are here; lest thou be consumed in the iniquity of the city. 16 And **while he lingered, the men laid hold upon his hand, and upon the hand of his wife, and upon the hand of his two daughters**; the LORD being merciful unto him: **and they brought him forth**, and set him without the city.... 24 Then the LORD rained upon Sodom and upon Gomorrah brimstone and fire from the LORD out of heaven;... 26 **But his wife looked back from behind him, and she became a pillar of salt.**

[7] Gen. 45:9 Haste ye, and go up to my father, and say unto him, Thus saith thy son Joseph, God hath made me lord of all Egypt: come down unto me, tarry not: 10 And thou shalt dwell in the land of Goshen, and **thou shalt be near unto me, thou, and thy children, and thy children's children**, and thy flocks, and thy herds, and all that thou hast: 11 And **there will I nourish thee**; for yet *there are* five years of famine; lest thou, and thy household, and all that thou hast, come to poverty.
(The story is told in Gen. 41-47.)

[8] Josh. 2:12 Now therefore, I pray you, swear unto me by the LORD, since I have shewed you kindness, that ye will also shew kindness unto my father's house, and give me a true token: 13 And *that* ye will **save alive my father, and my mother, and my brethren, and my sisters, and all that they have, and deliver our lives from death.**
(Read Josh. 2 and 6 for more details of the story.)

[9] Acts 10:24 And the morrow after they entered into Caesarea. And **Cornelius** waited for them, and had **called together his kinsmen and near friends**.... 27 And as he talked with him, he went in, and found many that were come together.... 44 While Peter yet spake these words, the **Holy Ghost fell on all them which heard the word.**
(See all of Acts 10.)

[10] Acts 16:13 And on the sabbath we went out of the city by a river side, where prayer was wont to be made; and we sat down, and spake unto the women which resorted *thither*. 14 And a certain woman named **Lydia**, a seller of purple, of the city of Thyatira, which **worshipped God**, heard *us*: **whose heart the Lord opened**, that she attended unto the things which were spoken of Paul. 15 And when **she was baptized, and her household**, she besought *us*, saying, If ye have judged me to be faithful to the Lord, come into my house, and abide *there*. And she constrained us.

[11] Acts 16:27 And the keeper of the prison awaking out of his sleep, and seeing the prison doors open, he drew out his sword, and would have killed himself, supposing that the prisoners had been fled. 28 But Paul cried with a loud voice, saying, Do thyself no harm: for we are all here. 29 Then he called for a light, and sprang in, and came trembling, and fell down before Paul

The Bible also mentions several examples of families who were destroyed because of the sin of the head of the family. I will not list those here, but I am mentioning this to make the point that leaders of a family can lead in either direction: toward fullness of life or toward destruction. Make sure you are leading yours in the right direction.

The Bible instructs us to honor our elders.[12] That includes elders in our own family. There is a wealth of wisdom in those who have lived longer than we have. If we would just spend time with them, we could be greatly rewarded. However, we should respect them simply in obedience to God, whether or not we receive of their wisdom.

Family members should work together, and not be contrary to one another. Jesus said that a house divided against itself will not stand.[13] Christians are likened to members of the body of Christ.[14] A family is also a body of members, and, I believe, God sets members in a **family** as it pleases Him. We are different parts with different functions, yet we all benefit one another. What a blessing to have varied abilities and talents in the same household! There should be no division, but we should care for one another. If one member suffers, all the other members suffer with him; if one member is honored, all rejoice with him. The family is a good place to practice unity, which is also necessary in the body of Christ.

---

and Silas, 30 And brought them out, and said, Sirs, **what must I do to be saved?** 31 And they said, **Believe on the Lord Jesus Christ, and thou shalt be saved, and thy house.** 32 And **they spake unto him the word of the Lord, and to all that were in his house.** 33 And he took them the same hour of the night, and washed *their* stripes; and **was baptized, he and all his**, straightway. 34 And when he had brought them into his house, he set meat before them, and rejoiced, **believing in God with all his house**.
    (Acts 16:19-34 tells more of the story.)

[12] Lev. 19:32 Thou shalt rise up before the hoary head, and honour the face of the old man, and fear thy God: I *am* the LORD.
    Prov. 17:6 Children's children *are* the crown of old men; and the glory of children *are* their fathers.

[13] Mark 3:25 And if a house be divided against itself, that house cannot stand.

[14] 1 Cor. 12:14 For **the body is not one member, but many**. 15 If the foot shall say, Because I am not the hand, I am not of the body; is it therefore not of the body? 16 And if the ear shall say, Because I am not the eye, I am not of the body; is it therefore not of the body? 17 If the whole body *were* an eye, where *were* the hearing? If the whole *were* hearing, where *were* the smelling? 18 But now hath **God set the members every one of them in the body, as it hath pleased him**. 19 And if they were all one member, where *were* the body? 20 But now *are they* many members, yet but one body. 21 And the eye cannot say unto the hand, I have no need of thee: nor again the head to the feet, I have no need of you. 22 Nay, much more those members of the body, which seem to be more feeble, are necessary: 23 And those *members* of the body, which we think to be less honourable, upon these we bestow more abundant honour; and our uncomely *parts* have more abundant comeliness. 24 For our comely *parts* have no need: but God hath tempered the body together, having given more abundant honour to that *part* which lacked: 25 That **there should be no schism** {division} **in the body; but** *that* **the members should have the same care one for another**. 26 And **whether one member suffer, all the members suffer with it; or one member be honoured, all the members rejoice with it.** 27 Now ye are the body of Christ, and members in particular.

Chapter 9

Widows and Fatherless

When my mother became a widow, I searched in the Bible to see what God says about widows. I found that He provides special care for them and their children. Within a few years after my father went home to be with the Lord, my mother became a testimony of the truth of God's Word concerning widows. Almost every time I spoke with her, she had a "praise report" of how the Lord had ministered to her with provision, guidance, comfort, protection, and whatever else she had needed.

It was about four years after I searched the Scriptures about widows that it dawned on me that those verses about the fatherless applied to me. Because I was married and had a family of my own, I had not really thought about the fact that when my mother became a widow, I qualified as a "fatherless." The period following my father's death was a very difficult one for me. Getting a revelation of God's promises to the fatherless brought healing and comfort to me. If I had gotten the revelation earlier, I believe that it would have eliminated much grief.

God has special grace for the fatherless and widows. He is a father of the fatherless and a judge of widows.[1] He establishes the border of the widow[2] and commands that others not remove old landmarks or enter the fields of the fatherless. He will plead their cause.[3] He gives instructions for others to defend the poor and fatherless.[4] He forbids anyone to oppress[5] or do wrong or violence to the fatherless and widow.[6]

If anyone afflicts a widow or a fatherless child, God will hear their cry.[7] He will relieve them[8] and execute judgment on their behalf.[9] He will be a swift witness against those that oppress the widow and fatherless.[10] Woe to those who devour widows' houses; for they shall receive greater damnation.[11]

---

[1] Psalm 68:5 A **father of the fatherless, and a judge of the widows,** *is* God in his holy habitation.

[2] Prov. 15:25 The LORD will destroy the house of the proud: but **he will establish the border of the widow.**

[3] Prov. 23:10 Remove not the old landmark; and enter not into the fields **of the fatherless:** 11 For their redeemer *is* mighty; he shall plead their cause with thee.

[4] Psalm 82:3 **Defend the poor and fatherless:** do justice to the afflicted and needy.

[5] Zech. 7:9 Thus speaketh the LORD of hosts, saying, Execute true judgment, and shew mercy and compassions every man to his brother: 10 And **oppress not the widow, nor the fatherless,** the stranger, nor the poor; and let none of you imagine evil against his brother in your heart.

[6] Jer. 22:3 Thus saith the LORD; Execute ye judgment and righteousness, and deliver the spoiled out of the hand of the oppressor: and **do no wrong, do no violence to the stranger, the fatherless, nor the widow,** neither shed innocent blood in this place.

[7] Exod. 22:22 Ye shall not afflict any **widow, or fatherless child.** 23 If thou afflict them in any wise, and they cry at all unto me, **I will surely hear their cry;** 24 And my wrath shall wax hot, and I will kill you with the sword; and your wives shall be widows, and your children fatherless.

[8] Psalm 146:9 The LORD preserveth the strangers; he **relieveth the fatherless and widow:** but the way of the wicked he turneth upside down.

Jesus told a parable about a widow who went to a judge to get him to carry out justice on her behalf. The judge did not fear God nor regard man; and for a while, he did nothing for the widow. Later, he changed his mind and decided to help her so she would not weary him by continually coming to him.[12] Even though he was not godly, and he had the wrong motivation; God made sure that the widow was given justice.

God makes special provision for the fatherless and widows. He said that part of the tithe was to be used to feed them.[13] Another channel of provision came through His instructions for harvesters to leave the gleanings in their fields, olive trees, and vineyards. The fatherless and widows were allowed to gather the leftovers for themselves.[14]

Ruth was a widow who took advantage of this provision. She gleaned in the fields of Boaz to get grain for herself and her widowed mother-in-law Naomi. Boaz gave instructions to his reapers to purposely leave extra grain in the fields for Ruth to gather.[15] She eventually married Boaz and became the grandmother of King David and part of the lineage of Jesus.

---

[9] Deut. 10:18 He doth execute the **judgment of the fatherless and widow**, and loveth the stranger, in giving him food and raiment.

[10] Mal. 3:5 And I will come near to you to judgment; and I will be a swift witness against the sorcerers, and against the adulterers, and against false swearers, and against those that oppress the hireling in *his* wages, the **widow**, and the **fatherless**, and that turn aside the stranger *from his right*, and fear not me, saith the LORD of hosts.

[11] Matt. 23:14 Woe unto you, scribes and Pharisees, hypocrites! for ye devour **widows' houses**, and for a pretence make long prayer: therefore ye shall receive the greater damnation.

[12] Luke 18:1 And he spake a parable unto them *to this end*, that men ought always to pray, and not to faint; 2 Saying, There was in a city a judge, which feared not God, neither regarded man: 3 And there was a **widow** in that city; and she came unto him, saying, Avenge me of mine adversary. 4 And he would not for a while: but afterward he said within himself, Though I fear not God, nor regard man; 5 Yet because this widow troubleth me, I will avenge her, lest by her continual coming she weary me. 6 And the Lord said, Hear what the unjust judge saith. 7 And shall not God avenge his own elect, which cry day and night unto him, though he bear long with them? 8 I tell you that he will avenge them speedily. Nevertheless when the Son of man cometh, shall he find faith on the earth?

[13] Deut. 14:28 At the end of three years thou shalt **bring forth all the tithe** of thine increase the same year, and shalt lay *it* up within thy gates: 29 And the Levite, (because he hath no part nor inheritance with thee,) and the stranger, and the **fatherless, and the widow**, which *are* within thy gates, **shall come, and shall eat and be satisfied**; that the LORD thy God may bless thee in all the work of thine hand which thou doest.

[14] Deut. 24:19 When thou cuttest down thine harvest in thy field, and hast forgot a sheaf in the field, thou shalt not go again to fetch it: it shall be for the stranger, **for the fatherless, and for the widow**: that the LORD thy God may bless thee in all the work of thine hands. 20 When thou beatest thine olive tree, thou shalt not go over the boughs again: it shall be for the stranger, **for the fatherless, and for the widow**. 21 When thou gatherest the grapes of thy vineyard, thou shalt not glean *it* afterward: it shall be for the stranger, **for the fatherless, and for the widow**.

[15] Ruth 2:2 And **Ruth** the Moabitess said unto Naomi, Let me now go to the field, and glean ears of corn after *him* in whose sight I shall find grace. And she said unto her, Go, my daughter. 3 And she went, and came, and **gleaned in the field after the reapers**: and her hap was to light on a part of the field *belonging* unto Boaz, who *was* of the kindred of Elimelech.... 7 And she said, I pray you, let me glean and gather after the reapers among the sheaves: so she came, and hath continued even from the morning until now, that she tarried a little in the house. 8 Then said Boaz unto Ruth, Hearest thou not, my daughter? **Go not to glean in another field, neither go from hence, but abide here fast by my maidens:**... 11 And Boaz answered and said unto her, It hath fully been shewed me, all that thou hast done unto thy mother in law since the death of thine husband: and *how* thou hast left thy father and thy mother, and the land of thy nativity, and art come unto a people which thou knewest not heretofore. 12 The LORD recompense thy work, and a full reward be given thee of the LORD God of Israel, under whose wings thou art come to trust.... 15 And when she was risen up to glean, Boaz commanded his young men, saying, **Let her glean even among the**

Another example of God's special provision involved the widow of Zarephath. She was preparing her last meal for herself and her son when Elijah asked her to make a cake for him first. She did this, and God caused her meal and oil to last until the drought was over. She, Elijah, and her household had enough to eat for many days.[16] This is a good lesson for widows not to hold back with what they have. When they give, even if they have only a little, it gives God a "seed" to multiply back to them.

This same widow got another miracle. When her son became sick and died, Elijah prayed for him; and God restored him to life.[17]

Another widow received a multiplication miracle. She was in debt, and her sons were about to be sold as slaves to pay for the debt. Elisha asked her what she had in her house. She did not think she had much, only a pot of oil. Elisha told her to ask for empty containers from her neighbors and not to be skimpy in how many she requested. Then she was to pour oil from her pot into the empty containers. When they were all full, the oil ran out. God miraculously provided enough oil for her to sell to pay her debt. There was enough left over for her and her children to live on the rest.[18]

---

sheaves, and reproach her not: 16 **And let fall also** *some* **of the handfuls of purpose for her, and leave** *them***, that she may glean** *them***, and rebuke her not.**

[16] 1 Kings 17:8 And the word of the LORD came unto him, saying, 9 Arise, get thee to Zarephath, which *belongeth* to Zidon, and dwell there: behold, I have commanded a widow woman there to sustain thee. 10 So he arose and went to Zarephath. And when he came to the gate of the city, behold, the widow woman *was* there gathering of sticks: and he called to her, and said, Fetch me, I pray thee, a little water in a vessel, that I may drink. 11 And as she was going to fetch *it*, he called to her, and said, Bring me, I pray thee, a morsel of bread in thine hand. 12 And she said, *As* the LORD thy God liveth, I have not a cake, but an handful of meal in a barrel, and a little oil in a cruse: and, behold, I *am* gathering two sticks, that I may go in and dress it for me and my son, that we may eat it, and die. 13 And Elijah said unto her, Fear not; go *and* do as thou hast said: but make me thereof a little cake first, and bring *it* unto me, and after make for thee and for thy son. 14 **For thus saith the LORD God of Israel, The barrel of meal shall not waste, neither shall the cruse of oil fail, until the day** *that* **the LORD sendeth rain upon the earth.** 15 And she went and did according to the saying of Elijah: and she, and he, and her house, did eat *many* days. 16 *And* **the barrel of meal wasted not, neither did the cruse of oil fail, according to the word of the LORD, which he spake by Elijah.**

[17] 1 Kings 17:17 And it came to pass after these things, *that* **the son of the woman, the mistress of the house, fell sick; and his sickness was so sore, that there was no breath left in him.** 18 And she said unto Elijah, What have I to do with thee, O thou man of God? art thou come unto me to call my sin to remembrance, and to slay my son? 19 And he said unto her, Give me thy son. And he took him out of her bosom, and carried him up into a loft, where he abode, and laid him upon his own bed. 20 And he cried unto the LORD, and said, O LORD my God, hast thou also brought evil upon the widow with whom I sojourn, by slaying her son? 21 And he stretched himself upon the child three times, and cried unto the LORD, and said, **O LORD my God, I pray thee, let this child's soul come into him again.** 22 And the LORD heard the voice of Elijah; and **the soul of the child came into him again, and he revived.** 23 And Elijah took the child, and brought him down out of the chamber into the house, and delivered him unto his mother: and Elijah said, See, **thy son liveth.** 24 And the woman said to Elijah, Now by this I know that thou *art* a man of God, *and* that the word of the LORD in thy mouth *is* truth.

[18] 2 Kings 4:1 Now there cried a certain woman of the wives of the sons of the prophets unto Elisha, saying, Thy servant **my husband is dead;** and thou knowest that thy servant did fear the LORD: and **the creditor is come to take unto him my two sons to be bondmen.** 2 And Elisha said unto her, What shall I do for thee? tell me, **what hast thou in the house?** And she said, Thine handmaid hath not any thing in the house, save **a pot of oil.** 3 Then he said, Go, borrow thee vessels abroad of all thy neighbours, *even* empty vessels; borrow not a few. 4 And when thou art come in, thou shalt shut the door upon thee and upon thy sons, and shalt pour out into all those vessels, and thou shalt set aside that which is full. 5 So she went from him, and shut the door upon her and upon her sons, who brought *the* vessels to her; and she poured out. 6 And it came to pass, when the vessels were full, that she said unto her son, Bring me yet a vessel. And he said unto her, *There is* not a vessel more. And the oil stayed. 7 Then she came and told the man of God. And he said, **Go, sell the oil, and pay thy debt, and live thou and thy children of the rest.**

In the New Testament, the widow Anna was being provided for in the temple. She was a prophetess and served God day and night with fastings and prayers. She had the special privilege of seeing baby Jesus the first time he was brought into the temple.[19]

Jesus had compassion on widows. When he came into the city of Nain, a funeral procession was coming out. The dead man was the only son of his mother, a widow. Jesus told her not to weep. He told the dead man to arise, and he was raised to life and restored to his mother.[20]

As Jesus sat in the temple watching people give into the treasury, he noticed a poor widow putting in two mites. She, like the widow who fed Elijah, had given all that she had. Jesus counted it as more than the rich had given.[21]

Even while Jesus was on the cross, He made arrangements for a widow: His own mother.[22] I assume that, as the firstborn son, He was responsible for his mother's care. Since Jesus was being crucified, He needed someone else to take over the care of His mother. He put His disciple John in charge of her care, and he took her into his home. The Bible does not specifically say why Jesus chose John instead of one of His own brothers. (He had at least four brothers and two sisters.) I think it could have been because His brothers still may not have believed in Him. John was probably His closest disciple, and Jesus could trust that His mother would be in a godly home. John was God's provision for Mary. God knew John would live long enough to care for her.

The early church ministered to widows daily. When there were reports of neglect of some of the widows, the disciples called a meeting to choose seven men to oversee the distribution. They were not chosen lightly, but had to meet certain qualifications: to be of honest report and full of the Holy Spirit and wisdom.[23] Churches today should appoint men with these same qualifications to distribute part of the tithe to provide for the widows for whom the church is responsible.

---

[19] Luke 2:36 And there was one **Anna**, a prophetess, the daughter of Phanuel, of the tribe of Aser: she was of a great age, and had lived with an husband seven years from her virginity; 37 And she *was* a **widow of about fourscore and four years**, which **departed not from the temple**, but **served** *God* **with fastings and prayers night and day**. 38 And she coming in that instant gave thanks likewise unto the Lord, and spake of him to all them that looked for redemption in Jerusalem.

[20] Luke 7:11 And it came to pass the day after, that he went into a city called Nain; and many of his disciples went with him, and much people. 12 Now when he came nigh to the gate of the city, behold, there was **a dead man** carried out, the **only son of his mother, and she was a widow**: and much people of the city was with her. 13 And when **the Lord** saw her, **he had compassion on her**, and said unto her, Weep not. 14 And he came and touched the bier: and they that bare *him* stood still. **And he said, Young man, I say unto thee, Arise.** 15 And **he that was dead sat up**, and began to speak. **And he delivered him to his mother.**

[21] Mark 12:41 And Jesus sat over against the treasury, and beheld how the people cast money into the treasury: and many that were rich cast in much. 42 And **there came a certain poor widow, and she threw in two mites**, which make a farthing. 43 And he called *unto him* his disciples, and saith unto them, Verily I say unto you, That **this poor widow hath cast more in, than all they which have cast into the treasury:** 44 For all *they* did cast in of their abundance; but **she of her want did cast in all that she had,** *even* **all her living.**

[22] John 19:25 Now there stood by the cross of Jesus his mother, and his mother's sister, Mary the *wife* of Cleophas, and Mary Magdalene. 26 **When Jesus therefore saw his mother, and the disciple standing by, whom he loved**, he saith unto his mother, **Woman, behold thy son!** 27 Then saith he to the disciple, **Behold thy mother! And from that hour that disciple took her unto his own** *home.*

[23] Acts 6:1 And in those days, when the number of the disciples was multiplied, there arose a murmuring of the Grecians against the Hebrews, because their **widows** were neglected in the daily ministration. 2 Then the twelve called the multitude of the disciples *unto them*, and said, It is not reason that we should leave the word of God, and serve tables. 3 Wherefore, brethren, look ye out among you seven men of honest report, full of the Holy Ghost and wisdom, whom we may appoint over this business. 4 But

Specific instructions were given to the church for the care of widows. However, if a widow has children or other relatives, they are expected to care for her. The Bible says the children should learn first to show piety at home, and to requite (repay) their parents. ("Piety" toward parents means to respect and support them.) This is good and acceptable before God; but if any provide not for those of his own house, he has denied the faith and is worse than an infidel (unbeliever). Any believers (men or women) who have widows are to relieve them and not expect the church to do it. This frees the church to relieve the widows who have no family to help them.[24]

A widow who is desolate is to be provided for by the church. She has to meet certain qualifications. She must trust in God and continue in supplications (humble petitions) and prayers night and day (as the widow Anna did that we mentioned earlier). She must be at least sixty years old and married only once. She must be well reported of for good works. She must have brought up children, lodged strangers, washed the saints' feet, relieved the afflicted, and diligently followed every good work. Younger widows are not to be taken in by the church, but encouraged to marry, bear children, and guide the house.[25]

The Bible says that pure religion includes visiting the fatherless and widows in their affliction.[26] All believers should have compassion on the fatherless and widows whether or not they have any in their own family. This reflects the heart of God toward them. He works through His people (us) to minister to them.

---

we will give ourselves continually to prayer, and to the ministry of the word. 5 And the saying pleased the whole multitude: and they chose Stephen, a man full of faith and of the Holy Ghost, and Philip, and Prochorus, and Nicanor, and Timon, and Parmenas, and Nicolas a proselyte of Antioch: 6 Whom they set before the apostles: and when they had prayed, they laid *their* hands on them.

[24] 1 Tim. 5:3 Honour widows that are widows indeed. 4 But if any widow have children or nephews, let them learn first to shew piety at home, and to requite their parents: for that is good and acceptable before God.... 8 But if any provide not for his own, and specially for those of his own house, he hath denied the faith, and is worse than an infidel.... 16 If any man or woman that believeth have widows, let them relieve them, and let not the church be charged; that it may relieve them that are widows indeed.

[25] 1 Tim. 5:5 Now she that is a widow indeed, and desolate, trusteth in God, and continueth in supplications and prayers night and day. 6 But she that liveth in pleasure is dead while she liveth. 7 And these things give in charge, that they may be blameless.... 9 Let not a widow be taken into the number under threescore years old, having been the wife of one man, 10 Well reported of for good works; if she have brought up children, if she have lodged strangers, if she have washed the saints' feet, if she have relieved the afflicted, if she have diligently followed every good work. 11 But the younger widows refuse: for when they have begun to wax wanton against Christ, they will marry; 12 Having damnation, because they have cast off their first faith. 13 And withal they learn *to be* idle, wandering about from house to house; and not only idle, but tattlers also and busybodies, speaking things which they ought not. 14 I will therefore that the younger women marry, bear children, guide the house, give none occasion to the adversary to speak reproachfully. 15 For some are already turned aside after Satan.

[26] James 1:27 Pure religion and undefiled before God and the Father is this, To **visit the fatherless and widows in their affliction**, *and* to keep himself unspotted from the world.

Part Four

Choices Affect Relationships

Chapter 10

Choose Life

Much of our lives consists of making choices. Following God is a choice; love is a choice; forgiveness is a choice. The paths to health and prosperity begin with choices. In fact, every path of life begins with a choice. How we live our lives is largely the result of our choices. What kind of family life we have can be the result of our choices. God has given us that freedom of choice. When He created man, He gave him dominion over the earth. That means we are the ones to make the decisions concerning our areas of God-given authority and responsibility. Sometimes there is a tendency to blame others when we do not like the way things are going. However, we must take responsibility for our own choices. Although there are situations in our lives that seem beyond our control, there are many that are the result of what we ourselves have done or what we have allowed others to do. It makes a big difference when we ask for God's help rather than try to do everything by ourselves.

It may seem that we have only two choices in a given situation, so we think we must choose one of them. An example might be in the area of sickness or disease. A doctor may offer the choice of two different treatments: surgery or drugs. Either one of these could bring other problems or side effects. There really are other choices. God offers the choice of divine healing, but that requires faith. He has also designed natural healing into our bodies, but that requires letting go of destructive habits and changing to a healthy lifestyle. When we make choices, there is a path we must follow to bring us to the desired end. It requires commitment to walk that path, and it takes time and patience to see the desired outcome.

Satan tries to deceive us by offering us his choices and making us think that we must choose one of them. I have heard people say, "I had no choice." They could see only the choices the devil was offering, and none of them were good; so they settled for what they considered to be the lesser of two evils. It reminds me of a game we used to play as children. One would ask the other, "Would you rather have a broken arm or be blind?" or "Would you rather die by freezing or drowning?" This was really the devil's game. He starts deceiving us when we are young and continues working on us as adults if we let him.

God says we have a choice. He calls heaven and earth as witness that He has set before us life and death, blessing and cursing. Just in case we have trouble making the decision, God even tells us what to choose: **life**! Why? So that we and our seed (children) may live.[1] Notice there is no in-between, no "gray" area. It is either one or the other. The path we choose will lead either to life or to death. The choice is up to us. If the only choices we see before us are greater or lesser degrees of death, then it is time to seek the Lord for the life choices. We can do this by praying and studying His Word.

Once we have discovered the choice or provision that God offers in any given situation, that is what we should choose, no matter how impossible it looks in the natural. He is supernatural! When we choose His way, He is given a channel to work in to fulfill that decision. He has a host of angels at His disposal to help bring to pass our decisions that are based on His Word. The devil cannot stop it. He is only a fallen angel; he is not equal with God.

---

[1] Deut. 30:19 I call heaven and earth to record this day against you, *that* I have set before you life and death, blessing and cursing: therefore **choose life**, that both thou and thy seed may live:

On the other hand, if we choose contrary to God's Word, we cut Him off from helping us. We are on our own, and we, in ourselves, are no match for the devil and his demons. Therefore, we must make choices based on God's Word, not on natural circumstances. In other words, we must choose life and blessing for every situation.

God makes it clear what brings the blessing and what brings the curse. The blessing comes if we obey God; the curse comes if we disobey Him.[2] Deuteronomy 28 gives a list of blessings and curses.[3] If we choose to obey God, we are choosing life and blessing. If we choose to disobey Him, we are choosing death and cursing. If we have made the wrong choice in the past by turning away from the Lord, we can repent (turn around) and come back to Him. Jesus has redeemed us from the curse that we might receive the blessing.[4]

As parents, our children are under our authority and responsibility. Whether we have wise or foolish children[5] will depend, in part, on whether or not we choose to train them according to God's instruction. God also gives them freedom of choice, but we can train them to make wise choices. Even when they are away from us, we can pray for them. (See Part Six for more on child training.)

Speak Life

When we choose life and blessing, we must also speak life and blessing. Our words must agree with our choice. Otherwise, they negate our choice. We cannot be successful if we choose life, but speak death. Death and life are in the power of the tongue, and we will eat the fruit of what we speak.[6]

---

[2] Deut. 11:26 Behold, **I set before you this day a blessing and a curse**; 27 **A blessing, if ye obey** the commandments of the LORD your God, which I command you this day: 28 And **a curse, if ye will not obey** the commandments of the LORD your God, but turn aside out of the way which I command you this day, to go after other gods, which ye have not known.

[3] Deut. 28:1 And it shall come to pass, if thou shalt hearken diligently unto the voice of the LORD thy God, to observe *and* to do all his commandments which I command thee this day, that the LORD thy God will set thee on high above all nations of the earth: 2 And all these blessings shall come on thee, and overtake thee, if thou shalt hearken unto the voice of the LORD thy God.... 15 But it shall come to pass, if thou wilt not hearken unto the voice of the LORD thy God, to observe to do all his commandments and his statutes which I command thee this day; that all these curses shall come upon thee, and overtake thee:

[4] Gal. 3:13 Christ hath redeemed us from the curse of the law, being made a curse for us: for it is written, Cursed *is* every one that hangeth on a tree: 14 That the blessing of Abraham might come on the Gentiles through Jesus Christ; that we might receive the promise of the Spirit through faith.

[5] Prov. 10:1 The proverbs of Solomon. A wise son maketh a glad father: but a foolish son *is* the heaviness of his mother.
Prov. 10:5 He that gathereth in summer *is* a wise son: *but* he that sleepeth in harvest *is* a son that causeth shame.
Prov. 15:20 A wise son maketh a glad father: but a foolish man despiseth his mother.
Prov. 17:21 He that begetteth a fool *doeth it* to his sorrow: and the father of a fool hath no joy.
Prov. 17:25 A foolish son *is* a grief to his father, and bitterness to her that bare him.
Prov. 19:13a A foolish son *is* the calamity of his father....
Prov. 19:26 He that wasteth *his* father, *and* chaseth away *his* mother, *is* a son that causeth shame, and bringeth reproach.
Prov. 23:15 My son, if thine heart be wise, my heart shall rejoice, even mine. 16 Yea, my reins shall rejoice, when thy lips speak right things.
Prov. 23:24 The father of the righteous shall greatly rejoice: and he that begetteth a wise *child* shall have joy of him. 25 Thy father and thy mother shall be glad, and she that bare thee shall rejoice.
Prov. 27:11 My son, be wise, and make my heart glad, that I may answer him that reproacheth me.
Prov. 29:3a Whoso loveth wisdom rejoiceth his father....
Prov. 30:11 *There is* a generation *that* curseth their father, and doth not bless their mother.

[6] Prov. 18:21 Death and life *are* in the power of the tongue: and they that love it shall eat the fruit thereof.

You may wonder how your words could have such power. In the beginning God framed the worlds by His Word[7] ("And God said...."). After that, He created man in His own image and likeness. This included the ability to create with words. In addition to that, God has a heavenly host of angels that listen to and obey the voice of His Word.[8] When we speak God's Word, we give it voice. His mighty angels get on the job of bringing that Word to pass on our behalf. When we speak life, God's heavenly host is there to bring it forth. On the other hand, if we speak death (things contrary to God's Word), then the devil has his angels working to bring forth death in that situation.

An example of speaking forth death is found in Genesis 31 where Jacob had left Laban, his father-in-law, whom he had served for years. Laban pursued and searched Jacob's stuff for his stolen idols. Jacob, unaware that his wife Rachel had stolen them, said that with whomsoever Laban found his gods, let him not live.[9] Soon afterward, Rachel died in childbirth.[10]

An example of speaking forth life is found in 2 Kings 4 where it tells that a certain woman's son died. She told her husband she was going to the man of God, Elisha. When he questioned her, she simply said, "It shall be well."[11] When Elisha saw her coming, he sent his servant to meet her. Her response was again, "It is well."[12] This woman's son had died, yet she refused to speak death over him. She only spoke her desired outcome. Her words came to pass as Elisha prayed for the child, and the Lord raised him up.

The tongue is like a bit in a horse's mouth that can turn its whole body or like a small helm on a big ship that can turn the whole ship.[13] What we say can set the course for ourselves and for our children. I have heard testimonies of people who said that words of encouragement had changed the direction of their lives from hopelessness to success. On the other hand, words of criticism have wrecked people's lives.

Our words can create an atmosphere for those around us. Have you ever noticed how enjoyable it is to be in the presence of someone who has only pleasant things to say?[14] On the other hand, a person who constantly speaks negatively seems to carry with them a dark, heavy cloud that drives us away.

---

[7] Heb. 11:3 Through faith we understand that the worlds were framed **by the word of God**, so that things which are seen were not made of things which do appear.

[8] Psalm 103:20 Bless the LORD, ye **his angels**, that excel in strength, that do his commandments, **hearkening unto the voice of his word**.

[9] Gen. 31:32 With whomsoever thou findest thy gods, **let him not live**: before our brethren discern thou what *is* thine with me, and take *it* to thee. For Jacob knew not that Rachel had stolen them.

[10] Gen. 35:19 And Rachel died, and was buried in the way to Ephrath, which *is* Bethlehem.

[11] 2 Kings 4:23 And he said, Wherefore wilt thou go to him to day? *it is* neither new moon, nor sabbath. And she said, *It shall be* **well**.

[12] 2 Kings 4:26 Run now, I pray thee, to meet her, and say unto her, *Is it* well with thee? *is it* well with thy husband? *is it* well with the child? And she answered, *It is* **well**.

[13] James 3:3 Behold, we put bits in the horses' mouths, that they may obey us; and we turn about their whole body. 4 Behold also the ships, which though *they be* so great, and *are* driven of fierce winds, yet are they turned about with a very small helm, whithersoever the governor listeth. 5 Even so the tongue is a little member, and boasteth great things. Behold, how great a matter a little fire kindleth!

[14] Prov. 16:24 Pleasant words *are as* an honeycomb, sweet to the soul, and health to the bones.

Jesus said that what we put into our hearts determines what we speak. Whatever is abundant in our hearts will come forth, whether it is evil or good.[15] The way to speak good things is to put good things in our hearts and keep evil things out.

What we believe and what we speak must agree in order for those things to come to pass. With this combination, Jesus said that we could remove mountains. When we pray, if we believe that we receive what we prayed for, it shall come to pass.[16] Be warned, though, that this will also happen in the negative: if we believe something bad will come to pass and we speak that way, we will have what we say.

Jesus warned against speaking idle words. He said we would give account of them in the day of judgment. By our words we will be either justified or condemned.[17] Our prayer should be:

"Set a watch, O LORD, before my mouth; keep the door of my lips." (Psalm 141: 3)

Names and Nicknames

Another area of speaking life over our children has to do with what we call them and the names we give them. God sometimes changed people's names to reflect what He had for them. God changed Abram's name to Abraham because of His promise to give him a son. From then on, when Abraham's name was called, the promise that he would be "father of a multitude" was spoken forth.

The Bible speaks of the value of a good name; it says that a good name is better than great riches and precious ointment.[18] "A good name" may refer to a person's reputation, but it could also apply to the name they are called.

God can give you names for your children. He gave us the first names for our last two children, but we did not really think about asking Him for names for our first two children. However, we did take seriously the responsibility of naming them and considered the meanings of the names before we chose them.

Nicknames should also be considered. Make sure anything that you call your children (or anyone else) is speaking forth life and good, not death and evil. I have heard parents call their children "brats," "monsters," "stupid," and other such degrading names. What you call them is what you get. We made a

---

[15] Luke 6:43 For a good tree bringeth not forth corrupt fruit; neither doth a corrupt tree bring forth good fruit. 44 For every tree is known by his own fruit. For of thorns men do not gather figs, nor of a bramble bush gather they grapes. 45 A good man out of the good treasure of his heart bringeth forth that which is good; and an evil man out of the evil treasure of his heart bringeth forth that which is evil: for **of the abundance of the heart his mouth speaketh.**

[16] Mark 11:22 And Jesus answering saith unto them, Have faith in God. 23 For verily I say unto you, That whosoever shall **say** unto this mountain, Be thou removed, and be thou cast into the sea; and shall not doubt in his heart, but shall **believe** that those things which he **saith** shall come to pass; **he shall have whatsoever he saith**. 24 Therefore I **say** unto you, What things soever ye desire, **when ye pray, believe** that ye receive *them*, and **ye shall have *them***.

[17] Matt. 12:36 But I say unto you, That every idle word that men shall speak, they shall give account thereof in the day of judgment. 37 For by thy words thou shalt be justified, and by thy words thou shalt be condemned.

[18] Prov. 22:1a A *good* name *is* rather to be chosen than great riches....
Eccl. 7:1 A good name *is* better than precious ointment....

decision in our family that we would never call one another "stupid." Because of our ban on this word, our children used to think it was a "cuss" word.

Another name for children that is commonly used today (and I do mean "commonly") is "**kids**." If you sometimes wonder why your children act like wild goats, maybe it is because of what you have been calling them. We decided that we would not call our children "kids." I do not believe children should be called "kids" any more than adults should call one another "turkeys." Both sound disrespectful. Another reason I do not like calling children "kids" is because of what Jesus said about separating the sheep from the goats. He said the "goats" would have to depart from Him, cursed, into everlasting fire that was prepared for the devil and his angels.[19] (The symbol of a goat is used today as a satanic symbol.) Kids grow up to be goats. I would rather not call my children anything associated with those that will be separated from Jesus. I would rather they be associated with the "sheep" that will go with Him into life eternal.

Sowing and Reaping

Whatever we sow, we will reap.[20] This is a natural law. Gardeners and farmers know about this law. When we look at things in nature we can learn about spiritual things because they both are God's design. Sowing and reaping is also a spiritual law. We should not deceive ourselves to think that we can break this law. Our lives now are the result of what has been sown into it by ourselves or others. The seeds sown into our children determine how they will turn out.[21]

There are some principles that we should keep in mind as we study sowing and reaping. One is that **seeds are designed to produce more** than the amount sown. If we planted one tomato seed, we would expect to get a plant that produced a number of tomatoes. Likewise, if we sow good seed into our family, God will multiply it. When people have complimented us on our children's good behavior, we have told them that God has multiplied the good seed we sowed into them. We could never on our own have produced such good results, but God honored the part we did and increased it. By God's increase, our families can turn out better than what we could produce on our own. However, this principle of increase also works with bad seed. If bad seed is sown, it multiplies and produces more seeds, which get replanted and multiplied again. This is why a situation in the family can keep getting worse and worse.

Another principle is that we will **reap in proportion to the amount sown**. If we sow a little, we will reap a smaller harvest than if we sowed more.[22] To reap a greater harvest, we must sow more good seed!

The third principle is that **there are seasons**. Seeds are sown in one season, but the harvest comes in another season. The growing season comes in between.[23] The challenge for us is to be patient during the

---

[19] Matt 25:32 And before him shall be gathered all nations: and he shall separate them one from another, as a shepherd divideth *his* sheep from the **goats**: 33 And he shall set the sheep on his right hand, but the **goats on the left**.... 41 Then shall he say also unto **them on the left** hand, Depart from me, ye cursed, into everlasting fire, prepared for the devil and his angels:... 46 And these shall go away into everlasting punishment: but the righteous into life eternal.

[20] Gal. 6:7 Be not deceived; God is not mocked: for whatsoever a man soweth, that shall he also reap.

[21] Prov. 22:6 Train up a child in the way he should go: and when he is old, he will not depart from it.

[22] 2 Cor. 9:6 But this *I say*, He which soweth sparingly shall reap also sparingly; and he which soweth bountifully shall reap also bountifully.

growing season. We must not "dig up" the seed to see if it is sprouting, lest we damage it. The harvest will come in its due season.[24]

The fourth principle is that the **condition of the ground determines the harvest**. Jesus told the parable of the sower to illustrate this principle.[25] As the sower sowed seed, some fell by the wayside, but was eaten up by the birds. Some seed fell on rocky places and sprung up, but without depth of earth it had no root and withered from the sun. Some seed fell among thorns and was choked. The only ground that brought forth fruit to maturity was the good ground. Jesus went on to explain how this natural principle also applies spiritually.[26] The seed represents the Word of God, and the ground represents the heart. Those by the wayside are those who hear the Word, but do not understand, and Satan immediately takes it away to keep them from believing. Those on stony places hear the Word and receive it with gladness, but have no root in themselves. They endure for a while, but fall away when temptation, tribulation, or persecution comes. Those among thorns hear the Word, but are choked by cares, riches, and pleasures of this life. Those on the good ground hear and keep the Word and bring forth fruit with patience.

As mentioned earlier in this chapter, there are only two basic choices: life or death. In the same way, there are only two basic kinds of seeds: seeds of life and seeds of death.[27] There are no neutral seeds because there are no neutral sources. All seeds come either from God or from Satan.

Many people seem confused about what comes from God and what comes from Satan. When something good happens to them, they say, "This is too good to be true," and they do not give God the glory for it. When something bad happens to them, they blame God and say, "Why is God letting this happen to me?" Their thinking is that God is in control of everything; therefore, everything that happens to them is from Him. Remember that God gave man dominion in the earth, and He set before us two choices: life or death. Sometimes we choose the path that leads to death; but when the consequences start showing up, we start blaming God.

---

[23] Mark 4:26 And he said, So is the kingdom of God, as if a man should cast seed into the ground; 27 And should sleep, and rise night and day, and the seed should spring and grow up, he knoweth not how. 28 For the earth bringeth forth fruit of herself; **first the blade, then the ear, after that the full corn in the ear.** 29 But when the fruit is brought forth, immediately he putteth in the sickle, because the harvest is come.

[24] Gal. 6:9 And let us not be weary in well doing: for **in due season we shall reap**, if we faint not.

[25] Luke 8:4 And when much people were gathered together, and were come to him out of every city, he spake by a parable: 5 A sower went out to sow his seed: and as he sowed, some fell by the way side; and it was trodden down, and the fowls of the air devoured it. 6 And some fell upon a rock; and as soon as it was sprung up, it withered away, because it lacked moisture. 7 And some fell among thorns; and the thorns sprang up with it, and choked it. 8 And other fell on good ground, and sprang up, and bare fruit an hundredfold. And when he had said these things, he cried, He that hath ears to hear, let him hear.
(See also Matt. 13:3-9 and Mark 4:2-9.)

[26] Luke 8:11 Now the parable is this: The seed is the word of God. 12 Those by the way side are they that hear; then cometh the devil, and taketh away the word out of their hearts, lest they should believe and be saved. 13 They on the rock *are they*, which, when they hear, receive the word with joy; and these have no root, which for a while believe, and in time of temptation fall away. 14 And that which fell among thorns are they, which, when they have heard, go forth, and are choked with cares and riches and pleasures of *this* life, and bring no fruit to perfection. 15 But that on the good ground are they, which in an honest and good heart, having heard the word, keep *it*, and bring forth fruit with patience.
(See also Matt. 13:18-23 and Mark 4:13-20.)

[27] Gal. 6:8 For he that soweth to his flesh shall of the flesh reap corruption; but he that soweth to the Spirit shall of the Spirit reap life everlasting.

I used to be confused on this issue myself until John 10:10 was pointed out to me. It gives the dividing line for what is from Satan and what is from God. Satan comes only to steal, kill, and destroy. Jesus came to give abundant life.[28] This verse makes it clear that the seeds that produce death are from Satan, but the seeds that produce life are from God.

Looking at the natural example of a farmer, we see that first he considers what kind of harvest he would like. Then he prepares the ground to receive the seed. Next he plants the seeds that will produce the desired harvest. In the same way, we should first consider what kind of family life we would like to have. Then we should prepare our own and our children's hearts and plant seeds to produce our desired harvest. If you are now reaping a bad harvest, ask God to show you what seeds produced that crop. Then stop sowing those seeds. (In other words, repent!) Pray for crop failure on those bad seeds already sown. Ask God what seeds to sow to produce a good harvest. Then plant so much of those good seeds that they will choke out anything remaining from the bad seeds. For example: if you now have strife in your family, but you desire peace, ask God to show you what seeds produced the strife and stop planting them. Ask God what seeds to sow to produce peace in your family and begin sowing them.

Of course, the best seed to sow is the Word of God. The Bible says that God will give seed to the sower and multiply the seed sown and increase the fruits. His Word will accomplish that purpose for which He sent it forth.[29] The Bible is like a seed catalog, and a concordance is like an index to help us find the seed we are looking for in the Bible. We can sow God's Word by speaking it and by obeying it. We should be continually sowing it into our hearts.

We must realize, however, that **anything** sown into our hearts will produce fruit. Everything we say and do is a seed. Whatever we put in is what will come out. Those are the things we will think about, talk about, and act on. That is why it is so important to guard our own and our children's hearts. Training our children is not a one-time cycle of sowing and reaping. It is a process that is repeated over and over. It is like the process of bringing forth a beautiful flower garden. It takes years of diligent work continually sowing, watering, nurturing, and weeding. But great are the rewards!

(In Part Eight, we will deal with getting bad seed out of our families, and putting in good seed.)

Vision

Considering what harvest we would like to see in our family life is like getting a vision (direction or goal) for it. It is important to have a vision for our family, especially when it agrees with the vision God has for our family. Where there is no vision, people perish.[30] They just get pushed along their lives by whatever

---

[28] John 10:10 The thief cometh not, but for to steal, and to kill, and to destroy: I am come that they might have life, and that they might have *it* more abundantly.

[29] 2 Cor. 9:10 Now he that **ministereth seed to the sower** both minister bread for *your* food, and **multiply your seed sown**, and **increase the fruits** of your righteousness;
Isa. 55:10 For as the rain cometh down, and the snow from heaven, and returneth not thither, but watereth the earth, and maketh it bring forth and bud, that it may **give seed to the sower**, and bread to the eater: 11 So shall **my word** be that goeth forth out of my mouth: it shall not return unto me void, but it **shall accomplish that which I please**, and it shall prosper *in the thing* whereto I sent it.

[30] Prov. 29:18 Where *there is* no vision, the people perish: but he that keepeth the law, happy *is* he.

comes their way. They are usually "**under** the circumstances" instead of on top of them. When there is no vision, there is no hope. Without hope, there is no faith because faith is the substance of things hoped for. Without faith, it is impossible to please God.[31]

God will give us a vision for ourselves, our spouse, our children, our home, and whatever other vision we may seek from Him.[32] His vision is above and beyond anything that we could think of on our own.[33] We must be willing to spend time in His Word because much of His vision for families is already written there. This book is designed to gather Scriptures together about the family to help readers get a vision of God's plan for families.

As we receive God's vision for our family, we should write it down[34] and keep it before our eyes. The vision becomes what we hope for. The hope is the blueprint, and faith is the substance. The vision God has given must become more real to us than the natural circumstances that we may see around us.[35] They are temporary, but God's Word is eternal.[36] His Word will change the circumstances.

We should speak forth the vision God has given us.[37] We must be patient and let nothing pull us off the vision. There must be no wavering.[38] Faith requires corresponding action.[39] If God has given you a vision of peace in your home, keep that picture before you. Speak peace over your home and start **acting** like you would if you already had a peaceful home.

---

[31] Heb. 11:1 Now **faith** is the substance of things **hoped** for, the evidence of things not seen.... 6 But without **faith** *it is* impossible to please *him*: for he that cometh to God must believe that he is, and *that* he is a rewarder of them that diligently seek him.

[32] Ezra 8:21 Then I proclaimed a fast there, at the river of Ahava, that we might afflict ourselves before our God, to seek of him a right way for us, and for our little ones, and for all our substance.

[33] Jer. 33:3 Call unto me, and I will answer thee, and shew thee great and mighty things, which thou knowest not.
Isa. 55: 8 For my thoughts *are* not your thoughts, neither *are* your ways my ways, saith the LORD. 9 For *as* the heavens are higher than the earth, so are my ways higher than your ways, and my thoughts than your thoughts.

[34] Hab. 2:2 And the LORD answered me, and said, Write the vision, and make *it* plain upon tables, that he may run that readeth it. 3 For the vision *is* yet for an appointed time, but at the end it shall speak, and not lie: though it tarry, wait for it; because it will surely come, it will not tarry. 4b ... the just shall live by his faith.

[35] 2 Cor. 5:7 (For we walk by faith, not by sight:)

[36] 2 Cor. 4:18 While we look not at the things which are seen, but at the things which are not seen: for the things which are seen *are* temporal; but the things which are not seen *are* eternal.

[37] Luke 17:5 And the apostles said unto the Lord, Increase our faith. 6 And the Lord said, If ye had faith as a grain of mustard seed, ye might **say** unto this sycamine tree, Be thou plucked up by the root, and be thou planted in the sea; and it should obey you.

[38] James 1:3 Knowing *this*, that the trying of your faith worketh patience. 4 But let patience have *her* perfect work, that ye may be perfect and entire, wanting nothing. 5 If any of you lack wisdom, let him ask of God, that giveth to all *men* liberally, and upbraideth not; and it shall be given him. 6 But let him ask in faith, nothing wavering. For he that wavereth is like a wave of the sea driven with the wind and tossed. 7 For let not that man think that he shall receive any thing of the Lord. 8 A double minded man *is* unstable in all his ways.

[39] James 2:20 But wilt thou know, O vain man, that faith without works is dead?

The Bible gives many examples of visions brought forth through faith. One example is of Abraham. God had promised him a son when it seemed impossible in the natural. Abraham hoped when the circumstances seemed hopeless. He did not consider the natural fact that he and his wife were past child-bearing age, and that Sarah had always been barren. He did not consider God's promise to be impossible, but believed it because God said it. He was persuaded that God was able to do what He had promised.[40] Isaac was brought forth by faith.

Let's look unto Jesus, who is the author and finisher of our faith!

---

[40] Rom. 4:18 Who against hope believed in hope, that he might become the father of many nations, according to that which was spoken, So shall thy seed be. 19 And being not weak in faith, he considered not his own body now dead, when he was about an hundred years old, neither yet the deadness of Sara's womb: 20 He staggered not at the promise of God through unbelief; but was strong in faith, giving glory to God; 21 And being fully persuaded that, what he had promised, he was able also to perform.

Part Five

Partner Relationship with Our Creator

Chapter 11

Fruit of the Womb

Be Fruitful and Multiply

God's first command to man and his wife were to be fruitful and multiply.[1] He repeated it to Noah and his sons when they came out of the ark after the flood.[2] One of the purposes of marriage is to produce godly seed. God made husband and wife one so that He might have godly seed.[3]

In the Bible, bringing forth children is counted as a blessing. Being plenteous in the fruit of your body is included in the list of blessings in Deuteronomy 28.[4] Psalms also speaks of having children as being a blessing. Children are a heritage of the Lord, and the fruit of the womb is His reward. Children are as arrows in the hand of a mighty man, and happy is the man who has his quiver full of them.[5] The man that fears the Lord shall be blessed with a wife who is as a fruitful vine and with children like olive plants around his table.[6]

Many people today have a different attitude toward children. Some think they are more of a burden than a blessing. I remember back in the 1970's after we had our first two children, that I was thinking we would be doing well just to bring up these two. After all, I had heard people say that the world was no fit place to bring up children. Well, God has blessed us since then with two more children, and all four are blessings indeed! I found that my earlier way of thinking was not supported by the Bible.

Instead of limiting the birth of children because of troublesome times, the Bible speaks of multiplying and increasing! During the time the Israelites were slaves in Egypt, they multiplied and increased abundantly

---

[1] Gen. 1:28a And God blessed them, and God said unto them, **Be fruitful, and multiply**, and replenish the earth, and subdue it:...

[2] Gen. 9:1 And God blessed Noah and his sons, and said unto them, **Be fruitful, and multiply**, and replenish the earth.... 7 And you, **be ye fruitful, and multiply; bring forth abundantly in the earth, and multiply** therein.... 19 These *are* the three sons of Noah: and **of them was the whole earth overspread.**

[3] Mal. 2:15a And did not he make one? Yet had he the residue of the spirit. And wherefore one? That he might seek a **godly seed**....

[4] Deut. 28:11a And the LORD shall make thee plenteous in goods, in the fruit of thy body....

[5] Psalm 127:3 Lo, **children** *are* an heritage of the LORD: *and* the **fruit of the womb** *is his* reward. 4 As arrows are in the hand of a mighty man; so *are* children of the youth. 5 **Happy** *is* the man that hath his **quiver full of them**: they shall not be ashamed, but they shall speak with the enemies in the gate.

[6] Psalm 128:1 Blessed *is* every one that feareth the LORD; that walketh in his ways. 2 For thou shalt eat the labour of thine hands: happy *shalt* thou *be*, and *it shall be* well with thee. 3 Thy **wife** *shall be* **as a fruitful vine** by the sides of thine house: thy **children like olive plants round about thy table**. 4 Behold, that thus shall the man be blessed that feareth the LORD.

and became mighty,[7] even stronger than their enemies.[8] Another example of increasing in troublesome times was when the Israelites were taken captive by Babylon. God told the captives to marry and have children. When their children were grown, they, too, were to marry and have children. This command was so that they might increase and not be diminished. God told them to seek the peace of the place where they were living and to pray unto Him for it. That is the way they would have peace.[9]

With all the emphasis in the Bible on the blessedness of having children, I found only one instance of an attempt to **prevent** conception. Judah's second son Onan was told to marry his older brother's widow and raise up seed to his brother. Onan married her, but tried to prevent pregnancy because he knew the seed would be counted as his brother's. This displeased the Lord.[10]

Freed from Barrenness

I hear of many couples today who have been told that they cannot have children. Some couples resign themselves to that as the final word in their situation. Others seek help from the medical profession or others who, they think, might be able to help them. Since God is the giver of life, it would be wise to seek Him first for answers.

Barrenness can be caused by other than physical reasons, such as is mentioned in Genesis 20. Abraham and Sarah were traveling to Gerar, and king Abimelech took Sarah because he was led to believe that she was Abraham's sister. God came to him in a dream and told him to give Sarah back to her husband. He did, and Abraham prayed for his household. They had all been barren because Abimelech had taken Abraham's wife. When Sarah was returned to her husband, Abimelech's wife and maidservants were able to bear children.[11]

Most of the barren women mentioned in the Bible were freed from barrenness: Sarah, Rebekah, Manoah's wife (Samson's mother), Hannah, the Shunammite woman, and Elisabeth. Sarah and Elisabeth were also considered past the age of childbearing. (The Bible says the righteous shall still bring forth fruit in

---

[7] Exod. 1:5 And all the souls that came out of the loins of Jacob were seventy souls: for Joseph was in Egypt *already*. 6 And Joseph died, and all his brethren, and all that generation. 7 And the children of Israel were **fruitful**, and **increased abundantly**, and **multiplied**, and **waxed exceeding mighty**; and the **land was filled with them**.

[8] Psalm 105:24 And he increased his people greatly; and made them stronger than their enemies.

[9] Jer. 29:4 Thus saith the LORD of hosts, the God of Israel, unto all that are carried away captives, whom I have caused to be carried away from Jerusalem unto Babylon; 5 Build ye houses, and dwell *in them*; and plant gardens, and eat the fruit of them; 6 Take ye wives, and **beget sons and daughters**; and **take wives for your sons**, and **give your daughters to husbands**, that they may **bear sons and daughters**; that ye may **be increased** there, and **not diminished**. 7 And seek the peace of the city whither I have caused you to be carried away captives, and pray unto the LORD for it: for in the peace thereof shall ye have peace.

[10] Gen. 38:6 And Judah took a wife for Er his firstborn, whose name *was* Tamar. 7 And Er, Judah's firstborn, was wicked in the sight of the LORD; and the LORD slew him. 8 And Judah said unto Onan, Go in unto thy brother's wife, and marry her, and raise up seed to thy brother. 9 And Onan knew that the seed should not be his; and it came to pass, when he went in unto his brother's wife, that he spilled *it* on the ground, lest that he should give seed to his brother. 10 And the thing which he did **displeased the LORD**: wherefore he slew him also.

[11] Gen. 20:17 So Abraham prayed unto God: and God healed Abimelech, and his wife, and his maidservants; and they bare *children*. 18 For the LORD had fast closed up all the wombs of the house of Abimelech, because of Sarah Abraham's wife.

old age.)[12] God enabled all of these barren women to bear a child; some had more than one. Some of the children born to these women had special calls to fulfill.

We ended the last chapter with the example of Abraham and Sarah, whose son Isaac was brought forth by faith. God had promised them a son in their old age. Abraham had to be so convinced of God's promise that he could overlook their old age and the deadness of Sarah's womb.[13] Sarah herself received strength through faith to conceive seed when she was past age because she judged that God would be faithful to His promise.[14]

Rebekah was Isaac's wife. She, too, was barren, but her husband intreated the Lord for her. She conceived and had twins.[15]

Manoah's wife became the mother of Samson. The angel of the Lord appeared to her and told her that even though she was barren, she would conceive and bear a son.[16] God had a special call on her son's life. He was to be a deliverer for Israel. God gave him strength above that of ordinary men. The Bible says that after his death his brothers helped bury him.[17] This indicates that more children were born into that family after Samson's birth.

Hannah prayed for a son and promised that she would give him to the Lord. Eli the priest heard her praying and agreed with her prayer. Samuel was born; when he was weaned, she brought him to the house of the Lord.[18] Eli asked the Lord to give Elkanah and Hannah more seed because of their giving Samuel to the Lord. Hannah had five more children, and Samuel became a great prophet in Israel.[19]

---

[12] Psalm 92:12 The righteous shall flourish like the palm tree: he shall grow like a cedar in Lebanon. 13 Those that be planted in the house of the LORD shall flourish in the courts of our God. 14 They shall **still bring forth fruit in old age**; they shall be fat and flourishing; 15 To shew that the LORD *is* upright: *he is* my rock, and *there is* no unrighteousness in him.

[13] Rom. 4:19 And being not weak in faith, he considered not **his own body now dead**, when he was about an **hundred years old**, neither yet the **deadness of Sara's womb**: 20 He staggered not at the promise of God through unbelief; but was strong in faith, giving glory to God; 21 And being fully persuaded that, what he had promised, he was able also to perform.

[14] Heb. 11:11 Through faith also Sara herself received strength to **conceive seed**, and was **delivered of a child** when **she was past age**, because she judged him faithful who had promised. 12 Therefore sprang there even of one, and him **as good as dead**, *so many* as the stars of the sky in multitude, and as the sand which is by the sea shore innumerable.

[15] Gen. 25:21 And Isaac intreated the LORD for his wife, because she *was* **barren**: and the LORD was intreated of him, and Rebekah his wife **conceived**.

[16] Judges 13:2 And there was a certain man of Zorah, of the family of the Danites, whose name *was* Manoah; and his wife *was* **barren**, and bare not. 3 And the angel of the LORD appeared unto the woman, and said unto her, Behold now, thou *art* **barren, and bearest not**: but thou **shalt conceive**, and **bear a son**.

[17] Judges 16:31 Then his {Samson's} brethren and all the house of his father came down, and took him, and brought *him* up, and buried him between Zorah and Eshtaol in the buryingplace of Manoah his father. And he judged Israel twenty years.

[18] 1 Sam. 1:2 And he had two wives; the name of the one *was* Hannah, and the name of the other Peninnah: and Peninnah had children, but Hannah **had no children**.... 6 And her adversary also provoked her sore, for to make her fret, because the LORD had **shut up her womb**.... 10 And she *was* in bitterness of soul, and **prayed unto the LORD**, and wept sore. 11 And she vowed a vow, and said, O LORD of hosts, if thou wilt indeed look on the affliction of thine handmaid, and remember me, and not forget thine handmaid, but wilt give unto thine handmaid a man child, then I will give him unto the LORD all the days of his life, and there shall no razor come upon his head.... 17 Then Eli answered and said, Go in peace: and the **God of Israel grant *thee* thy petition** that thou hast asked of him.... 19 And they rose up in the morning early, and worshipped before the LORD, and returned, and came to their house to Ramah: and Elkanah knew Hannah his wife; and the LORD remembered her. 20 Wherefore

The Shunammite woman and her husband had offered hospitality to the prophet Elisha. They had even added on a room for him to use when he was in their area. Elisha was looking for a way to repay her for her kindness to him. His servant Gehazi told him that she had no child, and her husband was old. Elisha prophesied that she would have a son.[20] (When her son was grown, he died. We mentioned in the last chapter that his mother spoke only life over him, and he was raised from the dead.)

Elisabeth became the mother of John the Baptist. She and her husband were both old. An angel of the Lord appeared to her husband Zacharias while he was burning incense in the temple. The angel said that his prayer had been heard, and Elisabeth would bear him a son. His name would be John, and he would prepare the way before the Lord. God took away Elisabeth's reproach of barrenness and gave her a son.[21]

God freed these women from barrenness, and He can also free women from barrenness today. If you have been considered barren, ask God how to get in position to receive from Him. If He reveals an area where you need to repent, then repent. If He shows you changes to make in your lifestyle concerning your health, then make those adjustments. Be willing to be obedient to whatever He tells you. Here is a promise for you:

"He maketh the barren woman to keep house, *and to be* a joyful mother of children.
Praise ye the LORD." (Psalm 113: 9)

In the Old Testament, the barren are told to **sing**.[22] This Scripture quoted in the New Testament says to **rejoice**.[23] In Psalms a promise is given that the Lord will give you the desires of your heart if you trust in

---

it came to pass, when the time was come about after Hannah had **conceived**, that she **bare a son**, and called his name Samuel, *saying*, Because I have asked him of the LORD.... 27 **For this child I prayed**; and the **LORD hath given me my petition** which I asked of him: 28 Therefore also I have lent him to the LORD; as long as he liveth he shall be lent to the LORD. And he worshipped the LORD there.

[19] 1 Sam. 2:20 And Eli blessed Elkanah and his wife, and said, **The LORD give thee seed of this woman for the loan which is lent to the LORD**. And they went unto their own home. 21 And the LORD visited Hannah, so that **she conceived, and bare three sons and two daughters**. And the child Samuel grew before the LORD.

[20] 2 Kings 4:14 And he said, What then *is* to be done for her? And Gehazi answered, Verily **she hath no child**, and **her husband is old**. 15 And he said, Call her. And when he had called her, she stood in the door. 16 And he said, About this season, according to the time of life, thou shalt embrace a son. And she said, Nay, my lord, *thou* man of God, do not lie unto thine handmaid. 17 And the woman **conceived, and bare a son** at that season that Elisha had said unto her, according to the time of life.

[21] Luke 1:7 And **they had no child**, because that **Elisabeth was barren**, and they **both were** *now* **well stricken in years**.... 13 But the angel said unto him, Fear not, Zacharias: for thy **prayer is heard**; and thy wife **Elisabeth shall bear thee a son**, and thou shalt call his name John. 14 And thou shalt have joy and gladness; and many shall rejoice at his birth. 15 For he shall be great in the sight of the Lord, and shall drink neither wine nor strong drink; and he shall be filled with the Holy Ghost, even from his mother's womb. 16 And many of the children of Israel shall he turn to the Lord their God. 17 And he shall go before him in the spirit and power of Elias, to turn the hearts of the fathers to the children, and the disobedient to the wisdom of the just; to make ready a people prepared for the Lord. 18 And Zacharias said unto the angel, Whereby shall I know this? for I am an **old man**, and my **wife well stricken in years**.... 24 And after those days his wife **Elisabeth conceived**, and hid herself five months, saying, 25 Thus hath the Lord dealt with me in the days wherein he looked on *me*, **to take away my reproach** among men.

[22] Isa. 54:1 **Sing, O barren**, thou *that* didst not bear; break forth into singing, and cry aloud, thou *that* didst not travail with child: for more *are* the children of the desolate than the children of the married wife, saith the LORD.

[23] Gal. 4:27 For it is written, **Rejoice, *thou* barren** that bearest not; break forth and cry, thou that travailest not: for the desolate hath many more children than she which hath an husband.

Him, do good, and delight in Him. Commit your way unto Him, and He will bring it to pass.[24] So if you are barren, sing and rejoice and stand on the promises given in God's Word.

God Made Us

It is God who made us, and we are His.[25] He formed us from the womb.[26] His hands made and fashioned us.[27] We are fearfully and wonderfully made. Even before we could be seen, He was forming our parts in the womb.[28]

God also made our children, and they are His.[29] We have no right to abort a baby at any time after conception. God has a purpose for every person even before He forms each one in the womb.[30] When one's life is aborted, one's purpose is aborted.

God created us for His glory. He formed us for Himself to show forth His praise. We were created to please Him. He is worthy to receive glory and honor and power.[31] We should seek to please Him and to train our children to please Him.

---

[24] Psalm 37:3 Trust in the LORD, and do good; *so* shalt thou dwell in the land, and verily thou shalt be fed. 4 Delight thyself also in the LORD; and he shall give thee the desires of thine heart. 5 Commit thy way unto the LORD; trust also in him; and he shall bring *it* to pass.

[25] Psalm 100:3 **Know ye that the LORD he** *is* **God:** *it is* **he** *that* **hath made us**, and not we ourselves; *we are* his people, and the sheep of his pasture.

[26] Isa. 44:24 Thus saith the LORD, thy redeemer, and **he that formed thee from the womb**, I *am* the LORD that maketh all *things*; that stretcheth forth the heavens alone; that spreadeth abroad the earth by myself;

[27] Psalm 119:73 **Thy hands have made me and fashioned me:** give me understanding, that I may learn thy commandments.

[28] Psalm 139:13 For thou hast possessed my reins: thou hast covered me in my mother's womb. 14 I will praise thee; for I am fearfully *and* wonderfully made: marvellous *are* thy works; *and that* my soul knoweth right well. 15 My substance was not hid from thee, when I was made in secret, *and* curiously wrought in the lowest parts of the earth. 16 Thine eyes did see my substance, yet being unperfect; and in thy book all *my* members were written, *which* in continuance were fashioned, when *as yet there was* none of them.
Eccl. 11:5 As thou knowest not what *is* the way of the spirit, *nor* **how the bones** *do* **grow in the womb of her that is with child:** even so thou knowest not the works of **God who maketh all.**

[29] Isa. 29:23 But when he seeth **his children, the work of mine hands**, in the midst of him, they shall sanctify my name, and sanctify the Holy One of Jacob, and shall fear the God of Israel.

[30] Isa. 49:1 Listen, O isles, unto me; and hearken, ye people, from far; The **LORD hath called me from the womb**; from the bowels of my mother hath he made mention of my name.... 5 And now, saith the **LORD that formed me from the womb** *to be* **his servant**, to bring Jacob again to him, Though Israel be not gathered, yet shall I be glorious in the eyes of the LORD, and my God shall be my strength.
Jer. 1:4 Then the word of the LORD came unto me, saying, 5 **Before I formed thee in the belly** I knew thee; and before thou camest forth out of the womb **I sanctified thee,** *and* **I ordained thee** a prophet unto the nations.

[31] Isa. 43:7 *Even* every one that is called by my name: for **I have created him for my glory**, I have formed him; yea, I have made him.... 21 This people have I formed for myself; they shall shew forth my praise.
Rev. 4:11 Thou art worthy, O Lord, to receive glory and honour and power: for thou hast created all things, and for thy pleasure they are and were created.

Parents as Stewards

God gives children to parents.[32] Parents do not own the children, but are **stewards** over them. The children still belong to God (as do the parents), but God gives authority and responsibility to the parents to bring up the children according to His plan and purpose. God requires stewards to be faithful.[33]

My husband and I have always taken seriously the responsibility of bringing up our children. We purposed in our hearts that we would not have ordinary, "run-of-the-mill" children. We expect them to be as Daniel, ten times wiser than the children of the world.[34] We purposed that we would bring our children up in the nurture and admonition of the Lord. We would train them to love and serve Him, and we would help prepare them for the call God has on their lives.

There are more than ten years between the births of our second and third children. As I mentioned earlier, I thought we would be doing well just to bring two children to adulthood. However, I felt God was dealing with us about having more children, and He put that desire for more in our hearts. It was quite a consideration for us as another baby at this time would definitely change our lifestyle.

During this time, I was reading in the book of Esther where her cousin Mordecai had asked her to intercede to the king on behalf of her people, the Jews. He told her that if she kept quiet, God would provide deliverance from another place, and who knows whether she was come to the kingdom for such a time as this.[35] I felt the Lord was saying to me that He had a plan for a baby to be born on the earth, and He was offering us the privilege. If we refused, He would ask someone else. So they would be the ones to receive the blessing, but we would miss out. We felt honored to accept the offer and are now receiving the blessing of having her in our lives. I believe God led us to name her Esther. Over and over, I would say to her (before and after she was born) "Esther, you're come to the kingdom for such a time as this."

I do not believe Esther is any more special to God than any other child; neither are we any more special to God than any other parents. I am sharing this testimony because I believe God desires all parents to see each of their children as a special gift from Him. We all should be honored that He would entrust us with such a stewardship.

Childbearing and parenting are not always easy, but God rewards us.[36] No matter what other vocation or calling we may have in life, we (as parents) have a vocation (calling) to bring up our children in the

---

[32] Gen. 48:9 And Joseph said unto his father, They *are* **my sons, whom God hath given me** in this *place*. And he said, Bring them, I pray thee, unto me, and I will bless them.
Heb. 2:13b ... Behold I and the **children which God hath given me**.

[33] 1 Cor. 4:2 Moreover it is required in stewards, that a man be found faithful.

[34] Dan. 1:20 And in all matters of wisdom *and* understanding, that the king inquired of them, he found them ten times better than all the magicians *and* astrologers that *were* in all his realm.

[35] Esther 4:14 For if thou altogether holdest thy peace at this time, *then* shall there enlargement and deliverance arise to the Jews from another place; but thou and thy father's house shall be destroyed: and who knoweth whether thou art come to the kingdom for *such* a time as this?

[36] Psalm 126:5 They that sow in tears shall reap in **joy**. 6 He that goeth forth and weepeth, **bearing precious seed**, shall doubtless come again with **rejoicing**, bringing his sheaves *with him*.
Prov. 23:24 The father of the righteous shall greatly **rejoice**: and he that begetteth a wise *child* shall have **joy** of him. 25 Thy father and thy mother shall be **glad**, and she that bare thee shall **rejoice**.

nurture and admonition of the Lord. We must walk worthy of that calling, too.[37] We should develop the same attitude toward our children that Paul had toward those to whom he ministered. We should lay up for our children and gladly spend and be spent for them unconditionally.[38] Children start out small, but God has big plans for them.[39] We must help prepare our children to fulfil His plans.

---

[37] Eph. 4:1 I therefore, the prisoner of the Lord, beseech you that ye **walk worthy of the vocation wherewith ye are called**, 2 With all lowliness and meekness, with longsuffering, forbearing one another in love; 3 Endeavouring to keep the unity of the Spirit in the bond of peace.

[38] 2 Cor. 12:14b ... for the children ought not to lay up for the parents, but the parents for the children. 15 And I will very gladly spend and be spent for you; though the more abundantly I love you, the less I be loved.

[39] Job 8:7 Though thy beginning was small, yet thy latter end should greatly increase.

Chapter 12

Childbearing

Freed from the Curse

In Genesis, the curse was pronounced on Adam and Eve because of their disobedience to God in the Garden of Eden. God said to Eve that He would greatly multiply her **sorrow** and her conception, and that in **sorrow** she would bring forth children. He told Adam that the ground was cursed for his sake, and that in **sorrow** he would eat of it all the days of his life.[1] When I researched the word "sorrow," I found that it can mean toil and labor, as well as pain and sorrow. Adam and Eve both received the same curse, but Adam's was associated with laboring for food, and Eve's involved laboring to bring forth children.

Through many generations, women have expected to have painful childbirth experiences because of what happened in the Garden of Eden. What they have not realized is that, no matter what the curse, Jesus came to redeem us from it. Isaiah prophesied that Jesus bore our **griefs** and carried our **sorrows**.[2] In researching the words "griefs" and "sorrows," I discovered that what Jesus bore for us includes travail in childbirth. The New Testament also tells us that Christ has redeemed us from the curse of the law because He was made a curse for us.[3] In other words, He took our place and bore the punishment we deserved.

Jesus came to redeem the whole world, but redemption is not automatic. We must receive the freedom that Jesus has made available to us in each area of our lives. But how can we receive it if we do not know about it? In the rest of this chapter, we will look at what the Bible says about pregnancy and childbirth so that we can receive God's plan for us in these areas.

Inquire of the Lord

Many times we have problems concerning pregnancy and childbirth because we fail to inquire of the Lord. I like what Rebekah did when she was pregnant. She was evidently feeling quite a bit of activity inside, so she went straight to the Lord to find out what was going on. He told her that twins were in her womb and also gave her insight into the future of her two sons.[4] (No medical tests can give this much information!)

---

[1] Gen. 3:16 Unto the woman he said, I will greatly multiply thy **sorrow** and thy conception; in **sorrow** thou shalt bring forth children; and thy desire *shall be* to thy husband, and he shall rule over thee. 17 And unto Adam he said, Because thou hast hearkened unto the voice of thy wife, and hast eaten of the tree, of which I commanded thee, saying, Thou shalt not eat of it: cursed *is* the ground for thy sake; in **sorrow** shalt thou eat *of* it all the days of thy life;

[2] Isa. 53:4a Surely he hath borne our **griefs**, and carried our **sorrows**....

[3] Gal. 3:13a Christ hath redeemed us from the curse of the law, being made a curse for us....

[4] Gen. 25:22 And the children struggled together within her; and she said, If *it be* so, why *am* I thus? And she went to **enquire of the LORD**. 23 And the LORD said unto her, **Two nations *are* in thy womb**, and two manner of people shall be separated from thy bowels; and *the one* people shall be stronger than *the other* people; and the elder shall serve the younger. 24 And when her days to be delivered were fulfilled, behold, *there were* **twins** in her womb.

Samson's parents got even more instructions from the Lord. The angel gave his mother instructions concerning what she should not eat or drink during her pregnancy. He also told her what their son was called to do.[5] Manoah was not with his wife when the angel first appeared to her, but he asked the Lord to let the angel come back and teach them what they should do for the child that would be born. The angel returned and repeated the instructions and told Manoah to make sure his wife followed them.[6]

Difficulties during pregnancy, childbirth, and beyond would be relieved if we would inquire of the Lord concerning them. He designed us and knows what is best for us. We should establish good health habits involving diet, exercise, rest, and hygiene. These are important for both the mother and the baby. When these habits are established early, they will result in a much healthier life and will prevent many diseases. If you lack wisdom in this (or any other) area, ask God, and He will give it.[7] Then be obedient to His instructions as Samson's mother was.

Season of Gentle Care

The season of childbearing is a special time. Sometimes it can seem overwhelming. Too often, we try to cram too much into that time, not realizing that it is a **season**, and that there will be other seasons to do other things.[8] It is a time to gently lead with gentle care. When the wife is pregnant, nursing, or consumed with the care of a new baby, it is an especially good time for the husband to remember the instruction to dwell with his wife according to knowledge, giving honor unto her as unto the weaker vessel.[9] He should understand the extra demands on her body and her time and realize that she may not be able to do all the other things he usually expects her to do.

There are examples in God's Word about dealing gently with those who are with young. One example is when Esau came to meet Jacob on his return journey from serving Laban. Jacob told Esau to go on ahead, so Jacob could travel more slowly because of the children and the flocks with young that traveled with him.[10] Another example is when Joseph sent for his father and all his family to bring them into Egypt during the famine. He sent wagons for the little ones and their mothers to ride in.[11]

---

[5] Judges 13:3 And the angel of the LORD appeared unto the woman, and said unto her, Behold now, thou *art* barren, and bearest not: but thou shalt conceive, and bear a son. 4 Now therefore beware, I pray thee, and drink not wine nor strong drink, and eat not any unclean *thing*: 5 For, lo, thou shalt conceive, and bear a son; and no razor shall come on his head: for the child shall be a Nazarite unto God from the womb: and he shall begin to deliver Israel out of the hand of the Philistines.

[6] Judges 13:12 And Manoah said, Now let thy words come to pass. How shall we order the child, and *how* shall we do unto him? 13 And the angel of the LORD said unto Manoah, Of all that I said unto the woman let her beware.

[7] James 1:5 If any of you lack wisdom, let him ask of God, that giveth to all *men* liberally, and upbraideth not; and it shall be given him.

[8] Eccl. 3:1 To every *thing there is* a season, and a time to every purpose under the heaven:... 11a He hath made every *thing* **beautiful in his time**....

[9] 1 Pet. 3:7 Likewise, ye husbands, dwell with *them* according to knowledge, giving honour unto the wife, as unto the weaker vessel, and as being heirs together of the grace of life; that your prayers be not hindered.

[10] Gen. 33:13 And he said unto him, My lord knoweth that the **children *are* tender**, and the flocks and herds with young *are* with me: and if men should overdrive them one day, all the flock will die. 14 Let my lord, I pray thee, pass over before his servant: and I will **lead on softly, according as** the cattle that goeth before me and **the children be able to endure**, until I come unto my lord unto Seir.

My favorite example is the one that speaks of Jesus and His tender loving care. He is compared to a shepherd who gathers the lambs with His arms and carries them in his bosom. He **gently** leads those with young;[12] He does not drive them.

In this season of life, I often found myself staying behind to care for the little ones. We took them with us many times, but sometimes it just was not practical.

There were times mentioned in the Bible when someone had to stay behind to care for the little ones. During the time that the Israelites were in Egypt, Joseph and his brothers went to Canaan to bury their father. Their little ones were not required to make that trip, but stayed in Goshen.[13] Another instance was when the tribes of Reuben, Gad, and the half tribe of Manasseh left their little ones in the land of their inheritance on the east side of Jordan. The men had to go over to the west side of the Jordan and help the rest of the tribes possess their lands.[14]

There is a principle given in the Bible that those who "stay with the stuff" share in the rewards of those who go to the battle. David went to battle with about four hundred men and left two hundred men with their stuff.[15] After the battle, David made sure that those who were left behind shared in the spoils of the victory. Those who went to battle and those who stayed with the stuff shared **equally** in the rewards.[16]

This was a great encouragement to me because it helped me realize that "staying with the stuff" (taking care of the little ones) is just as important as going out and doing some great exploit. We share equally in the rewards.[17]

---

[11] Gen. 45:19 Now thou art commanded, this do ye; take you wagons out of the land of Egypt **for your little ones, and for your wives**, and bring your father, and come.

[12] Isa. 40:1 Comfort ye, comfort ye my people, saith your God.... 11 He shall feed his flock like a shepherd: he shall gather the lambs with his arm, and carry *them* in his bosom, *and* shall **gently lead those that are with young.**

[13] Gen. 50:7 And Joseph went up to bury his father: and with him went up all the servants of Pharaoh, the elders of his house, and all the elders of the land of Egypt, 8 And all the house of Joseph, and his brethren, and his father's house: **only their little ones, and their flocks, and their herds, they left in the land of Goshen.**

[14] Josh. 1:14 **Your wives, your little ones**, and your cattle, **shall remain in the land** which Moses gave you on this side Jordan; but ye shall pass before your brethren armed, all the mighty men of valour, and help them; 15 Until the LORD have given your brethren rest, as *he hath given* you, and they also have possessed the land which the LORD your God giveth them: then ye shall return unto the land of your possession, and enjoy it, which Moses the LORD'S servant gave you on this side Jordan toward the sunrising.

[15] 1 Sam. 25:13 And David said unto his men, Gird ye on every man his sword. And they girded on every man his sword; and David also girded on his sword: and there went up after David about four hundred men; and two hundred **abode by the stuff**.

[16] 1 Sam. 30:24b ... as his part *is* that goeth down to the battle, so *shall* his part *be* that tarrieth by the stuff: they shall part alike. 25 And it was *so* from that day forward, that he made it a statute and an ordinance for Israel unto this day.

[17] Psalm 68:11 The Lord gave the word: great *was* the company of those that published *it*. 12 Kings of armies did flee apace: and **she that tarried at home divided the spoil.** 13 Though ye have lien among the pots, *yet shall ye be as* the wings of a dove covered with silver, and her feathers with yellow gold.

Jesus and Little Ones

Jesus has a heart of love and tenderness for little ones. There are some special things He said about infants and children. He said that perfect praise comes out of the mouth of babes and sucklings.[18] He quoted this from the Psalms where it says that God has ordained strength out of the mouth of babes and sucklings. This indicates that praise to God will stop the enemy.[19] What a powerful weapon against Satan that can be used even by little ones!

Jesus rejoiced and thanked God that He had hidden some things from the wise and prudent, but had revealed them unto babes because it seemed good in His sight.[20] He used a little child to settle the issue of who would be greatest. He set a child beside Him and said that whoever would receive the child in His name would receive Him, and whoever would receive Him would receive God Who sent Him. He said that whoever is least shall be great.[21]

Jesus warned us not to despise any of these little ones. He said their angels always behold the face of our Father in heaven.[22] (That sounds to me like full-time guardian angels!) Jesus was displeased with his disciples when they tried to stop those who were bringing young children to Him. He told them to let the little children come to Him, and not to forbid them. He said the kingdom of God is made up of such as they are, and whoever would not receive the kingdom of God as a little child, would not enter in. He took the children in his arms, put His hands upon them, and blessed them.[23]

People have questioned whether or not babies who die before birth or at a young age are in heaven with Jesus. The only passage I found specific to this issue is the one about King David's first child he had with Bathsheba. After the child had died, David said he would go to the child, but the child would not return to him. This implies that the child went to heaven; and that when David's life on earth was over, he would go to heaven and be with his child.[24]

---

[18] Matt. 21:16 And said unto him, Hearest thou what these say? And Jesus saith unto them, Yea; have ye never read, Out of the mouth of **babes and sucklings** thou hast perfected praise?

[19] Psalm 8:2 Out of the mouth of **babes and sucklings** hast thou ordained strength because of thine enemies, that thou mightest still the enemy and the avenger.

[20] Luke 10:21 In that hour Jesus rejoiced in spirit, and said, I thank thee, O Father, Lord of heaven and earth, that thou hast hid these things from the wise and prudent, and hast revealed them unto **babes**: even so, Father; for so it seemed good in thy sight.

[21] Luke 9:47 And Jesus, perceiving the thought of their heart, took a **child**, and set him by him, 48 And said unto them, Whosoever shall receive this child in my name receiveth me: and whosoever shall receive me receiveth him that sent me: for he that is least among you all, the same shall be great.

[22] Matt. 18:10 Take heed that ye despise not one of these **little ones**; for I say unto you, That in heaven their angels do always behold the face of my Father which is in heaven.

[23] Mark 10:13 And they brought young children to him, that he should touch them: and *his* disciples rebuked those that brought *them*. 14 But when Jesus saw *it*, he was much displeased, and said unto them, Suffer the little children to come unto me, and forbid them not: for of such is the kingdom of God. 15 Verily I say unto you, Whosoever shall not receive the kingdom of God as a little child, he shall not enter therein. 16 And he took them up in his arms, put *his* hands upon them, and blessed them.

[24] 2 Sam. 12:22 And he said, While the child was yet alive, I fasted and wept: for I said, Who can tell *whether* GOD will be gracious to me, that the child may live? 23 But now he is dead, wherefore should I fast? can I bring him back again? **I shall go to him**, but he shall not return to me.

Chapter 13

Faith Builders during Pregnancy

This chapter is set up differently. It is simply a list of Scriptures that may be often referred to, especially by expectant mothers. During my fourth pregnancy, the Lord instructed me to search His Word for Scriptures relating to childbearing or that could be applied to childbearing. I found that God has an answer for any area of difficulty. In this chapter Bible verses are listed in different categories for ease of reference. I used some of these as daily confessions. They are good for building up faith in particular areas relating to childbearing.

BLESSING AND HEALING: The first passage from Exodus was one of my favorites because it promised so many things: blessing of food and drink, deliverance from sickness (which includes "morning sickness"), fulfillment of days, no miscarriage, and no barrenness. I believe the promise of fulfillment of days includes the number of days the baby requires in the womb and full lifetimes for mother and baby after the birth.

Exod. 23:25 And ye shall serve the LORD your God, and he shall bless thy bread, and thy water; and I will take sickness away from the midst of thee. 26 There shall nothing cast their young, nor be barren, in thy land: the number of thy days I will fulfil.

Deut. 7:12 Wherefore it shall come to pass, if ye hearken to these judgments, and keep, and do them, that the LORD thy God shall keep unto thee the covenant and the mercy which he sware unto thy fathers: 13 And he will love thee, and **bless thee**, and **multiply thee**: he will also **bless the fruit of thy womb**, and the fruit of thy land, thy corn, and thy wine, and thine oil, the increase of thy kine, and the flocks of thy sheep, in the land which he sware unto thy fathers to give thee. 14 Thou shalt be **blessed above all people**: there shall **not be male or female barren** among you, or among your cattle. 15 And the **LORD will take away from thee all sickness**, and will put none of the evil diseases of Egypt, which thou knowest, upon thee; but will lay them upon all *them* that hate thee.

Deut. 28:4 **Blessed** *shall be* the **fruit of thy body**, and the fruit of thy ground, and the fruit of thy cattle, the increase of thy kine, and the flocks of thy sheep.... 11 And the LORD shall make thee **plenteous in goods, in the fruit of thy body**, and in the fruit of thy cattle, and in the fruit of thy ground, in the land which the LORD sware unto thy fathers to give thee.

Psalm 147:13 For he hath strengthened the bars of thy gates; he hath **blessed thy children within thee.**

Isa. 53:4 Surely he hath borne our griefs, and carried our sorrows:... 5 But he *was* wounded for our transgressions, *he was* bruised for our iniquities: the chastisement of our peace *was* upon him; and **with his stripes we are healed**.

Isa. 58:8 Then shall thy light break forth as the morning, and **thine health shall spring forth speedily**: and thy righteousness shall go before thee; the glory of the LORD shall be thy rereward.

Isa. 61:9 And their seed shall be known among the Gentiles, and their offspring among the people: all that see them shall acknowledge them, that they *are* the **seed which the LORD hath blessed.**

Isa. 65:23 They shall **not labour in vain, nor bring forth for trouble**; for they *are* the **seed of the blessed of the LORD, and their offspring with them.**

3 John 2 Beloved, I wish above all things that thou mayest **prosper and be in health**, even as thy soul prospereth.

PEACE: During my pregnancies, I had difficulty controlling my emotions. I was offended far too easily. Keeping the right attitude and staying at peace was a real challenge. I had to continually put 1 Corinthians 13:4-8 (the "love chapter") into my heart, and the Holy Spirit would remind me of it when I would get offended. Following are other verses to help us stay at peace and keep the right attitude. God's peace includes not only peace of mind, but also wholeness where all is well and nothing is lacking in any area.

Psalm 29:11 The LORD will give strength unto his people; the LORD will bless his people with **peace**.

Isa. 26:3 Thou wilt keep *him* in **perfect peace**, *whose* mind *is* stayed *on thee*: because he trusteth in thee. 4 Trust ye in the LORD for ever: for in the LORD JEHOVAH *is* everlasting strength:

John 14:27 **Peace** I leave with you, **my peace** I give unto you: not as the world giveth, give I unto you. Let not your heart be troubled, neither let it be afraid.

Rom. 15:13 Now the God of hope fill you with all **joy and peace** in believing, that ye may abound in hope, through the power of the Holy Ghost.... 33 Now the **God of peace** *be* **with you** all. Amen.

Eph. 2:14 For he is our **peace**, who hath made both one, and hath broken down the middle wall of partition *between us*;

Phil. 4:6 Be careful for nothing; but in every thing by prayer and supplication with thanksgiving let your requests be made known unto God. 7 And the **peace of God**, which passeth all understanding, shall keep your hearts and minds through Christ Jesus. 8 Finally, brethren, whatsoever things are true, whatsoever things *are* honest, whatsoever things *are* just, whatsoever things *are* pure, whatsoever things *are* lovely, whatsoever things *are* of good report; if *there be* any virtue, and if *there be* any praise, think on these things. 9 Those things, which ye have both learned, and received, and heard, and seen in me, do: and the **God of peace** shall be with you.

Col. 3:15 And let the **peace of God rule in your hearts**, to the which also ye are called in one body; and be ye thankful.

1 Thess. 5:23 And the very **God of peace** sanctify you wholly; and *I pray God* your whole spirit and soul and body be preserved blameless unto the coming of our Lord Jesus Christ. 24 Faithful *is* he that calleth you, who also will do *it*.

2 Thess. 3:16 Now the **Lord of peace** himself **give you peace always** by all means. The Lord *be* with you all.

2 Cor. 10:3 For though we walk in the flesh, we do not war after the flesh: 4 (For the weapons of our warfare *are* not carnal, but mighty through God to the pulling down of strong holds;) 5 **Casting down imaginations**, and every high thing that exalteth itself against the knowledge of God, and **bringing into captivity every thought to the obedience of Christ**;

Eph. 6:12 For we **wrestle not against flesh and blood**, but against principalities, against powers, against the rulers of the darkness of this world, against spiritual wickedness in high *places*.

Phil. 2:14 Do all things without murmurings and disputings:

Heb. 12:14 Follow **peace** with all *men*, and holiness, without which no man shall see the Lord:

James 3:16 For where envying and strife *is*, there *is* confusion and every evil work.

James 4:7 Submit yourselves therefore to God. Resist the devil, and he will flee from you. 8a Draw nigh to God, and he will draw nigh to you....

SLEEP AND REST: I found that sleep and rest were not as easy to get during pregnancy and when there are babies in the household. I stood on these Scriptures.

Psalm 127:2 *It is* vain for you to rise up early, to sit up late, to eat the bread of sorrows: *for so* **he giveth his beloved sleep**.
Prov. 3:24 When thou liest down, thou shalt not be afraid: yea, thou shalt lie down, and thy **sleep shall be sweet**.

Matt. 11:28 Come unto me, all *ye* that labour and are heavy laden, and **I will give you rest**. 29 Take my yoke upon you, and learn of me; for I am meek and lowly in heart: and **ye shall find rest** unto your souls. 30 For my yoke *is* easy, and my burden is light.

HELP: Whatever you are dealing with, God will help you.

Psalm 46:5 God *is* in the midst of her; she shall not be moved: God shall **help** her, *and that* right early.

Psalm 55:22 Cast thy burden upon the LORD, and he shall **sustain** thee: he shall never suffer the righteous to be moved.

Psalm 116:6 The LORD **preserveth** the simple: I was brought low, and he **helped** me. 7 Return unto thy rest, O my soul; for the LORD hath dealt bountifully with thee. 8 For thou hast delivered my soul from death, mine eyes from tears, *and* my feet from falling.

Isa. 50:7 For the Lord GOD will **help** me; therefore shall I not be confounded: therefore have I set my face like a flint, and I know that I shall not be ashamed.

Heb. 13:5b ... for he hath said, **I will never leave thee, nor forsake thee**. 6 So that we may boldly say, **The Lord *is* my helper**, and I will not fear what man shall do unto me.

STRENGTH: God gives us strength.

Psalm 18:32 *It is* God that girdeth me with **strength**, and maketh my way perfect.

Psalm 84:7 They **go from strength to strength**, *every one of them* in Zion appeareth before God.

Isa. 25:4 For thou hast been a **strength** to the poor, a **strength** to the needy in his distress, a **refuge** from the storm, a shadow from the heat, when the blast of the terrible ones *is* as a storm *against* the wall.

Isa. 30:7 For the Egyptians shall help in vain, and to no purpose: therefore have I cried concerning this, Their **strength** *is* to sit still.... 15 For thus saith the Lord GOD, the Holy One of Israel; In returning and rest shall ye be saved; in quietness and in confidence shall be your **strength**: and ye would not.... 21 And thine ears shall hear a word behind thee, saying, This *is* the way, walk ye in it, when ye turn to the right hand, and when ye turn to the left.

Isa. 40:28 Hast thou not known? hast thou not heard, *that* the everlasting God, the LORD, the Creator of the ends of the earth, fainteth not, neither is weary? *there is* no searching of his understanding. 29 **He giveth power to the faint**; and to *them that have* no might **he increaseth strength**. 30 Even the youths shall faint and be weary, and the young men shall utterly fall: 3 But they that wait upon the LORD **shall renew *their* strength**; they shall mount up with wings as eagles; they shall run, and **not be weary**; *and* they shall walk, and **not faint**.

Joel 3:10b ... let the weak say, **I *am* strong**.

Hab. 3:19a **The LORD God *is* my strength**, and he will make my feet like hinds' *feet*, and he will make me to walk upon mine high places....

Zech. 4:6 Then he answered and spake unto me, saying, This *is* the word of the LORD unto Zerubbabel, saying, **Not by might, nor by power, but by my spirit**, saith the LORD of hosts.

2 Cor. 12:9 And he said unto me, My grace is sufficient for thee: for **my strength is made perfect** in weakness. Most gladly therefore will I rather glory in my infirmities, that the power of Christ may rest upon me. 10 Therefore I take pleasure in infirmities, in reproaches, in necessities, in persecutions, in distresses for Christ's sake: for when I am weak, then **am I strong**.

Eph. 3:16 That he would grant you, according to the riches of his glory, to **be strengthened with might by his Spirit in the inner man**;

Col. 1:10 That ye might walk worthy of the Lord unto all pleasing, being fruitful in every good work, and increasing in the knowledge of God; 11 **Strengthened with all might**, according to his glorious power, unto all patience and longsuffering with joyfulness;

OLD WIVES' TALES: It seemed that when I was pregnant, I heard more "old wives' tales" than I had ever heard before. I believe they were designed by the devil to put fear into the hearts of pregnant women. Those words can eat as a canker, and the Bible says to refuse them.

1 Tim. 4:7 But refuse profane and old wives' fables, and exercise thyself *rather* unto godliness.

2 Tim. 2:16 But shun profane *and* vain babblings: for they will increase unto more ungodliness. 17a And their word will eat as doth a canker….

FEAR: Fear may try to come in, especially if something may not seem quite right. The expectant mother may be afraid that something is wrong with her or the baby. Fear is believing an evil report or thought. It leads to worry. This kind of fear does not come from God. It is the opposite of faith, which is believing God. He says over and over in His Word to fear not!

Isa. 35:4a Say to them *that are* of a fearful heart, Be strong, **fear not**….

Isa. 41:10 **Fear thou not**; for I *am* with thee: be not dismayed; for I *am* thy God: I will strengthen thee; yea, I will help thee; yea, I will uphold thee with the right hand of my righteousness…. 13 For I the LORD thy God will hold thy right hand, saying unto thee, **Fear not**; I will help thee.

2 Tim. 1:7 For **God hath not given us the spirit of fear**; but of power, and of love, and of a sound mind.

1 John 4:18 There is **no fear in love**; but **perfect love casteth out fear**: because fear hath torment. He that feareth is not made perfect in love.

FULFILLMENT: There is a time to be born. Expectant mothers may get impatient for that time, especially in the last month or so of pregnancy. When it is time for your baby to be born, he (or she) will be born! Any other plans you have made will be interrupted.

Eccl. 3:1 To every *thing there is* a season, and a time to every purpose under the heaven: 2a A **time to be born**….

Psalm 138:8 The LORD will perfect *that which* concerneth me: thy mercy, O LORD, *endureth* for ever: forsake not the works of thine own hands.

Gal. 6:9 And let us not be weary in well doing: for in due season we shall reap, if we faint not.

Phil. 1:6 Being confident of this very thing, that he which hath begun a good work in you will perform *it* until the day of Jesus Christ:

Phil. 2:13 For it is God which worketh in you both to will and to do of *his* good pleasure.

LABOR: God is with us in labor. We are laborers with Him. We are in partnership with Him in bringing forth children into the earth.

Prov. 10:16a The **labour** of the righteous *tendeth* to life....

Prov. 14:23a In all **labour** there is profit....

Isa. 66:7 **Before she travailed, she brought forth**; before her pain came, she was delivered of a man child. 8b ... for as soon as Zion travailed, she brought forth her children. 9 Shall I bring to the birth, and not cause to bring forth? saith the LORD: shall I cause to bring forth, and shut *the womb*? saith thy God.

John 16:21 A woman when she is in **travail** hath sorrow, because her hour is come: but as soon as she is delivered of the child, she remembereth no more the anguish, for joy that a man is born into the world.

1 Cor. 3:9a For we are **labourers together with God**....

1 Cor. 15:57 But thanks *be* to God, which giveth us the victory through our Lord Jesus Christ. 58b ... your **labour is not in vain in the Lord**.

1 Tim. 5:18b The **labourer** *is* worthy of his reward.

Heb. 6:10a For God *is* not unrighteous to forget your work and **labour of love**....

DELIVERY: God is the deliverer; He takes the babies out of the womb and gives them breath.

Gen. 2:7 And the LORD God formed man *of* the dust of the ground, and **breathed into his nostrils the breath of life**; and man became a living soul.

Job 33:4 The spirit of God hath made me, and the **breath of the Almighty hath given me life**.

Psalm 18:2 The LORD *is* my rock, and my fortress, and **my deliverer**; my God, my strength, in whom I will trust; my buckler, and the horn of my salvation, *and* my high tower.

Psalm 22:9 But thou *art* he that **took me out of the womb**: thou didst make me hope *when I was* upon my mother's breasts. 10 I was cast upon thee from the womb: thou *are* my God from my mother's belly.

Psalm 40:17 But I *am* poor and needy; *yet* the Lord thinketh upon me: thou *art* my help and **my deliverer**; make no tarrying, O my God.

Psalm 71:5 For thou *art* my hope, O Lord GOD: *thou art* my trust from my youth. 6 By thee have I been holden up from the womb: **thou art he that took me out of my mother's bowels**: my praise *shall be* continually of thee.

Psalm 91:14 Because he hath set his love upon me, therefore **will I deliver him**: I will set him on high, because he hath known my name. 15 He shall call upon me, and I will answer him: I *will be* with him in trouble; **I will deliver him**, and honour him. 16 With long life will I satisfy him, and shew him my salvation.

Prov. 11:21b ... but the seed of the righteous shall be **delivered**.

Isa. 46:3 Hearken unto me, O house of Jacob, and all the remnant of the house of Israel, which are **borne *by me* from the belly**, which are **carried from the womb**: 4 And *even to your* old age I *am* he; and *even* to hoar hairs will I carry *you*: I have made, and I will bear; even I will carry, and **will deliver *you***.

Gal. 1:15 But when it pleased **God, who separated me from my mother's womb**, and called *me* by his grace,

1 Tim. 2:15 Notwithstanding she shall be **saved in childbearing**, if they continue in faith and charity and holiness with sobriety.

Part Six

Parent and Child Relationships

Chapter 14

Protecting Children

Good, Not Evil

In the Garden of Eden, God forbade Adam and Eve to partake of the tree of the knowledge of good and evil.[1] They already knew the good because of all that God had provided for them, including close fellowship with Him. It was the evil that would destroy them. The devil deceived Eve by telling her that when they ate the forbidden fruit, they would be as gods, knowing good and evil. When she saw that the tree was good for food, pleasant to the eyes, and to be desired to make one wise, she and her husband ate of it. God sent them out of the Garden of Eden so they would not eat of the tree of life and live forever.[2]

As Adam and Eve were responsible to keep the garden of Eden, so parents are responsible to keep evil out of their own homes and away from their families. When we allow evil in, we open the door that allows the curse in.

Not only does the devil try to destroy adults, but he also seeks to destroy children. Revelation 12 tells that the devil stood before a woman who was ready to give birth so that he could devour her child as soon as it was born.[3] The devil tries to destroy many children by aborting them **before** they are born. If he is unable to do that, he seeks to lead them astray as early as possible.

Jesus told a parable about the wheat and the tares. He sows the good seed (the children of the kingdom), and the devil sows the tares (the children of the wicked).[4] If we considered our children as the

---

[1] Gen. 2:15 And the LORD God took the man, and put him into the garden of Eden to dress it and to keep it. 16 And the LORD God commanded the man, saying, Of every tree of the garden thou mayest freely eat: 17 But of the tree of the knowledge of good and evil, thou shalt not eat of it: for in the day that thou eatest thereof thou shalt surely die.

[2] Gen. 3:4 And the serpent said unto the woman, Ye shall not surely die: 5 For God doth know that in the day ye eat thereof, then your eyes shall be opened, and ye shall be as gods, knowing good and evil. 6 And when the woman saw that the tree *was* good for food, and that it *was* pleasant to the eyes, and a tree to be desired to make *one* wise, she took of the fruit thereof, and did eat, and gave also unto her husband with her; and he did eat.... 22 And the LORD God said, Behold, the man is become as one of us, to know good and evil: and now, lest he put forth his hand, and take also of the tree of life, and eat, and live for ever: 23 Therefore the LORD God sent him forth from the garden of Eden, to till the ground from whence he was taken.

[3] Rev. 12:1 And there appeared a great wonder in heaven; a woman clothed with the sun, and the moon under her feet, and upon her head a crown of twelve stars: 2 And she being with child cried, travailing in birth, and pained to be delivered. 3 And there appeared another wonder in heaven; and behold a great red dragon, having seven heads and ten horns, and seven crowns upon his heads. 4 And his tail drew the third part of the stars of heaven, and did cast them to the earth: and the **dragon stood before the woman which was ready to be delivered, for to devour her child as soon as it was born.**

[4] Matt. 13:24 Another parable put he forth unto them, saying, The kingdom of heaven is likened unto a man which sowed good seed in his field: 25 But while men slept, his enemy came and sowed tares among the wheat, and went his way. 26 But when the blade was sprung up, and brought forth fruit, then appeared the tares also. 27 So the servants of the householder came and said unto him, Sir, didst not thou sow good seed in thy field? from whence then hath it tares? 28a He said unto them, An enemy hath done this....

"field" and have sown good seed into them, we may wonder why "tares" come forth in their lives. It is because of the enemy. We must be diligent to keep him from sowing evil into our children.

We should teach our children the difference between right and wrong[5] so they will cling to that which is good and avoid all appearance of evil.[6] The children of God can be recognized because they do not practice sin; the children of the devil are recognized by their lack of righteousness and love.[7] There should be no doubt as to which we are.

Some parents may think that the more experiences their children have, the better their children will be equipped to choose what is right for them. However, this is not what the Bible says. It says we should not learn the way of the ungodly, for their customs are vain.[8] In training our children, we should **not** try to broaden their experiences by allowing them to be involved in everything that is available to them. The devil has laid many traps, and unsuspecting parents can be deceived into allowing (or even leading) their children into them. Instead, we should narrow our children's experiences to include **only** those offered by God. He says that the broad gate leads to destruction, but the narrow way leads to life.[9] Let's make sure our children are with us on the narrow way.

Jesus is our example of refusing evil and choosing good.[10] The Bible says He loves righteousness and hates iniquity.[11]

Separate from the World

The Bible states very clearly that Christians must not conform to this world,[12] but wholly follow God and his Word.[13] We are not to make any covenants with unbelievers nor allow them to be a snare to us.[14]

---

[5] Ezek. 44:23 And they shall teach my people *the difference* between the holy and profane, and cause them to discern between the unclean and the clean.

[6] 1 Thess. 5:21 Prove all things; hold fast that which is good. 22 Abstain from all appearance of evil.

[7] 1 John 3:9 Whosoever is born of God doth not commit sin; for his seed remaineth in him: and he cannot sin, because he is born of God. 10 In this the children of God are manifest, and the children of the devil: whosoever doeth not righteousness is not of God, neither he that loveth not his brother.

[8] Jer. 10:2 Thus saith the LORD, **Learn not the way of the heathen,** and be not dismayed at the signs of heaven; for the heathen are dismayed at them. 3a For the **customs of the people** *are* **vain**....

[9] Matt. 7:13 Enter ye in at the strait gate: for wide *is* the gate, and broad *is* the way, that leadeth to destruction, and many there be which go in thereat: 14 Because strait *is* the gate, and narrow *is* the way, which leadeth unto life, and few there be that find it.

[10] Isa. 7:14 Therefore the Lord himself shall give you a sign; Behold, a virgin shall conceive, and bear a son, and shall call his name **Immanuel**. 15 Butter and honey shall he eat, that he may know to **refuse the evil, and choose the good**.

[11] Heb. 1:8 But unto the Son *he saith*, Thy throne, O God, *is* for ever and ever: a sceptre of **righteousness** *is* the sceptre of thy kingdom. 9 Thou hast **loved righteousness, and hated iniquity**; therefore God, *even* thy God, hath anointed thee with the oil of gladness above thy fellows.

[12] Rom. 12:1 I beseech you therefore, brethren, by the mercies of God, that ye present your bodies a living sacrifice, holy, acceptable unto God, *which is* your reasonable service. 2 And **be not conformed to this world**: but be ye transformed by the renewing of your mind, that ye may prove what *is* that good, and acceptable, and perfect, will of God.

Lot was vexed by the conversation and deeds of the wicked among whom he lived in Sodom and Gomorrah.[15] Genesis 13 tells why he moved into Sodom and Gomorrah in the first place. Lot and his uncle, Abraham, had so many cattle that they had to spread out to make room for them all. Abraham gave Lot first choice of the land. Lot chose the well-watered land that was toward Sodom and Gomorrah. It looked good to him economically, but the men of that place were wicked.

Eventually Lot moved into the city, and its wickedness became a snare to his family. Genesis 19 tells about a time when Lot offered his virgin daughters to the wicked men of the city. His other daughters had married men that lived there. Later, when Lot warned his sons-in-law to flee the city because the Lord was going to destroy it, they did not heed his warning. After Lot and his two daughters were delivered from Sodom and Gomorrah, it was destroyed. However, the influence of the city was still with them. His daughters caused Lot to become drunk and took turns having sexual intercourse with him. They each bore a son by their father.

Choices of where to live should not be based only on what is best economically, but consideration should also be given to how the area might influence the family. However, if God calls us to a certain area, He will give us what is necessary to live there. He knows how to deliver the godly out of temptations.[16] We should seek His direction and follow it.

We should not allow our relatives or close friends to turn us away from God.[17] They may be the ones who influence us the most. Our relatives and friends may have traditions, customs, or ways of doing things that we once followed, too. An example might be involvement in Halloween. Perhaps you celebrated Halloween until you found out that it is a satanic holiday. Your relatives may persist in trying to keep you or your children involved because they may think you are missing all the "fun." But you must stand against that pressure and not allow it to pull you back into those things from which you have separated yourself.

---

[13] Lev. 18:1 And the LORD spake unto Moses, saying, 2 Speak unto the children of Israel, and say unto them, I am the LORD your God. 3 After the doings of the land of Egypt, wherein ye dwelt, shall ye not do: and after the doings of the land of Canaan, whither I bring you, shall ye not do: neither shall ye walk in their ordinances. 4 Ye shall do my judgments, and keep mine ordinances, to walk therein: I *am* the LORD your God. 5 Ye shall therefore keep my statutes, and my judgments: which if a man do, he shall live in them: I *am* the LORD.

[14] Exod. 34:12 Take heed to thyself, lest thou make a covenant with the inhabitants of the land whither thou goest, lest it be for a snare in the midst of thee:

[15] 2 Pet. 2:6 And turning the cities of **Sodom and Gomorrha** into ashes condemned *them* with an overthrow, making *them* an ensample unto those that after should live ungodly; 7 And delivered **just Lot, vexed with the filthy conversation of the wicked**: 8 (For **that righteous man dwelling among them**, in seeing and hearing, **vexed** *his* righteous soul from day to day **with *their* unlawful deeds;**)

[16] 2 Pet. 2:9 The Lord knoweth how to deliver the godly out of temptations, and to reserve the unjust unto the day of judgment to be punished:

[17] Deut. 13:6 If thy brother, the son of thy mother, or thy son, or thy daughter, or the wife of thy bosom, or thy friend, which *is* as thine own soul, entice thee secretly, saying, Let us go and serve other gods, which thou hast not known, thou, nor thy fathers; 7 *Namely*, of the gods of the people which *are* round about you, nigh unto thee, or far off from thee, from the *one* end of the earth even unto the *other* end of the earth; 8 **Thou shalt not consent unto him, nor hearken unto him;**...

If you are a new Christian, your friends in the world may not understand why you no longer enjoy those things you liked before.[18] But it is time to come out from among them and get out from under their influence.[19] Those who are friends of the world are enemies of God.[20] You should no longer share their interest in ungodly things. Do not allow them to pull you back into the evil from which you have been freed.

The New Testament says not to keep company with someone who claims to be a Christian, but is acting wickedly.[21] This person not only dishonors the Lord, but also is a bad influence on others. The Old Testament speaks of a "mixed multitude."[22] This occurs when God's children mix with the children of the world so much that you cannot tell the difference between the Christians and the unbelievers. Christians should not allow their children to marry non-Christians.[23]

The writer of Psalm 144 asked God to deliver him from the hand of strange children who speak vainly and deal falsely, so that his sons may be as plants grown up and his daughters as polished cornerstones.[24] This speaks of the effect that our friends and acquaintances can have on our children. Both our own and our children's friends should be chosen wisely. Evil communications and conduct corrupt good manners.[25] Since children may be easily influenced by others, we should make sure that friends (ours and theirs) are good influences.

---

[18] 1 Pet. 4:3 For the time past of *our* life may suffice us to have wrought the will of the Gentiles, when we walked in lasciviousness, lusts, excess of wine, revellings, banquetings, and abominable idolatries: 4 Wherein **they think it strange that ye run not with *them*** to the same excess of riot, speaking evil of *you*:

[19] 2 Cor. 6:14 Be ye not unequally yoked together with unbelievers: for what fellowship hath righteousness with unrighteousness? and what communion hath light with darkness? 15 And what concord hath Christ with Belial? or what part hath he that believeth with an infidel? 16 And what agreement hath the temple of God with idols? for ye are the temple of the living God; as God hath said, I will dwell in them, and walk in *them*; and I will be their God, and they shall be my people. 17 Wherefore **come out from among them, and be ye separate**, saith the Lord, and touch not the unclean *thing*; and I will receive you, 18 And will be a Father unto you, and ye shall be my sons and daughters, saith the Lord Almighty.

[20] James 4:4 Ye adulterers and adulteresses, know ye not that the friendship of the world is enmity with God? whosoever therefore will be a friend of the world is the enemy of God.

[21] 1 Cor. 5:6b ... Know ye not that a little leaven leaveneth the whole lump?... 11 But now I have written unto you not to keep company, if any man that is called a brother be a fornicator, or covetous, or an idolater, or a railer, or a drunkard, or an extortioner; with such an one no not to eat.... 13b ... Therefore put away from among yourselves that wicked person.

[22] Exod. 12:37a And the children of Israel journeyed.... 38a And a **mixed multitude** went up also with them....
Num. 11:4a And the **mixt multitude** that *was* among them fell a lusting ....
Psalm 106:34 They did not destroy the nations, concerning whom the LORD commanded them: 35 But were **mingled among the heathen**, and learned their works. 36 And they served their idols: which were a snare unto them. 37 Yea, they sacrificed their sons and their daughters unto devils,

[23] Ezra 9:12 Now therefore give not your daughters unto their sons, neither take their daughters unto your sons, nor seek their peace or their wealth for ever: that ye may be strong, and eat the good of the land, and leave *it* for an inheritance to your children for ever.

[24] Psalm 144:11 Rid me, and **deliver me from the hand of strange children**, whose mouth speaketh vanity, and their right hand *is* a right hand of falsehood: 12 That our sons *may be* as plants grown up in their youth; *that* our daughters *may be* as corner stones, polished *after* the similitude of a palace:

[25] 1 Cor. 15:33 Be not deceived: evil communications corrupt good manners.

In the book of Proverbs, counsel is given to choose the right companions and avoid the wrong ones. Those who walk with wise men shall be wise;[26] they will sharpen each other.[27] On the other hand, we are warned not to walk with sinners nor follow their path.[28] We should not involve ourselves with those who are unstable.[29] It brings shame to a father when his son becomes a friend of riotous men.[30] We should get away from a foolish person when we realize he speaks without knowledge[31] because a companion of fools shall be destroyed.[32] The Bible's definition of a fool is one who says in his heart that there is no God.[33] In Proverbs, we can see many contrasts between the wise and foolish. (These are tips on how to recognize a fool, so you can stay away from them and not become one yourself.)

Jesus prayed **not** for us to be taken out of the world, but that God would keep us from evil. We are not **of** the world, but He has sent us **into** the world.[34] We should not allow the world to influence us for evil, but we should influence the world for good. Jesus commands us to love our enemies.[35] The kind of love He was talking about is described in 1 Corinthians 13. All people are made in the image of God even if they are not presently reflecting that image. We should allow God's love to flow through us in order to point others to Him.

Keep Abominations Out

God says not to bring abominations into our houses lest we be cursed. We are to detest and abhor things that are an abomination to the Lord.[36] Abominations are things that the Lord hates, that are disgusting to Him. We should not give any place to the devil;[37] we should not allow anything of him in our homes.

---

[26] Prov. 13:20a He that walketh with wise *men* shall be wise....

[27] Prov. 27:17 Iron sharpeneth iron; so a man sharpeneth the countenance of his friend.

[28] Prov. 1:10 My son, **if sinners entice thee, consent thou not**.... 15 My son, walk not thou in the way with them; refrain thy foot from their path:

[29] Prov. 24:21 My son, fear thou the LORD and the king: *and* **meddle not with them that are given to change**: 22 For their calamity shall rise suddenly; and who knoweth the ruin of them both?

[30] Prov. 28:7 Whoso keepeth the law *is* a wise son: but he that is a **companion of riotous *men* shameth his father**.

[31] Prov. 14:7 **Go from the presence of a foolish man**, when thou perceivest not *in him* the lips of knowledge.

[32] Prov. 13:20b ... but a companion of fools shall be destroyed.

[33] Psalm 14:1a The fool hath said in his heart, *There is* no God....

[34] John 17:15 I pray not that thou shouldest take them out of the world, but that thou shouldest keep them from the evil. 16 They are not of the world, even as I am not of the world. 17 Sanctify them through thy truth: thy word is truth. 18 As thou hast sent me into the world, even so have I also sent them into the world.

[35] Matt. 5:44 But I say unto you, **Love your enemies**, bless them that curse you, do good to them that hate you, and pray for them which despitefully use you, and persecute you;

[36] Deut. 7:26 **Neither shalt thou bring an abomination into thine house**, lest thou be a cursed thing like it: *but* thou shalt **utterly detest it**, and thou shalt **utterly abhor it**; for it *is* a cursed thing.

[37] Eph. 4:27 Neither give place to the devil.

Sometimes people come to our door with a spiritual purpose. They may witness to us about the Lord or invite us to a church meeting. If they are truly Christian, their visit should be a blessing to us. If you cannot tell if the visitors are Christian, you could ask them some basic questions, such as: Do you believe Jesus is the Son of God and Savior of the world? Do you believe Jesus is the **only** way to God? Do you believe there is a heaven and a hell? If they cannot answer yes to these questions, they could be involved in a religious cult and have come to bring false doctrine. If this is their purpose, you should not receive them into your house.[38]

Child sacrifice, occult activities, spiritism, and idolatry are all abominations to the Lord. We should not be involved in any of these ourselves nor seek direction from those who are. God has raised up Jesus, to Whom we should listen.[39] The abominable will have their part in the lake of fire.[40]

The occult includes magic and astrology. Magic includes sorcery, witchcraft, charms, and spells. Wizards and witches are men and women who have made pacts with the devil or evil spirits to give them supernatural power. Elves and fairies are also associated with magic. Astrology includes the signs of the zodiac and horoscopes. Those who seek direction through horoscopes, fortunetellers, palm readers, or ouija boards are actually looking to Satan to guide their lives instead of seeking God.

Spiritism (or necromancy) is based on the ungodly belief that living people can communicate with the spirits of dead people. When people die, their spirits go immediately to heaven or hell, depending on their relationship with Jesus. Those involved in spiritism are opening themselves up to demonic spirits. A demon spirit that was familiar with a person living on the earth can make itself appear or sound like that person after his (or her) death.

Idolatry can take many forms. It includes myths about gods and goddesses. Trolls, mermaids, and unicorns are associated with mythology. (The Philistine god Dagon mentioned in 1 Samuel 5:1-5 was half-man and half-fish.) I suppose that most Christians today would consider themselves free of idolatry. We do not make graven images and fall down before them and worship them, do we? Yet consider the time, money, and attention that is spent by adults and children on the things of the world. Many people idolize sports heroes or movie and music stars. Bodies and body parts are sacrificed for the sake of sports. Many parents, without realizing it, train their little ones to take comfort and security in inanimate objects, such as blankets, dolls, and stuffed animals. If a child becomes so attached to a blanket or an image of a person or animal that

---

[38] 2 John 2:9 Whosoever transgresseth, and abideth not in the doctrine of Christ, hath not God. He that abideth in the doctrine of Christ, he hath both the Father and the Son. 10 If there come any unto you, and bring not this doctrine, receive him not into *your* house, neither bid him God speed: 11 For he that biddeth him God speed is partaker of his evil deeds.

[39] Deut. 18:9 When thou art come into the land which the LORD thy God giveth thee, thou shalt not learn to do after the **abominations** of those nations. 10 There shall not be found among you *any one* that **maketh his son or his daughter to pass through the fire,** *or* that useth **divination,** *or* an **observer of times,** or an **enchanter,** or a **witch,** 11 Or a **charmer,** or a **consulter with familiar spirits,** or a **wizard,** or a **necromancer.** 12 For all that do these things *are* an **abomination unto the LORD**: and because of **these abominations** the LORD thy God doth drive them out from before thee. 13 Thou shalt be perfect with the LORD thy God. 14 For these nations, which thou shalt possess, hearkened unto observers of times, and unto diviners: but as for thee, the LORD thy God hath not suffered thee so *to do.* 15 The LORD thy God will raise up unto thee a Prophet from the midst of thee, of thy brethren, like unto me; unto him ye shall hearken;

[40] Rev. 21:8 But the fearful, and unbelieving, and the **abominable,** and murderers, and whoremongers, and **sorcerers,** and **idolaters,** and all **liars,** shall have their part in the lake which burneth with fire and brimstone: which is the second death.

he objects to going anywhere or doing anything without it, then that thing has become an idol to that child. We must not allow **anything** to become an idol in our lives or our children's lives.[41]

As our understanding is opened to realize these things, it becomes clear how Satan has targeted the children. Items associated with these abominable things are marketed especially for children. They come in many different forms. There are books, magazines, posters, and comic books in printed form. Many games, movies, videos, tapes, television and computer programs for children have themes involving magic and other abominations. Many dolls and toys are made in the image of some fairy tale character, superhero, or mythological creature. Some toy creatures, especially those that do not represent something in God's natural creation, may be replicas of demons. Some may even appear cute, cuddly, and harmless; but that is Satan's way of causing children to become familiar and trusting of things with which he is associated. Even clothes, bedspreads and curtains may have on them pictures or symbols of abominable things.

We have had to purge our house of some of these things. It has not been a one-time purging; as we learn more, we purge more. We try to keep things out of our home that do not belong in it.

Some things are blatantly evil; others are not as easy to discern. Sometimes good and evil are mixed together as in a storybook that has both Bible stories and fairy tales. Parents must be discerning and seek the Lord for His guidance. I have found that whenever I have an uneasy feeling about a certain thing (even if I am not sure why), it is best for me to avoid that thing. My uneasy feeling is usually a warning prompted by the Holy Spirit. Learning to be sensitive to His promptings can keep us out of trouble.

It is better if you never allow your children to become fascinated with the occult, mythology, and fantasy. Fascination with these things causes confusion. When you allow your children to believe things that are not true, they cannot trust your word. How will they know that the Gospel is true if other things you have told them were not true? Imagination is good, but it must be channeled in the right direction. In Genesis 11, the people used their imagination to try to build a tower to heaven, the tower of Babel. God was not pleased with this, and He stopped it. Do not allow ungodly things to steal time from your child that should be spent on godly things. Teach them to go to the Lord for their needs and desires, not to Santa Claus or some other imaginary source.

If you still have doubts about what I have presented in this section, I encourage you to read Joshua 7. The Israelites had just won the battle of Jericho, but when they fought the battle with Ai (who had fewer people than Jericho), they were defeated. When Joshua sought the Lord to find out why, He told him that someone had taken an accursed thing into the camp.[42] Achan had taken a garment and some silver and gold from the spoils of Jericho. These items were accursed because God had forbidden the Israelites to take them. God told them to keep from the accursed thing, lest they make themselves and the camp of Israel accursed.[43]

If you have been involved in any abominations or have allowed abominable things in your house, the door has been opened to release demonic activity into your life and into your family. To close the door, you

---

[41] 1 John 5:21 Little children, keep yourselves from idols. Amen.

[42] Josh. 7:13 Up, sanctify the people, and say, Sanctify yourselves against to morrow: for thus saith the LORD God of Israel, *There is* an accursed thing in the midst of thee, O Israel: **thou canst not stand before thine enemies, until ye take away the accursed thing from among you.**

[43] Josh. 6:18 And ye, in any wise keep *yourselves* from the accursed thing, lest ye make *yourselves* accursed, when ye take of the accursed thing, and make the camp of Israel a curse, and trouble it.

must repent and ask God's forgiveness. Refuse any further association with these abominations. Do not hesitate to destroy occult paraphernalia. Maybe you think you have made too big an investment in the wrong things, and to get rid of them would be a waste of your money. However, the New Testament tells that some new believers who had used "curious arts" (magic) brought their books and burned them publicly. The price of them amounted to fifty thousand pieces of silver. The Word of God grew mightily and prevailed.[44] It is certainly worth getting rid of abominations to have the Word of God grow and prevail in your life and home. It is the Word of God that prompts you to get rid of the abominations in the first place; when you do, there is even more freedom for the Word to operate in your life.

It is not enough just to purge all evil out of your home. That would leave your home empty. You must replace the evil with good. When you take away unacceptable things from your children, you must replace them with acceptable things. Do not leave their lives empty. Jesus told a story about an unclean spirit that had gone out of a man. It was looking for another place to dwell, but found none. It decided to return and found the "house" empty. Then it gathered seven other spirits more wicked than itself, and they all entered in and dwelt in the man. Of course, the man was worse off then than at the first when he had only one demon.[45] Emptiness seems to draw evil. Fill your children's lives with things of the Lord, so there will be no empty places left for evil. There is much good that has been crowded out by the wrong things. Purging out the evil makes room to bring back the good.

Do Not Sacrifice Your Children

Jesus said not to give that which is holy unto the dogs and not to cast your pearls before swine, lest they trample them under foot and turn and destroy you.[46] I believe this verse can apply to our children because they are pearls (precious), and they are holy (set apart for God). Many parents are quick to give their children over to someone else to entertain, teach, and care for them. Many children are "trampled under foot" as a result. Make sure that you do not sacrifice your children by entrusting them to the ungodly.

There are parents today who depend too much on the world system to teach and train their children. People may think that children need prolonged socialization with children their own age, but much of the socialization offered by worldly institutions does more harm than good. Some parents are deceived into thinking they themselves are not as qualified to train their own children as the institutions are. In studying the Bible concerning families, I have found no Scriptural basis for turning our children over to any institution for training. The Bible repeatedly says it is the parents' responsibility to train their children. When God gives us the responsibility, He certainly will also give us the ability.

---

[44] Acts 19:18 And many that believed came, and confessed, and shewed their deeds. 19 Many of them also which used curious arts brought their books together, and burned them before all *men:* and they counted the price of them, and found *it* fifty thousand *pieces* of silver. 20 So mightily grew the word of God and prevailed.

[45] Matt. 12:43 When the unclean spirit is gone out of a man, he walketh through dry places, seeking rest, and findeth none. 44 Then he saith, I will return into my house from whence I came out; and when he is come, he findeth *it* empty, swept, and garnished. 45 Then goeth he, and taketh with himself seven other spirits more wicked than himself, and they enter in and dwell there: and the last *state* of that man is worse than the first. Even so shall it be also unto this wicked generation.

[46] Matt. 7:6 Give not that which is holy unto the dogs, neither cast ye your pearls before swine, lest they trample them under their feet, and turn again and rend you.

Many parents **expect** the government to train their children for them. However, children do not belong to the government; they belong to God. When questioned about paying taxes, Jesus answered that we should give to the government what belongs to it, but also give to God what belongs to Him.[47] As stewards over God's children, parents are responsible for training them God's way, not the government's way.

Parents must make sure that their children learn from the right source. The fear of the Lord is the beginning of both knowledge and wisdom.[48] If there is no fear of the Lord, there will be no true knowledge or wisdom. If your children are being taught by someone who believes there is no God, they are being taught by a fool.[49] Neither our children nor we should walk in the counsel of the ungodly.[50] The Bible says to beware lest anyone spoil you through philosophy and vain deceit based on traditions of men and the world, and not after Christ.[51] It warns that evil men and seducers will get worse and worse; those who are deceived will deceive others.[52]

In Proverbs it says to stop hearing instruction that causes you to err from the words of knowledge.[53] This verse convicted me when I was sending my children to be educated by the ungodly. I realized that I could no longer allow my children to receive instruction from them. It can be very confusing to a child when his parents teach him one way at home, yet send him to be educated by those with an opposing perspective. The verse that I stand on now says that all our children shall be taught of the Lord, and great shall be the peace of our children.[54] We see this now working in our family.

I found **many** Scriptures about people sacrificing their children by passing them through the fire, offering them as a burnt offering to their gods.[55] We shudder to even think of such a thing. God called it an abomination. Yet, today a lot of child sacrifice is still going on. It may be a different kind of sacrifice and

---

[47] Luke 20:25 And he said unto them, Render therefore unto Caesar the things which be Caesar's, and unto God the things which be God's.

[48] Prov. 1:7a The fear of the LORD *is* the beginning of knowledge....
Psalm 111:10 The fear of the LORD *is* the beginning of wisdom: a good understanding have all they that do *his commandments*: his praise endureth for ever.

[49] Psalm 53:1a The fool hath said in his heart, *There is* no God....

[50] Psalm 1:1 Blessed *is* the man that **walketh not in the counsel of the ungodly**, nor standeth in the way of sinners, nor sitteth in the seat of the scornful. 2 But his delight *is* in the law of the LORD; and in his law doth he meditate day and night.

[51] Col. 2:8 Beware lest any man spoil you through philosophy and vain deceit, after the tradition of men, after the rudiments of the world, and not after Christ.

[52] 2 Tim. 3:13 But evil men and seducers shall wax worse and worse, deceiving, and being deceived. 14 But continue thou in the things which thou hast learned and hast been assured of, knowing of whom thou hast learned *them*;

[53] Prov. 19:27 Cease, my son, to hear the instruction *that causeth* to err from the words of knowledge.

[54] Isa. 54:13 And all thy children *shall be* **taught of the LORD**; and great *shall be* the **peace** of thy children.

[55] Jer. 32:35 And they built the high places of Baal, which *are* in the valley of the son of Hinnom, to cause their sons and their daughters to pass through *the fire* unto Molech; which I commanded them not, neither came it into my mind, that they should do this **abomination**, to cause Judah to sin.
Ezek. 16:20 Moreover thou hast taken **thy sons and thy daughters**, whom **thou hast borne unto me**, and **these hast thou sacrificed unto them** to be devoured. *Is this* of thy whoredoms a small matter, 21 That **thou hast slain my children**, and delivered them to cause them to pass through *the fire* for them?

different names for the gods; but either way, the children are sacrificed. Abortion is definitely child sacrifice. This kind of child sacrifice is given for the gods of money, convenience, or whatever else has become an idol in the parents' lives.

There are other ways children are being sacrificed short of physical death. They are being "passed through the fire" of a different sort. One way is by our neglect of them. This may result in turning them over to the ungodly for care and instruction (as we have already mentioned). It may be that we are just leaving our children to themselves. Very often the god that is served is covetousness.

The Bible says covetousness is idolatry.[56] Covetousness is one of the signs of the perilous times that come in the last days.[57] People, whether great or small or anywhere in between, can become covetous.[58] Christians must not get caught up in this. The love of money is the root of all evil, and those who covet after it are seduced from the faith and reap many sorrows.[59] Covetousness adversely affects families. Those who are greedy of gain trouble their own houses.[60] Covetousness should never be found among Christians. No covetous person, who is an idolater, has any inheritance in the kingdom of God.[61] Beware of covetousness; realize that your life is not measured by what you possess.[62] Be content with what you have, and realize God is always with you and will provide for you.[63] When you hate covetousness, you prolong your days.[64]

Our family has a testimony of God's provision. My husband and I purposed in our hearts that I would stay home and care for our children. When I was pregnant with our first child, my husband and I were both working at jobs outside the home. Shortly after I became pregnant, my husband won a college scholarship. I quit my job two months before our daughter was born. My husband left his job and started school when she was about three months old. People wondered how we would make it financially, but God provided for us and carried us through. I have been home with our children ever since. God has honored our commitment to take the responsibility to train our children.

---

[56] Col. 3:5 Mortify therefore your members which are upon the earth; fornication, uncleanness, inordinate affection, evil concupiscence, and **covetousness, which is idolatry**:

[57] 2 Tim. 3:1 This know also, that in the last days perilous times shall come. 2 For **men shall be lovers of their own selves, covetous**, boasters, proud, blasphemers, disobedient to parents, unthankful, unholy,

[58] Jer. 6:13 For from the least of them even unto the greatest of them **every one *is* given to covetousness**; and from the prophet even unto the priest every one dealeth falsely.

[59] 1 Tim. 6:10 For the love of money is the root of all evil: which while some **coveted** after, they have erred from the faith, and pierced themselves through with many sorrows.

[60] Prov. 15:27a He that is greedy of gain **troubleth his own house**....

[61] Eph. 5:3 But fornication, and all uncleanness, or **covetousness**, let it not be once named among you, as becometh saints;... 5 For this ye know, that no whoremonger, nor unclean person, nor **covetous** man, **who is an idolater**, hath any inheritance in the kingdom of Christ and of God.

[62] Luke 12:15 And he said unto them, Take heed, and **beware of covetousness**: for a man's life consisteth not in the abundance of the things which he possesseth.

[63] Heb. 13:5 *Let your* conversation *be* **without covetousness**; *and be* content with such things as ye have: for he hath said, I will never leave thee, nor forsake thee.

[64] Prov. 28:16 The prince that wanteth understanding *is* also a great oppressor: *but* he that **hateth covetousness** shall prolong *his* days.

Your family may be in a situation where it seems that both parents must work at outside jobs, and someone else is caring for your children. I would encourage you to seek the Lord on this issue. Check your heart to make sure you are not acting out of covetousness. If you are committed to taking responsibility for your children's care, I believe God will show you how and will uphold your commitment.

However, just being at home with your children does not guarantee that they will not be neglected. Training and caring for children involves work, and we must be willing to do it.

Chapter 15

Training Children

There are many voices competing for our children. There is much advice available today on how to deal with our children. Some are worldly sources; some are Christian. The only valid source of advice is God's Word. He designed families, and He knows how they are to function. His instructions for us are written in the Bible. Any other advice, whether "secular" or "Christian," must line up with all of God's Word, or there is no guarantee of success. Parents must make the choice of how they will rear their children.

God told the Israelites not to go to Egypt (a type of the world) for counsel nor trust them for help. He said that would bring shame and confusion.[1] This applies to going to the "world" for counsel and help with our children. If we will commit to train and discipline our children according to God's way, He will direct us and enable us to do it. We can be confident that He will bring forth success.[2]

Parents' Responsibility

The Bible says that parents are responsible to care for and train their children. It says that if you train them up in the way they should go, they will not depart from it when they are old.[3] Notice that this verse does **not** say that the child will go away from his good training during his teen years, but will come back to it when he gets old. It **does** say he will **not depart** from his training. That means he will stay with it all his life and not turn away.

On becoming a parent, you are given the call to **bring up** your children in the nurture and admonition of the Lord.[4] If you are going to "bring" your children up, **you** have to be "up." Bringing means you are taking "with" you. "Sending" is not bringing. Bringing them up implies leading the way by example.[5]

---

[1] Isa. 30:1 Woe to the rebellious children, saith the LORD, that take counsel, but not of me; and that cover with a covering, but not of my spirit, that they may add sin to sin: 2 That walk to go down into Egypt, and **have not asked at my mouth**; to strengthen themselves in the strength of Pharaoh, and to trust in the shadow of Egypt! 3 Therefore shall the strength of Pharaoh be your **shame**, and the trust in the shadow of Egypt *your* **confusion**.... 7a For the **Egyptians shall help in vain**, and to no purpose....

[2] Isa. 30:7b ... therefore have I cried concerning this, Their strength *is* to sit still.... 15 For thus saith the Lord GOD, the Holy One of Israel; In returning and rest shall ye be saved; in quietness and in confidence shall be your strength: and ye would not.... 21 And thine ears shall hear a word behind thee, saying, **This *is* the way, walk ye in it**, when ye turn to the right hand, and when ye turn to the left.

[3] Prov. 22:6 Train up a child in the way he should go: and when he is old, he will **not depart** from it.

[4] Eph. 6:4 And, ye fathers, provoke not your children to wrath: but **bring them up** in the nurture and admonition of the Lord.

[5] Prov. 23:26 My son, give me thine heart, and let thine eyes observe my ways.
Psalm 101:2 I will behave myself wisely in a perfect way. O when wilt thou come unto me? **I will walk within my house with a perfect heart.** 3 I will set no wicked thing before mine eyes: I hate the work of them that turn aside; *it* shall not cleave to me.

Your children will reflect you. There can be no double standard; the Word of God must be the standard (absolute authority) for your children and for you.

Even though we are examples to our children, we cannot set ourselves up as the ultimate example. We make mistakes and should be willing to admit them, repent, and ask our children's forgiveness when we have failed them. Jesus is the supreme example for our children and us.

We should not provoke our children to anger. It can discourage them.[6] There are many ways parents can provoke their children to anger or cause them to be discouraged. Three ways that will be noted here are demanding too much of them, being inconsistent, and showing indifference.

We can overburden our children with too many demands. Sometimes it seems that no matter how hard our children try or how well they do, we are never quite satisfied. There is always something we can find fault with. Parents should not be like the lawyers and Pharisees Jesus rebuked. He said that they laid on others burdens that were too heavy, yet they would not even lift a finger to help.[7] He also said that they strain at a gnat and swallow a camel.[8] We should not be so concerned with little mistakes that we miss the big improvements our children are making. We should be generous with praise and encouragement.

Even when our children are not performing up to our standards, we should not give up on them, but give them another chance to improve. In Luke 13:6-9 Jesus told a parable about a man who had planted a fig tree, but found no fruit on it. After three years, he was ready to give up on it. But the caretaker requested another year in which he would give the fig tree special care. If our children are not meeting our expectations, perhaps we should focus on this area and give them extra care and attention to help them through it.

Inconsistency can show up in our training and lifestyle. Sometimes we tell our children one thing and then change our minds about it, or we may not follow through on what we have told them. When we set boundaries or rules or answer their requests, we should not do it lightly or hastily or according to our mood at the time. We should carefully consider and think things through before setting rules or answering requests. We should first of all make sure the rules we set line up with God's Word. We should be fair and just and not lay unnecessary burdens on the children. We must be prepared to back up our word and follow through on it. When we are consistent, our children can trust our word.

It helps with consistency when our household rules apply also to our children's visitors. God told the children of Israel that the same laws apply to the homeborn and the stranger that dwelt among them.[9] When our children's friends are in our home, they should be expected to abide by our household rules. If we require our children to pick up their toys after playing, their friends should help pick up toys they have used. If we do not allow our children to run while inside our house, neither should their friends.

---

[6] Col. 3:21 Fathers, provoke not your children *to anger*, lest they be discouraged.

[7] Luke 11:46 And he said, Woe unto you also, *ye* lawyers! for ye lade men with burdens grievous to be borne, and ye yourselves touch not the burdens with one of your fingers.

[8] Matt. 23:24 *Ye* blind guides, which strain at a gnat, and swallow a camel.

[9] Exod. 12:49 **One law** shall be to him that is **homeborn, and** unto the **stranger** that sojourneth **among you.**

Probably one of the most difficult inconsistencies for children is when parents give contrary orders. Which do they obey? My grandmother said that her parents always showed a united front before their children. If they disagreed, they worked it out privately. This unity between the parents provides great security for the children. Jesus promised to be in the midst of such unity.[10] On the other hand, He said that division can cause a house to fall.[11] Parents must get a vision for being laborers **together** to bring up God's children according to His way.[12]

Parents can be indifferent to a child's disobedience and rebellion. Some parents do not set boundaries for their children. Boundaries give a child a sense of security, even though he may test them. Parents can also expect too little of their children and not challenge them to do better. Parents can also be indifferent to their child's interests. It can be very discouraging to a child when his parents are not available to him or do not truly listen to him. Jesus is very clear about not offending little ones.[13] Parents, take heed!

Parents are like ministers to their children. We should follow the advice and example of Paul, one of the great ministers of the early church. He kept back nothing that was profitable to those for whom he was responsible.[14] He encouraged and comforted them and charged them to walk worthy of God.[15] Paul said that the servant of the Lord must not strive, but be gentle, apt to teach, and patient.[16]

The Bible places a high priority on providing for one's own family. It says that anyone who does not provide for his own, and especially those of his own household is worse than an unbeliever.[17] We should give good gifts to our children as God gives good gifts to us.[18]

We should not neglect our children. God says we should not hide ourselves from our own flesh.[19] We should make ourselves available to our own families. Proverbs says to be diligent to know the state of

---

[10] Matt. 18:19 Again I say unto you, That if **two of you shall agree** on earth as touching any thing that they shall ask, it shall be done for them of my Father which is in heaven. 20 For where **two or three are gathered together in my name**, there am **I in the midst** of them.

[11] Mark 3:25 And if a house be divided against itself, that house cannot stand.

[12] 1 Cor. 3:9 For we are **labourers together** with God: ye are God's husbandry, *ye are* God's building.

[13] Luke 17:1 Then said he unto the disciples, It is impossible but that offences will come: but woe *unto him*, through whom they come! 2 It were better for him that a millstone were hanged about his neck, and he cast into the sea, than that he should **offend one of these little ones**.

[14] Acts 20:20 *And* how I **kept back nothing that was profitable *unto you***, but have shewed you, and have taught you publickly, and from house to house,

[15] 1 Thess. 2:11 As ye know how we **exhorted** and **comforted** and **charged** every one of you, **as a father** *doth* **his children**, 12 That ye would walk worthy of God, who hath called you unto his kingdom and glory.

[16] 2 Tim. 2:24 And the servant of the Lord must **not strive**; but **be gentle** unto all *men*, **apt to teach, patient**,

[17] 1 Tim. 5:8 But if any **provide not for his own**, and specially for those of his own house, he hath denied the faith, and is **worse than an infidel**.

[18] Matt. 7:9 Or what man is there of you, whom if his son ask bread, will he give him a stone? 10 Or if he ask a fish, will he give him a serpent? 11 If ye then, being evil, know how to give good gifts unto your children, how much more shall your Father which is in heaven give good things to them that ask him?

[19] Isa. 58:7b … and that thou hide not thyself from thine own flesh?

your flocks and to look well to your herds.[20] Since we should do that for our animals, how much more should we do it for our own families!

Proverbs says that a man who wanders from his place is as a bird that wanders from her nest.[21] I used to wonder what that meant until I saw a revelation of that verse. One time we were looking at a house for rent and noticed a bird on a nest in a nearby tree. A few days later, we went back again and noticed the eggs had hatched, but the mother bird was gone. When we moved into the house a few days later, the baby birds had died. The revelation of the verse is that as the bird deserted her nest and left her babies without nourishment and vulnerable to the cold, so a man that deserts his home and neglects to care for his family opens the door to destruction.

Sometimes we feel justified in neglecting our family because we are ministering to others. Jesus gave an example of people who did that. He said that people were taking what they should have been giving to their parents and instead were giving it away as a gift to God. By doing that, they felt they were justified in not giving it to their parents. Jesus said they were replacing God's commandment with their own tradition.[22]

Another time, an outsider came to Jesus for help. He said the children's needs should be filled first; it was not suitable to take what belongs to the children and give it to others.[23] The woman pressed Jesus to give her the "crumbs" that fell from the children's "bread." For this saying, Jesus granted her request.[24] We should trust God to give us enough for our children and **extra** for others who need our help.

What profit is there if you gain the whole world and lose your own soul[25] (or the souls of your own children)? Following the Great Commission[26] begins at home. If every Christian parent made sure that all their children were born again and taught in God's Word, how much sooner could the rest of the world be evangelized? When the man from the country of the Gadarenes was delivered from the legion of demons,

---

[20] Prov. 27:23 Be thou diligent to know the state of thy flocks, *and* look well to thy herds.

[21] Prov. 27:8 As a bird that wandereth from her nest, so *is* a man that wandereth from his place.

[22] Matt. 15:3 But he answered and said unto them, Why do ye also transgress the commandment of God by your tradition? 4 For God commanded, saying, Honour thy father and mother: and, He that curseth father or mother, let him die the death. 5 But ye say, Whosoever shall say to *his* father or *his* mother, *It is* a gift, by whatsoever thou mightest be profited by me; 6 And honour not his father or his mother, *he shall be free*. Thus have ye made the commandment of God of none effect by your tradition.

[23] Mark 7:26 The woman was a Greek, a Syrophenician by nation; and she besought him that he would cast forth the devil out of her daughter. 27 But Jesus said unto her, **Let the children first be filled:** for **it is not meet to take the children's bread, and to cast** *it* **unto the dogs.**

[24] Mark 7:28 And she answered and said unto him, Yes, Lord: yet the dogs under the table eat of the children's crumbs. 29 And he said unto her, For this saying go thy way; the devil is gone out of thy daughter. 30 And when she was come to her house, she found the devil gone out, and her daughter laid upon the bed.

[25] Mark 8:36 For what shall it profit a man, if he shall gain the whole world, and lose his own soul? 37 Or what shall a man give in exchange for his soul?

[26] Matt. 28:18 And Jesus came and spake unto them, saying, All power is given unto me in heaven and in earth. 19 Go ye therefore, and teach all nations, baptizing them in the name of the Father, and of the Son, and of the Holy Ghost: 20 Teaching them to observe all things whatsoever I have commanded you: and, lo, I am with you alway, *even* unto the end of the world. Amen.

Jesus told him to return to **his own house** and show what God had done.[27] We should not neglect to show our own children the great things God has done for us.

This whole idea of parenting according to God's plan may seem overwhelming at first, especially if you have never really taken it seriously before. Just remember that when we commit it unto the Lord, He is there to help us. We cannot do it in our own strength anyway. When we are in yoke with Jesus and learn His way, everything becomes easier.[28] I like the way God led Joseph (Jesus' stepfather) step by step. After the wise men's visit, God warned Joseph to take his family and flee to Egypt. Then God let him know when it was time to return and where to go. Joseph obeyed at every step.[29] We parents should be so tuned in to God's leading and so obedient to Him that we, too, can be led as Joseph was.

As children grow, parents are also growing in their parenting skills. It does not happen overnight. It is a training process for both parents and children. We must start where we are and continue to move **forward**. As we become better at managing our households, God can entrust us with responsibilities beyond our own homes. At the same time we will be training our children (by our example) how to become good parents when they grow up.

Authority

Both parents are responsible for their children. God has given **both** parents authority over their children. This is all the more reason for **both** parents to be in agreement in bringing up their children.

In this day and time, some families seem to have the authority backwards. It appears that the children are ruling over the parents. The Bible says that is a woeful and oppressive situation.[30] Just as we (God's

---

[27] Luke 8:38 Now the man out of whom the devils were departed besought him that he might be with him: but Jesus sent him away, saying, 39 Return to thine own house, and shew how great things God hath done unto thee. And he went his way, and published throughout the whole city how great things Jesus had done unto him.

[28] Matt. 11:28 Come unto me, all *ye* that labour and are heavy laden, and I will give you rest. 29 Take my yoke upon you, and learn of me; for I am meek and lowly in heart: and ye shall find rest unto your souls. 30 For my yoke *is* easy, and my burden is light.

[29] Matt. 2:13 And when they were departed, behold, the **angel of the Lord appeareth to Joseph in a dream**, saying, Arise, and take the young child and his mother, and flee into Egypt, and be thou there until I bring thee word: for Herod will seek the young child to destroy him. 14 When he arose, he took the young child and his mother by night, and departed into Egypt: ... 19 But when Herod was dead, behold, an **angel of the Lord appeareth in a dream to Joseph** in Egypt, 20 Saying, Arise, and take the young child and his mother, and go into the land of Israel: for they are dead which sought the young child's life. 21 And he arose, and took the young child and his mother, and came into the land of Israel. 22 But when he heard that Archelaus did reign in Judaea in the room of his father Herod, he was afraid to go thither: notwithstanding, **being warned of God in a dream**, he turned aside into the parts of Galilee:

[30] Eccl. 10:16a **Woe to thee, O land, when thy king *is* a child**....
Isa. 3:4 And I will **give children *to be* their princes, and babes shall rule over them.** 5 **And the people shall be oppressed**, every one by another, and every one by his neighbour: **the child shall behave himself proudly against the ancient, and the base against the honourable.**

creatures) should not strive with our Maker, so children should not strive against their parents.[31] We and our children should recognize who is in authority.

Eli, a priest during the time of Samuel, was an example of a father who did not exercise his authority over his sons. The Bible says his sons did not know the Lord, and they did not listen to their father.[32] Eli had not trained them to know the Lord, nor had he trained them to respect his authority as their father. He also failed in that he honored his sons above God.[33] God judged Eli's house because he did not restrain his sons even when he knew "his sons made themselves vile."[34] "Vile" as used in this verse can mean accursed. In other words, Eli's sons brought a curse upon themselves. This is a lesson to us to restrain our children from evil and not allow them to draw a curse upon themselves.

There are examples of parents in the Bible who **did** recognize their authority over their children. There are several mentioned in the New Testament who came to Jesus to get help for their children. Jairus came to Jesus on behalf of his daughter for restoration of her life and health.[35] A father is mentioned who came to Jesus to deliver his son from demonic oppression.[36] A nobleman came to Jesus for healing for his

---

[31] Isa. 45:9 **Woe unto him that striveth with his Maker!** *Let* the potsherd *strive* with the potsherds of the earth. Shall the clay say to him that fashioneth it, What makest thou? or thy work, He hath no hands? 10 **Woe unto him that saith unto *his* father**, What begettest thou? **or to the woman**, What hast thou brought forth?

[32] 1 Sam. 2:12 Now the sons of Eli *were* sons of Belial; **they knew not the LORD**.... 17 Wherefore the sin of the young men was very great before the LORD: for men abhorred the offering of the LORD.... 22 Now Eli was very old, and heard all that his sons did unto all Israel; and how they lay with the women that assembled *at* the door of the tabernacle of the congregation. 23 And he said unto them, Why do ye such things? for I hear of your evil dealings by all this people. 24 Nay, my sons; for *it is* no good report that I hear: ye make the LORD'S people to transgress. 25 If one man sin against another, the judge shall judge him: but if a man sin against the LORD, who shall intreat for him? Notwithstanding **they hearkened not unto the voice of their father**, because the LORD would slay them.

[33] 1 Sam. 2:27 And there came a man of God unto Eli, and said unto him, Thus saith the LORD, Did I plainly appear unto the house of thy father, when they were in Egypt in Pharaoh's house? 28 And did I choose him out of all the tribes of Israel *to be* my priest, to offer upon mine altar, to burn incense, to wear an ephod before me? and did I give unto the house of thy father all the offerings made by fire of the children of Israel? 29 Wherefore kick ye at my sacrifice and at mine offering, which I have commanded *in my* habitation; and **honourest thy sons above me**, to make yourselves fat with the chiefest of all the offerings of Israel my people?

[34] 1 Sam. 3:11 And the LORD said to Samuel, Behold, I will do a thing in Israel, at which both the ears of every one that heareth it shall tingle. 12 In that day I will perform against Eli all *things* which I have spoken concerning his house: when I begin, I will also make an end. 13 For I have told him that I will judge his house for ever for the iniquity which he knoweth; **because his sons made themselves vile, and he restrained them not.**

[35] Matt. 9:18 While he spake these things unto them, behold, there came a certain ruler, and worshipped him, saying, My daughter is even now dead: but come and lay thy hand upon her, and she shall live. 19 And Jesus arose, and followed him, and *so did* his disciples.... 23 And when Jesus came into the ruler's house, and saw the minstrels and the people making a noise, 24 He said unto them, Give place: for the maid is not dead, but sleepeth. And they laughed him to scorn. 25 But when the people were put forth, he went in, and took her by the hand, and the maid arose.
(See also Mark 5:22-24, 35-43 and Luke 8:41-42, 49-56)

[36] Matt. 17:14 And when they were come to the multitude, there came to him a *certain* man, kneeling down to him, and saying, 15 Lord, have mercy on my son: for he is lunatick, and sore vexed: for ofttimes he falleth into the fire, and oft into the water. 16 And I brought him to thy disciples, and they could not cure him. 17 Then Jesus answered and said, O faithless and perverse generation, how long shall I be with you? how long shall I suffer you? bring him hither to me. 18 And Jesus rebuked the devil; and he departed out of him: and the child was cured from that very hour.
(See also Mark 9:17-27 and Luke 9: 37-42)

son.[37] Whenever we face any problem with our children, we should go to Jesus on behalf of our children for help in the situation.

All people who are **in authority** are also **under authority**.[38] Parents are **in authority** over their children, but they are **under the authority** of God and His Word. Jesus said that He spoke what His Father told Him to speak.[39] The people noticed that Jesus spoke with authority.[40] Parents can also speak with authority when they speak in line with God's Word.

We must train our children to respect authority. They must respect God's authority and also all those God has placed in authority over them, such as: parents, church leaders, and government leaders.[41] As you train your children to respect your authority as parents, you are setting a pattern of respect for others that will be in authority over them.

We should not allow our children to despise those in positions of authority. We should not set an example before them of criticizing church leaders, government leaders, or any others in authority. The Bible says that those who despise government will be punished.[42]

---

[37] John 4:46 So Jesus came again into Cana of Galilee, where he made the water wine. And there was a certain nobleman, whose son was sick at Capernaum. 47 When he heard that Jesus was come out of Judaea into Galilee, he went unto him, and besought him that he would come down, and heal his son: for he was at the point of death. 48 Then said Jesus unto him, Except ye see signs and wonders, ye will not believe. 49 The nobleman saith unto him, Sir, come down ere my child die. 50 Jesus saith unto him, Go thy way; thy son liveth. And the man believed the word that Jesus had spoken unto him, and he went his way. 51 And as he was now going down, his servants met him, and told *him*, saying, Thy son liveth. 52 Then enquired he of them the hour when he began to amend. And they said unto him, Yesterday at the seventh hour the fever left him. 53 So the father knew that *it was* at the same hour, in the which Jesus said unto him, Thy son liveth: and himself believed, and his whole house.

[38] Luke 7:8 For I also am a **man set under authority**, having under me soldiers, and I say unto one, Go, and he goeth; and to another, Come, and he cometh; and to my servant, Do this, and he doeth *it*.

[39] John 12:49 For I have not spoken of myself; but the Father which sent me, he gave me a commandment, what I should say, and what I should speak.

[40] Matt. 7:28 And it came to pass, when Jesus had ended these sayings, the people were astonished at his doctrine: 29 For he taught them as *one* having **authority**, and not as the scribes.

[41] Heb. 13:7 **Remember them which have the rule over you,** who have spoken unto you the word of God: whose faith follow, considering the end of *their* conversation.... 17 **Obey them that have the rule over you, and submit yourselves**: for they watch for your souls, as they that must give account, that they may do it with joy, and not with grief: for that *is* unprofitable for you.
Prov. 24:21 My son, **fear thou the LORD and the king**: *and* meddle not with them that are given to change:
1 Pet. 2:17 Honour all *men*. Love the brotherhood. **Fear God. Honour the king.** 18 Servants, *be* subject to *your* masters with all fear; not only to the good and gentle, but also to the froward.
Rom. 13:1 Let every soul **be subject unto the higher powers.** For there is no power but of God: the **powers that be are ordained of God.** 2 Whosoever therefore resisteth the power, resisteth the ordinance of God: and they that resist shall receive to themselves damnation. 3 For rulers are not a terror to good works, but to the evil. Wilt thou then not be afraid of the power? do that which is good, and thou shalt have praise of the same: 4 For he is the minister of God to thee for good. But if thou do that which is evil, be afraid; for he beareth not the sword in vain: for he is the minister of God, a revenger to *execute* wrath upon him that doeth evil. 5 Wherefore *ye* must needs be subject, not only for wrath, but also for conscience sake. 6 For for this cause pay ye tribute also: for they are God's ministers, attending continually upon this very thing. 7 Render therefore to all their dues: tribute to whom tribute *is due*; custom to whom custom; fear to whom fear; honour to whom honour.
Titus 3:1 Put them in mind to **be subject to principalities and powers**, to obey magistrates, to be ready to every good work,

[42] 2 Pet. 2:9 The Lord knoweth how to deliver the godly out of temptations, and to reserve the **unjust** unto the day of judgment to be punished: 10 But chiefly them that walk after the flesh in the lust of uncleanness, and **despise government**. Presumptuous *are they*, selfwilled, they are not afraid to speak evil of dignities.

Instead of criticizing, we should pray for those in authority.[43] If you think someone in authority over you is not right or fair, then pray that his heart be turned according to God's will.[44] Our daughter has prayed this prayer many times for us, and God has turned our hearts in the right direction. Sometimes He changed her heart to realize that we were already making the right choice on her behalf.

Jude 8 Likewise also these *filthy* dreamers defile the flesh, **despise dominion**, and speak evil of dignities.

[43] 1 Tim. 2:1 I exhort therefore, that, first of all, supplications, prayers, intercessions, *and* giving of thanks, be made for all men; 2 For **kings**, and *for* **all that are in authority**; that we may lead a quiet and peaceable life in all godliness and honesty.

[44] Prov. 21:1 The king's heart *is* in the hand of the LORD, *as* the rivers of water: he turneth it whithersoever he will.

Chapter 16

God's Word as Foundation

Wisdom and Understanding

There is a wealth of wisdom in the book of Proverbs[1] that instructs parents in training their children. The book is made up of thirty-one chapters, which makes it convenient to read one chapter a day every month. Not only will reading Proverbs increase your own wisdom; but if your children are old enough, they should also be encouraged to read a chapter a day. If your children are younger, you could select parts to discuss with them each day.

The fear of the Lord is the beginning of both wisdom and knowledge. Knowing God and His ways is understanding. Departing from evil is also understanding. The fear of the Lord is to hate evil, and by the fear of the Lord we depart from evil.[2] Since the fear of the Lord is involved with wisdom, knowledge, understanding, and departing from evil; it is foundational for us to learn to fear (reverence) the Lord. We must also teach our children to fear the Lord.[3] When parents and children have understanding, they will be drawn to what is holy and will shun what is evil.

Wisdom and understanding should be sought after.[4] The same wisdom that was with God at creation calls **us** to receive instruction. How awesome! Notice where wisdom stands and calls to us: in the top of the high places, by the way of the paths, at the gates, at the entries of cities and doors.[5] I believe this represents places of decision. Which path do I take? Where should I enter? Wisdom has the answers for you.

---

[1] Prov 1:1 The proverbs of Solomon the son of David, king of Israel; 2 To know **wisdom** and **instruction**; to perceive the words of **understanding**; 3 To receive the **instruction of wisdom**, justice, and judgment, and equity;

[2] Prov 1:7 The **fear of the LORD** *is* **the beginning of knowledge:** *but* fools despise wisdom and instruction.
Prov. 15:33 The **fear of the LORD** *is* **the instruction of wisdom**; and before honour *is* humility.
Prov. 9:9 Give *instruction* to a wise *man*, and he will be yet wiser: teach a just *man*, and he will increase in learning. 10 The **fear of the LORD** *is* **the beginning of wisdom:** and **the knowledge of the holy** *is* **understanding.** 11 For by me thy days shall be multiplied, and the years of thy life shall be increased.
Job. 28:28 And unto man he said, Behold, the **fear of the Lord, that** *is* **wisdom**; and **to depart from evil** *is* **understanding.**
Prov. 8:13a The **fear of the LORD** *is* **to hate evil:**...
Prov. 16:6 By mercy and truth iniquity is purged: and **by the fear of the LORD men depart from evil.**

[3] Psalm 34:11 Come, ye children, hearken unto me: I will teach you the **fear of the LORD.**

[4] Prov. 4:7 Wisdom *is* the principal thing; *therefore* get **wisdom**: and with all thy getting get **understanding.**
Prov. 2:1 My son, if thou wilt receive my words, and hide my commandments with thee; 2 So that thou incline thine ear unto **wisdom**, *and* apply thine heart to **understanding**; 3 Yea, if thou criest after **knowledge**, *and* liftest up thy voice for **understanding**; 4 If thou seekest her as silver, and searchest for her as *for* hid treasures; 5 Then shalt thou **understand the fear of the LORD, and find the knowledge of God.**

[5] Prov. 8:1 Doth not **wisdom** cry? and **understanding** put forth her voice? 2 She standeth in the **top of high places, by the way in the places of the paths.** 3 She crieth **at the gates, at the entry of the city, at the coming in at the doors.**... 10 Receive my instruction, and not silver; and knowledge rather than choice gold.... 22 The LORD possessed me in the beginning of his way, before his works of old. 23 I was set up from everlasting, from the beginning, or ever the earth was.... 32 Now therefore hearken unto me, O ye children: for blessed *are they that* keep my ways. 33 Hear instruction, and be wise, and refuse it not. 34

The Holy Spirit and the Bible have been given to us today as our source of wisdom in the earth. The Holy Spirit reveals God's Word to us and gives us understanding of it.

Receiving instruction brings forth wisdom and understanding.[6] We must train our children to hear and pay attention to instruction. Even a child who receives instruction can be wiser and better than an old king who refuses instruction and correction.[7]

Teaching

The foundation for teaching our children is the Word of God. What God has given us in His Word are the things that He desires to reveal to us. They belong to us and to our children.[8] His Word is profitable for teaching, conviction, correction, and instruction to bring us to maturity and to thoroughly furnish us.[9]

God's Word is spirit and life to us.[10] His Word is forever settled in heaven; His faithfulness is to all generations. His Word can cleanse our way and help us to avoid sin. His Word is a lamp and light to direct our way and give us understanding. His Word gives us peace and keeps us from being offended.[11]

Blessed *is* the man that heareth me, watching daily at my gates, waiting at the posts of my doors. 35 For whoso findeth me findeth life, and shall obtain favour of the LORD. 36 But he that sinneth against me wrongeth his own soul: all they that hate me love death.

[6] Prov. 1:5 A **wise** *man* will hear, and will increase learning; and a man of **understanding** shall attain unto wise counsels:
Prov. 5:1 My son, attend unto my **wisdom**, *and* bow thine ear to my **understanding**: 2 That thou mayest regard discretion, and *that* thy lips may keep knowledge.... 7 Hear me now therefore, O ye children, and depart not from the words of my mouth.
Prov. 7:1 My son, keep my words, and lay up my commandments with thee. 2 Keep my commandments, and live; and my law as the apple of thine eye. 3 Bind them upon thy fingers, write them upon the table of thine heart. 4 Say unto **wisdom**, Thou *art* my sister; and call **understanding** *thy* kinswoman:... 24 Hearken unto me now therefore, O ye children, and attend to the words of my mouth.
Prov. 16:21 The **wise** in heart shall be called prudent: and the sweetness of the lips increaseth learning. 22 **Understanding** *is* a wellspring of life unto him that hath it: but the instruction of fools *is* folly. 23 The heart of the **wise** teacheth his mouth, and addeth learning to his lips.

[7] Eccl. 4:13 Better *is* a poor and a **wise child** than an old and foolish king, who will no more be admonished.

[8] Deut. 29:29 The secret *things belong* unto the LORD our God: but those *things which are* revealed *belong* unto us and to our children for ever, that *we* may do all the words of this law.

[9] 2 Tim. 3:16 All scripture *is* given by inspiration of God, and *is* profitable for doctrine, for reproof, for correction, for instruction in righteousness: 17 That the man of God may be perfect, throughly furnished unto all good works.

[10] John 6:63 It is the spirit that quickeneth; the flesh profiteth nothing: the words that I speak unto you, *they* are spirit, and *they* are life.

[11] Psalm 119:9 Wherewithal shall a young man **cleanse his way**? by taking heed *thereto* according to thy word. 10 With my whole heart have I sought thee: O let me not wander from thy commandments. 11 Thy word have I hid in mine heart, that I might **not sin against thee**. 12 Blessed *art* thou, O LORD: teach me thy statutes.... 29 Remove from me the way of lying: and grant me thy law graciously. 30 I have chosen the way of truth: thy judgments have I laid *before me*.... 89 **For ever, O LORD, thy word is settled in heaven**. 90 Thy faithfulness *is* unto all generations: thou hast established the earth, and it abideth.... 99 I have more understanding than all my teachers: for thy testimonies *are* my meditation. 100 I understand more than the ancients, because I keep thy precepts. 101 I have refrained my feet from every evil way, that I might keep thy word.... 105 Thy word *is* a **lamp unto my feet**, and a **light unto my path**.... 130 The entrance of thy words **giveth light**; it **giveth understanding** unto the simple.... 133 Order my steps in thy word: and let not any iniquity have dominion over me. 134 Deliver me from the oppression

Following God's Word adds long life and peace to us. It gives us mercy, truth, favor, understanding, and direction.[12] These benefits of knowing and obeying God's Word can motivate us to teach our children so they will also receive the benefits.

However, God has **commanded** us to teach our children His Word. He says to talk of His Word to our children when we sit in our house, when we walk by the way, when we lie down, and when we rise up.[13] In other words, teaching our children God's Word is to be a continual process. There is no backing off or idle time if we teach them when we sit, walk, lie down, and rise up. We must lay a foundation for God's Word to be working in their hearts at all times so that following His Word becomes a way of life for them.[14]

When our first two children came along, instead of being ready to teach them, I was in the position mentioned in Hebrews 5 where I still needed to be taught myself.[15] I was still a baby Christian on "milk" and not yet ready for the "strong meat" of God's Word. Yet if we desire the milk of God's Word and feed on it, we will grow.[16] We can teach our children what we already know; then our family can continue to study God's Word and grow together.

Children are never too young for their spirits to receive God's Word. The Bible gives examples of children who started early in the things of God. The angel told Zacharias that his son (who became John the Baptist) would be filled with the Holy Ghost even from his mother's womb.[17] Jesus said that even babes and

---

of man: so will I keep thy precepts.... 164 Seven times a day do I praise thee because of thy righteous judgments. 165 **Great peace** have they which love thy law: and **nothing shall offend** them.

[12] Prov. 3:1 My son, forget not my law; but let thine heart keep my commandments: 2 For **length of days**, and **long life**, and **peace**, shall they add to thee. 3 Let not **mercy** and **truth** forsake thee: bind them about thy neck; write them upon the table of thine heart: 4 So shalt thou find **favour** and **good understanding** in the sight of God and man. 5 Trust in the LORD with all thine heart; and lean not unto thine own understanding. 6 In all thy ways acknowledge him, and **he shall direct thy paths**.

[13] Deut. 4:9 Only take heed to thyself, and keep thy soul **diligently**, lest thou forget the things which thine eyes have seen, and lest they depart from thy heart all the days of thy life: but **teach** them thy sons, and thy sons' sons; 10 *Specially* the day that thou stoodest before the LORD thy God in Horeb, when the LORD said unto me, Gather me the people together, and I will make them **hear** my words, that they may **learn** to fear me all the days that they shall live upon the earth, and *that* they may **teach their children**.
Deut. 6:4 Hear, O Israel: The LORD our God *is* one LORD: 5 And thou shalt love the LORD thy God with all thine heart, and with all thy soul, and with all thy might. 6 And these words, which I command thee this day, shall be in thine heart: 7 And thou shalt **teach them diligently unto thy children**, and shalt talk of them **when thou sittest** in thine house, and **when thou walkest** by the way, and **when thou liest down**, and **when thou risest up**. 8 And thou shalt bind them for a sign upon thine hand, and they shall be as frontlets between thine eyes. 9 And thou shalt **write them upon the posts of thy house, and on thy gates**.

[14] Prov. 6:20 My son, keep thy father's commandment, and forsake not the law of thy mother: 21 Bind them continually upon thine heart, *and* tie them about thy neck. 22 When thou goest, it shall lead thee; when thou sleepest, it shall keep thee; and *when* thou awakest, it shall talk with thee. 23 For the commandment *is* a lamp; and the law *is* light; and reproofs of instruction *are* the way of life:

[15] Heb. 5:12 For when for the time ye ought to be teachers, ye have need that one teach you again which *be* the first principles of the oracles of God; and are become such as have need of milk, and not of strong meat. 13 For every one that useth milk *is* unskilful in the word of righteousness: for he is a babe. 14 But strong meat belongeth to them that are of full age, *even* those who by reason of use have their senses exercised to discern both good and evil.

[16] 1 Peter 2:2 As newborn babes, desire the sincere milk of the word, that ye may grow thereby:

[17] Luke 1:15 For he shall be great in the sight of the LORD, and shall drink neither wine nor strong drink; and he shall be filled with the Holy Ghost, even from his mother's womb.

sucklings can praise God.[18] Timothy learned the Scriptures as a child.[19] He grew up to be an assistant to the Apostle Paul and later became a pastor. Samuel's parents took him to the temple and left him with Eli the priest from the time he was weaned. There the child Samuel ministered to the Lord.[20] God began speaking to Samuel when he was a child.[21] When Samuel grew up, he was established as a prophet of the Lord, and all that he said came to pass.[22] From childhood to old age, Samuel walked in integrity.[23]

In our own experience, we started reading the Bible regularly **as a family** when our first child was between two and three years old, and we were expecting our second child. My husband and I were already established in our own **personal** Bible reading. At that time we were teaching a young couples' Sunday School class. In one of the lessons, it was recommended that families have a regular devotion time. We felt that if we were going to tell others to do this, we should be doing it ourselves. We began family devotions then and have continued over twenty years. There have been many days during those years that we have missed our devotion time. Yet, there have been more days that we have not missed. Our family has been blessed to have this pattern established early in the lives of our children.

At first we used simple Bible stories from a children's book; later we read a chapter straight from the Bible. We would also pray together. When the children learned to read, they took their turns reading a chapter. Even before our third and fourth child could read, we would let them say a word that was repeated several times in the chapter we were reading. When we came to the word in our reading, we would stop and let them fill it in. They could hardly wait until they could really read it for themselves. As they were learning to read, we would let them read the simple words they knew when we came to them in a chapter. Family Bible and prayer time also gave us opportunity to train our children to sit quietly and pay attention.

God holds parents responsible for teaching His Word to their children. We should not expect Sunday Schools or children's ministries to do it for us. We should teach our children Bible stories and spiritual applications. We should teach them about salvation, our covenant with God, and what Jesus has done for us.

---

[18] Matt. 21:15 And when the chief priests and scribes saw the wonderful things that he did, and the children crying in the temple, and saying, Hosanna to the Son of David; they were sore displeased, 16 And said unto him, Hearest thou what these say? And Jesus saith unto them, Yea; have ye never read, Out of the mouth of **babes and sucklings** thou hast **perfected praise**?

[19] 2 Tim. 3:14 But continue thou in the things which thou hast learned and hast been assured of, knowing of whom thou hast learned *them*; 15 And that **from a child thou hast known the holy scriptures**, which are able to make thee wise unto salvation through faith which is in Christ Jesus.

[20] 1 Sam. 2:11 And Elkanah went to Ramah to his house. And the child did minister unto the LORD before Eli the priest.... 18 But Samuel ministered before the LORD, *being* a child, girded with a linen ephod.... 21b ... And the child Samuel grew before the LORD.... 26 And the child Samuel grew on, and was in favour both with the LORD, and also with men.

[21] 1 Sam. 3:1 And the child Samuel ministered unto the LORD before Eli. And the word of the LORD was precious in those days; *there was* no open vision.... 10 And the LORD came, and stood, and called as at other times, Samuel, Samuel. Then Samuel answered, Speak; for thy servant heareth.

[22] 1 Sam. 3:19 And Samuel grew, and the LORD was with him, and did let none of his words fall to the ground. 20 And all Israel from Dan even to Beersheba knew that Samuel *was* established *to be* a prophet of the LORD. 21 And the LORD appeared again in Shiloh: for the LORD revealed himself to Samuel in Shiloh by the word of the LORD.

[23] 1 Sam. 12:2 And now, behold, the king walketh before you: and I am old and grayheaded; and, behold, my sons *are* with you: and **I have walked before you from my childhood unto this day**.... 4 And they said, Thou hast not defrauded us, nor oppressed us, neither hast thou taken ought of any man's hand.

God has promised to pour out His Spirit on our sons and daughters.[24] We should teach them about the Holy Spirit and how He operates through us today. Our children should learn about spiritual warfare, how to recognize the enemy, and resist him.[25] We should teach our children to praise and worship God. They should learn how to minister to the Lord and to others. We should do all that we can to train and prepare them to fulfill God's call upon their lives.

There are many rewards for teaching our children God's Word. It is life to them and us, and it will prolong our days.[26] When we obey and teach God's commandments, we will be called great in the kingdom of heaven.[27] We will have the joy of knowing that our children walk in truth,[28] and that they have become doers of the Word.[29] We will be working toward presenting them mature in Christ Jesus.[30]

---

[24] Isa. 44:3 For I will pour water upon him that is thirsty, and floods upon the dry ground: **I will pour my spirit upon thy seed, and my blessing upon thine offspring**:

Joel 2:28 And it shall come to pass afterward, *that* I will pour out my spirit upon **all flesh**; and **your sons and your daughters shall prophesy**, your old men shall dream dreams, **your young men shall see visions**: 29 And also upon the servants and upon the handmaids in those days will I pour out my spirit.

Acts 2:16 But this is that which was spoken by the prophet Joel; 17 And it shall come to pass in the last days, saith God, I will pour out of my Spirit upon **all flesh**: and **your sons and your daughters shall prophesy, and your young men shall see visions**, and your old men shall dream dreams: 18 And on my servants and on my handmaidens I will pour out in those days of my Spirit; and they shall prophesy:... 38 Then Peter said unto them, Repent, and be baptized every one of you in the name of Jesus Christ for the remission of sins, and ye shall receive the **gift of the Holy Ghost**. 39 For the **promise is unto you, and to your children**, and to all that are afar off, *even* as many as the Lord our God shall call. 40 And with many other words did he testify and exhort, saying, Save yourselves from this untoward generation.

[25] 1 Pet. 5:8 Be sober, be vigilant; because your adversary the devil, as a roaring lion, walketh about, seeking whom he may devour: 9 Whom resist stedfast in the faith, knowing that the same afflictions are accomplished in your brethren that are in the world.

2 Cor. 10:3 For though we walk in the flesh, we do not war after the flesh: 4 (For the weapons of our warfare *are* not carnal, but mighty through God to the pulling down of strong holds;) 5 Casting down imaginations, and every high thing that exalteth itself against the knowledge of God, and bringing into captivity every thought to the obedience of Christ;

[26] Deut. 32:46 And he said unto them, Set your hearts unto all the words which I testify among you this day, which ye shall **command your children to observe to do**, all the words of this law. 47 For it *is* not a vain thing for you; because **it *is* your life**: and through this thing ye **shall prolong *your* days** in the land, whither ye go over Jordan to possess it.

[27] Matt 5:19 Whosoever therefore shall break one of these least commandments, and shall teach men so, he shall be called the least in the kingdom of heaven: but whosoever shall do and teach *them*, the same shall be called great in the kingdom of heaven.

[28] 3 John 4 I have no greater joy than to hear that **my children walk in truth**.

[29] James 1:22 But be ye **doers of the word**, and not hearers only, deceiving your own selves.

[30] Col. 1:28 {Christ} Whom we preach, warning every man, and teaching every man in all wisdom; **that we may present every man perfect in Christ Jesus:**

Chapter 17

Obedience and Disobedience

Instruction and Correction

There are several words that can be used when talking about instruction and correction. The word "instruct" as we use it today involves teaching and education. "Reproof" is rebuke or showing disapproval. "Correction" is changing something that is wrong to make it right. "Punish" has to do with imposing a penalty on the wrongdoer, such as paying a fine or being deprived of something. It may involve restitution, paying for the wrong in some way (such as restoring or replacing something that was stolen or broken). "Chastisement" usually means corporal punishment, such as using the "rod."

If we used an example of a student taking a spelling test, we might use these words this way. The teacher "instructed" the student on how to spell the words correctly. The student refused to study and did poorly on the spelling test. The teacher checked the test and "reproved" the student for the misspelled words. The student had to "correct" the test by erasing all the misspelled words and writing them correctly. The student was "punished" by having to write the misspelled words ten times each. The parent "chastised" the child for his refusal to study.

In most of the verses we will mention from the book of Proverbs, the words "instruction," "reproof," "rebuke," "correction," and "chasten" are all interrelated. These words are translated from Hebrew words that include all of these meanings.

Proverbs tells the benefits of receiving instruction and the consequences of not receiving it.[1] People who are willing to receive instruction are wise and prudent. They love knowledge and are in the way of life. They get knowledge, understanding, and honor. On the other hand, those who refuse instruction show themselves to be scornful, foolish, and brutish. They have erred and despise their own souls; they get poverty and shame. They have forsaken the way and are headed for death. They shall suddenly be destroyed without remedy.

---

[1] Prov. 13:1 A wise son *heareth* his father's instruction: but a scorner heareth not rebuke.
Prov. 15:5 A fool despiseth his father's instruction: but he that regardeth reproof is prudent.
Prov. 10:17 He *is in* the way of life that keepeth instruction: but he that refuseth reproof erreth.
Prov. 13:18 Poverty and shame *shall be to* him that refuseth instruction: but he that regardeth reproof shall be honoured.
Prov. 12:1 Whoso loveth instruction loveth knowledge: but he that hateth reproof *is* brutish.
Prov. 19:20 Hear counsel, and receive instruction, that thou mayest be wise in thy latter end.
Prov. 15:31 The ear that heareth the reproof of life abideth among the wise. 32 He that refuseth instruction despiseth his own soul: but he that heareth reproof getteth understanding.
Prov. 19:25 Smite a scorner, and the simple will beware: and reprove one that hath understanding, *and* he will understand knowledge.
Prov. 21:11 When the scorner is punished, the simple is made wise: and when the wise is instructed, he receiveth knowledge.
Prov. 29:1 He, that being often reproved hardeneth *his* neck, shall suddenly be destroyed, and that without remedy.
Prov. 15:10 Correction *is* grievous unto him that forsaketh the way: *and* he that hateth reproof shall die.

Honor and Obey Parents

God's specific command to children is that they honor and obey their parents.[2] Even a child is known by what he does, whether it is pure and right.[3] The child Jesus was a perfect example. He was subject to his parents as He grew strong in body and spirit and increased in wisdom and favor with both God and man.[4]

When children honor and obey their parents, they are obeying and pleasing God.[5] That is why it is so important for parents to train their children to honor and obey them. If our children do not honor and obey us when they are young, how can we expect them to honor and obey God when they are grown?

The command to honor parents comes with a promise for those who are obedient. They are promised long life on the earth, and things will go well with them.[6] You can help your children get in position to receive these promises when you train them to honor and obey you.

Diligence is required for receiving instruction from parents; rewards are also promised. Children must apply their hearts and ears to instruction and give their attention to it. They must hear, receive, and keep God's commandments. They must take hold of His instruction, keep it in their hearts, and not let it go. Godly instruction is an ornament of grace. It is good teaching in wisdom and leads in right paths. The rewards for those who heed instruction are that their steps will not be restricted, and they will not stumble. They will have health and long life.[7]

---

[2] Exod. 20:12 **Honour** thy father and thy mother: **that** thy days may be long upon the land which the LORD thy God giveth thee.
Lev. 19:3 Ye shall **fear every man his mother, and his father**, and keep my sabbaths: I *am* the LORD your God.
Eph. 6:1 Children, **obey** your parents in the Lord: **for** this is right. 2 **Honour** thy father and mother; (which is the first commandment with promise;) 3 **That** it may be well with thee, and thou mayest live long on the earth.

[3] Prov. 20:11 Even a child is known by his doings, whether his work *be* pure, and whether *it be* right.

[4] Luke 2:40 And the child grew, and waxed strong in spirit, filled with wisdom: and the grace of God was upon him.... 51 And he went down with them, and came to Nazareth, and **was subject unto them**: but his mother kept all these sayings in her heart. 52 And Jesus increased in wisdom and stature, and in favour with God and man.

[5] Col. 3:20 Children, **obey** *your* parents in all things: **for** this is well pleasing unto the Lord.

[6] Deut. 5:16 **Honour** thy father and thy mother, **as** the LORD thy God hath commanded thee; **that** thy days may be prolonged, **and that** it may go well with thee, in the land which the LORD thy God giveth thee.

[7] Prov. 1:8 **My son, hear the instruction of thy father, and forsake not the law of thy mother**: 9 For they *shall be* an ornament of grace unto thy head, and chains about thy neck.
Prov. 23:12 Apply thine heart unto **instruction**, and thine ears to the words of knowledge.... 22 **Hearken unto thy father that begat thee, and despise not thy mother when she is old**. 23 Buy the truth, and sell *it* not; *also* wisdom, and instruction, and understanding.
Prov. 4:1 **Hear, ye children, the instruction of a father**, and attend to know understanding. 2 For I give you good doctrine, forsake ye not my law. 3 For I was my father's son, tender and only *beloved* in the sight of my mother. 4 He taught me also, and said unto me, Let thine heart retain my words: keep my commandments, and live.... 10 **Hear, O my son, and receive my sayings**; and the years of thy life shall be many. 11 I have taught thee in the way of wisdom; I have led thee in right paths. 12 When thou goest, thy steps shall not be straitened; and when thou runnest, thou shalt not stumble. 13 Take fast hold of instruction; let *her* not go: keep her; for she *is* thy life.... 20 **My son, attend to my words**; incline thine ear unto my sayings. 21 Let them not depart from thine eyes; keep them in the midst of thine heart. 22 For they *are* life unto those that find them, and health to all their flesh. 23 Keep thy heart with all diligence; for out of it *are* the issues of life.

On the other hand, there are serious consequences for dishonoring parents. Disobedient children are not promised the blessings of obedience. Just consider the opposites to the blessings and rewards that we have just mentioned. Then you will know what disobedient children have in store for them. In the Old Testament, the penalty for dishonoring parents was death.[8]

Thank God we are living under the New Testament where Jesus has paid the death penalty for us. Even so, we can see that God considers dishonoring parents as a serious matter. In the New Testament, "disobedient to parents" is included in a list of unrighteous works[9] and also in a list describing the perilous times that shall come in the last days.[10] Although disobedience is a sign of the times in these last days, it should not be among Christians. God still has a law against it,[11] and we should not allow our children to disobey or dishonor us.

Dealing with Disobedience

Disobedience opens the door to Satan and the curse. When I was a child, I did not understand that; but I did realize that I usually got in some kind of trouble after I had been disobedient. As parents, it is important for us to require obedience of our children **every** time. Children must not be allowed to pick and choose which rules they will obey. If they obey consistently, they can avoid much trouble and even be delivered from danger by prompt obedience.

Obedience is the main issue, not the particular incidence. Disobedience is breaking a law or rule that has been set. I think of it as if disobedience breaks a string or a circuit. No matter how "little" or "big" you may think the offense was; the connection is still broken, and the power does not flow. It is not a matter of "little" or "big" sin.[12]

---

[8] Exod. 21:15 And he that smiteth his father, or his mother, shall be surely put to death.... 17 And he that curseth his father, or his mother, shall surely be put to death.
Lev. 20:9 For every one that curseth his father or his mother shall be surely put to death: he hath cursed his father or his mother; his blood *shall be* upon him.
Deut. 27:16 Cursed *be* he that setteth light by his father or his mother. And all the people shall say, Amen.
Prov. 20:20 Whoso curseth his father or his mother, his lamp shall be put out in obscure darkness.
Prov. 28:24 Whoso robbeth his father or his mother, and saith, *It is* no transgression; the same *is* the companion of a destroyer.
Prov. 30:11 *There is* a generation *that* curseth their father, and doth not bless their mother.... 17 The eye *that* mocketh at *his* father, and despiseth to obey *his* mother, the ravens of the valley shall pick it out, and the young eagles shall eat it.

[9] Rom. 1:30 Backbiters, haters of God, despiteful, proud, boasters, inventors of evil things, **disobedient to parents**,

[10] 2 Tim. 3:1 This know also, that in the last days perilous times shall come. 2 For men shall be lovers of their own selves, covetous, boasters, proud, blasphemers, **disobedient to parents**, unthankful, unholy,

[11] 1 Tim. 1:9 Knowing this, that the **law** is not made for a righteous man, but **for the lawless and disobedient**, for the ungodly and for sinners, for unholy and profane, **for murderers of fathers and murderers of mothers**, for manslayers,

[12] James 2:10 For whosoever shall keep the whole law, and yet offend in one *point*, he is guilty of all. 11 For he that said, Do not commit adultery, said also, Do not kill. Now if thou commit no adultery, yet if thou kill, thou art become a transgressor of the law.
1 John 3:4 Whosoever committeth sin transgresseth also the law: for sin is the transgression of the law.

When Saul was king, the Lord gave him instructions through the prophet Samuel to destroy the Amalekites and all the spoils of the battle. After the battle, Saul allowed the people to take of the best of the spoils to sacrifice unto the Lord. When Samuel found out Saul had taken of the spoils, he rebuked him. Samuel said that obedience is better than sacrifice. He said that rebellion is as the sin of witchcraft, and stubbornness is as idolatry. Saul's disobedience cost him his throne.[13]

We may find our children doing the same type of thing. For example, we tell them it is time to clean up a project they are working on. Later, when we check on them, we find they have not even started. Their explanation is that they were trying to finish a pretty card they were making for us. It is easy for a parent to be swayed by that, but the truth is that the child was disobedient, and that must be dealt with. It is better to obey than to disobey and then offer a sacrifice to make up for the disobedience.

We should not allow our children to be rebellious and stubborn any more than we would allow them to be involved in witchcraft and idolatry. It is the same because if they are not obeying God, then they are obeying the devil. Sometimes rebellion is open and easy to recognize, but it can be subtler. Children may act like the ones in a parable Jesus told. The first son was openly rebellious at first, but repented and obeyed his father. The other said he would obey, but never did.[14] When children do not obey **promptly**, they may forget or just never get around to obeying. This passive rebellion is subtler, but it must also be dealt with. Setting time limits may be necessary for training in prompt obedience.

It is important to train your children to obey you the first time you give instruction and not to wait until you raise your voice or get angry. If you are allowing them to put off obeying until you repeat the instruction several times, then you are actually training them to procrastinate. If they do not obey the first time, then you should take action immediately. Be consistent so they will know what to expect from you, and they will not be tempted to see how far they can push you. Do not wait until you become angry before you take action.[15] Anger can lead to abuse. Often your child will reflect your anger, and strife will result.[16] Do not allow yourself or your child to be out of control.

Recently, when I was talking to the Lord about our family, I asked Him why we had to "put up with" certain things. I realized there had been issues in our lives that were not issues anymore. We had victory in those areas. Yet there were other situations that kept coming up over and over again. Why had we not gotten

---

[13] 1 Sam. 15:22 And Samuel said, Hath the LORD *as great* delight in burnt offerings and sacrifices, as in **obeying** the voice of the LORD? Behold, to **obey** *is* better than sacrifice, *and* to hearken than the fat of rams. 23 For **rebellion *is as* the sin of witchcraft**, and **stubbornness** *is as* **iniquity and idolatry**. Because thou hast rejected the word of the LORD, he hath also rejected thee from *being* king.

[14] Matt. 21:28 But what think ye? A *certain* man had two sons; and he came to the first, and said, Son, go work to day in my vineyard. 29 He answered and said, I will not: but afterward he repented, and went. 30 And he came to the second, and said likewise. And he answered and said, I *go*, sir: and went not. 31 Whether of them twain did the will of *his* father? They say unto him, The first. Jesus saith unto them, Verily I say unto you, That the publicans and the harlots go into the kingdom of God before you.

[15] Prov. 19:11a The discretion of a man deferreth his anger;…
Psalm 37:8 Cease from anger, and forsake wrath: fret not thyself in any wise to do evil.
James 1:20 For the wrath of man worketh not the righteousness of God.

[16] Prov. 29:22 An **angry man stirreth up strife**, and a furious man aboundeth in transgression.
Prov. 30:33 Surely the churning of milk bringeth forth butter, and the wringing of the nose bringeth forth blood: so the **forcing of wrath bringeth forth strife**.

victory over them? The answer came very clearly: you have to deal with what you have not dealt with. In other words, you have to "put up with" what you allow to continue. What you do not allow, you do not have to continue dealing with. Now when I find myself having to "put up with" something that is not right, I know it is time to deal with it. If we do not deal with it immediately, it gets worse.[17] Do not try to smooth things over and pretend everything is all right. It is better to rebuke the wrong and get rid of it.[18]

When a child does wrong, his tendency may be to hide the sin or blame others. This has been going on since the fall of man when Adam ate the forbidden fruit and hid from God. When God confronted him, he blamed Eve for giving him the fruit. Eve, in turn, blamed the serpent.[19] Another tendency is to make excuses like Aaron did when Moses came down from Mt. Sinai and found that the people had made a golden calf. Aaron said he cast the gold into the fire and out came the calf.[20] He tried to make it sound like he was not responsible for the sin. However, excuses do not justify the wrong. Do not allow excuses from your child. The child must learn to take responsibility for his own behavior.

Whether a child tries to hide his sin, blame others, or make excuses; he can always be sure that his sin will find him out.[21] Things done in secret will be made known.[22] Covering sins will not prosper anyone, but there is mercy for those who confess and forsake the sin.[23]

Parents do not always see when their children misbehave. There is a principle in the Bible that requires two or three witnesses to establish a matter. One witness is not enough.[24] If a sibling tends to be a "tattletale," his witness is not enough to convict. If he gives a false witness, he should be given the same punishment that he expected the one he accused to receive. This is also a Bible principle and is designed to stop the false accuser and to discourage anyone else from false accusations.[25]

---

[17] Eccl. 8:11 Because **sentence against an evil work is not executed speedily**, therefore the heart of the sons of men is fully set in them to do evil.

[18] Prov. 28:23 He that rebuketh a man afterwards shall find more favour than he that flattereth with the tongue.

[19] Gen. 3:9 And the LORD God called unto Adam, and said unto him, Where *art* thou? 10 And he said, I heard thy voice in the garden, and I was afraid, because I *was* naked; and I hid myself. 11 And he said, Who told thee that thou *wast* naked? Hast thou eaten of the tree, whereof I commanded thee that thou shouldest not eat? 12 And the man said, The woman whom thou gavest *to be* with me, she gave me of the tree, and I did eat. 13 And the LORD God said unto the woman, What *is* this *that* thou hast done? And the woman said, The serpent beguiled me, and I did eat.

[20] Exod. 32:21 And Moses said unto Aaron, What did this people unto thee, that thou hast brought so great a sin upon them? 22 And Aaron said, Let not the anger of my lord wax hot: thou knowest the people, that they *are set* on mischief. 23 For they said unto me, Make us gods, which shall go before us: for *as for* this Moses, the man that brought us up out of the land of Egypt, we wot not what is become of him. 24 And I said unto them, Whosoever hath any gold, let them break *it* off. So they gave *it* me: then I cast it into the fire, and there came out this calf.

[21] Num. 32:23 But if ye will not do so, behold, ye have sinned against the LORD: and **be sure your sin will find you out**.

[22] Luke 8:17 For nothing is secret, that shall not be made manifest; neither *any thing* hid, that shall not be known and come abroad.

[23] Prov. 28:13 He that covereth his sins shall not prosper: but whoso confesseth and forsaketh *them* shall have mercy.

[24] Deut. 19:15 One witness shall not rise up against a man for any iniquity, or for any sin, in any sin that he sinneth: at the mouth of two witnesses, or at the mouth of three witnesses, shall the matter be established.

[25] Deut. 19:16 If a false witness rise up against any man to testify against him *that which is* wrong; 17 Then both the men, between whom the controversy *is*, shall stand before the LORD, before the priests and the judges, which shall be in those

There is much controversy today about parents' using corporal punishment on their children. Instead of getting confused by what the world has to say, we must look to God's Word. The Bible speaks of using the "rod," which basically means a stick. A rod could be used by a king as a symbol of authority, like a scepter.[26] Another use of a rod is for punishment and correction.

While I was growing up, I often heard the following quotation: "Spare the rod and spoil the child." I was sure it was from the Bible; but when I did my first Bible search for child-training Scriptures, I could not find it. That quotation was not in the Bible! What I did find in the Bible was an even stronger statement. The parent who withholds the rod from his child **hates** him. Parents who love their children chasten them "betimes."[27] This word "betimes" includes early and diligently. It gives the idea of someone who is diligent enough to start early. They are earnest about what they are doing and not willing to just wait until they "get around to it." Early can mean immediately after the child does wrong, which is especially necessary with very young children. (If you wait until later, they may not remember why you are punishing them.) Early can also mean to start discipline when the child is young. How young depends on when the child first disobeys on purpose.

One of the first times we noticed disobedience in our children occurred when they were around six months old. They would purposely try to roll over while I was changing their diaper. I would move them back into the right position, and they would roll over again. I found that a light swat on their behind with an empty cardboard tube from a paper towel roll got their attention. They soon got the message; just **seeing** the cardboard tube was enough to get their cooperation. A swat with a cardboard tube for discipline is less painful than accidentally sticking the baby with a diaper pin or sticking disposable diaper tapes to his skin because he rolled while he was being diapered. Worse yet, he could roll off the changing table if he was not trained to lie still. The discipline is for the child's immediate safety and the beginning of his long-term training to be obedient.

(Please note: I am not advocating any kind of child abuse or beating of infants. I do not believe infants should be spanked for crying. Crying is their way of letting us know they need something. It is not their fault if we cannot figure out what they need or if we fail to meet their needs.)

Children are born with a sin nature. The rod helps to control their behavior from the outside until they can get God's laws into their hearts.[28] The rod of correction drives out foolishness.[29] Using the rod on our children should be done with an attitude of love, not anger. It is the rod **and** reproof that give wisdom.[30] We should make sure our children know what they have done wrong and what the Bible says about it. We

---

days; 18 And the judges shall make diligent inquisition: and, behold, *if* the witness *be* a false witness, *and* hath testified falsely against his brother; 19 Then shall ye do unto him, as he had thought to have done unto his brother: so shalt thou put the evil away from among you. 20 And those which remain shall hear, and fear, and shall henceforth commit no more any such evil among you.

[26] Psalm 45:6 Thy throne, O God, *is* for ever and ever: the **sceptre** of thy kingdom *is* a right sceptre.

[27] Prov. 13:24 He that spareth his rod **hateth** his son: but he that loveth him chasteneth him **betimes**.

[28] Prov. 10:13 In the lips of him that hath understanding wisdom is found: but a rod *is* for the back of him that is void of understanding.

[29] Prov. 22:15 Foolishness *is* bound in the heart of a child; *but* the rod of correction shall drive it far from him.

[30] Prov. 29:15a The **rod and reproof** give wisdom:...

can explain what the proper behavior would have been or what they can do to correct the situation. After administering the rod, we should confirm our love to the child. This helps keep the relationship open and prevents bitterness from coming in.

The second part of Proverbs 29:15, the verse referred to in the above paragraph, says that a child left brings his mother to shame.[31] I have thought about how true this is. How often does a mother regret neglecting her child? Perhaps she neglected to spank the child for a "minor" offense, and later he went on to "major" offenses. Maybe she was not watching, and he was hurt or got into some kind of trouble. The word "left" in this verse can mean send or give over. How many times have mothers sent their children away or given them over to someone else's care or training, and something went wrong? Maybe those caring for or teaching her child were not doing it the way she would have, and the gap widens between the mother and her child. On the other hand, maybe someone else was privileged to witness certain milestones in the child's life, but the mother missed them. This, too, could make her ashamed and disappointed.

Anything can grow in untended ground, but weeds are kept out of ground that is tended. In the same way, leaving a child to himself gives opportunity for undesirable things to come into his life. We use the rod in obedience to God. The rod helps to keep children from destruction.[32] It helps them resist temptation even at a young age. When they know they will get the rod if they disobey, it is a deterrent to keep them from evil. The rod may hurt temporarily, but not nearly as bad as the destruction to which children would be headed if they were not restrained.

When you use the rod early and consistently, you will soon notice that it will be needed less and less as your child's training progresses. Instead of having to be restrained from the outside, they will receive God's Word into their hearts. This will give them the motivation from within to do what is right. When our children were two or three years old, they sometimes needed spankings several times a day. Their behavior seemed to improve for a while, and the spankings decreased. When I became slack, their misbehavior increased; and the cycle would begin again. By the time they were five or six, the spankings were needed only occasionally.

The Bible does not set an age limit for using the rod. It says a rod is for the fool's back,[33] and a fool can be any age. I think that when an older son or daughter (who is still living in your household) acts like a foolish child, they deserve to be treated like one. We have used the rod on our teenagers occasionally.

It is wonderful to have obedient children. You can take them with you wherever you go and not be embarrassed by their behavior. I remember times when I have been blessed by someone's comment on how well behaved our children were. Correcting our children is hard work, but the reward is rest and delight.[34] After children have been trained in the right way, it will take only a reproof to get them back in line when

---

[31] Prov. 29:15b ... but a child left *to himself* bringeth his mother to shame.

[32] Prov. 19:18 Chasten thy son while there is hope, and let not thy soul spare for his crying.
Prov. 23:13 Withhold not correction from the child: for *if* thou beatest him with the rod, he shall not die. 14 Thou shalt beat him with the rod, and shalt deliver his soul from hell.
Prov. 20:30 The blueness of a wound cleanseth away evil: so *do* stripes the inward parts of the belly.

[33] Prov. 26:3 A whip for the horse, a bridle for the ass, and a rod for the fool's back.

[34] Prov. 29:17 Correct thy son, and he shall give thee rest; yea, he shall give delight unto thy soul.

they miss it.[35] Sometimes all it takes is a look. When a child is attentive to his parent, he can be corrected simply by a look of disapproval from his parent.[36]

If you have older children in your household, and you are just now learning how to train them God's way, you must start right where you are. You should ask their forgiveness for your neglect of godly training in the past. Begin to put Bible principles into practice; God will honor your commitment. His Word will work for any age.

If your older children are rebellious and refuse to submit to your authority, then they will have to reap the consequences of their actions. This may include punishment by authorities that God has set up. If parents always bail their children out of trouble every time they get into it, the children never reap their consequences, so there is no incentive for them to change their behavior or their hearts. In the Old Testament, if parents had a rebellious son, they were required to turn him over to the elders, who would stone him.[37] In the New Testament God has ordained authorities to punish evildoers.[38]

You should always intercede for your children and believe God's promises for them. Do not ever give up. God can restore the wasted years.[39]

---

[35] Prov. 17:10 A reproof entereth more into a wise man than an hundred stripes into a fool.

[36] Prov. 20:8 A king that sitteth in the throne of judgment scattereth away all evil **with his eyes**.

[37] Deut. 21:18 If a man have a **stubborn and rebellious son**, which **will not obey** the voice of his father, or the voice of his mother, and *that,* **when they have chastened him, will not hearken unto them**: 19 Then shall **his father and his mother** lay hold on him, and **bring him out unto the elders** of his city, and unto the gate of his place; 20 And they shall say unto the elders of his city, This our son *is* stubborn and rebellious, he will not obey our voice; *he is* a glutton, and a drunkard. 21 And all the men of his city shall stone him with stones, that he die: so shalt thou put evil away from among you; and all Israel shall hear, and fear.

[38] Rom. 13:3 For rulers are not a terror to good works, but to the evil. Wilt thou then not be afraid of the power? do that which is good, and thou shalt have praise of the same: 4 For he is the minister of God to thee for good. But if thou do that which is evil, be afraid; for he beareth not the sword in vain: for he is the minister of God, a revenger to *execute* wrath upon him that doeth evil.

[39] Joel 2:25 And I will restore to you the years that the locust hath eaten, the cankerworm, and the caterpiller, and the palmerworm, my great army which I sent among you.

Chapter 18

Preparing Youth for Adulthood

Many parents think they must take a "hands off" approach when their children become teenagers. They think their job is over, and now it is up to their teenagers to decide how they will live their lives. This is a serious error. It is not wise to "dump" total independence and responsibility on our youth all at once. This should be a **gradual process** that begins in early childhood. It is true that many teenagers push for independence, but it should be given **only as** they prove they are trustworthy of responsibility.

This gradual giving of responsibility can be done in at least two ways. One way can be likened to letting out more and more rope. As the child can handle it, more is given. An example would be that of giving the child certain chores around the house. As he becomes proficient in doing them, more responsibilities can be given him. The other way is like tossing a ball back and forth. The child is fully responsible for it while it is in his hands, but he can give it back to the parent (or the parent can take it back) if it becomes too difficult. An example of this would be allowing the teen to use the family car. He is responsible to drive it and care for it properly while he is using it. However, he is not fully responsible for it at all times. As he becomes more and more responsible, he is allowed to get a car of his own. He that is faithful in little things will be faithful in greater things. Being faithful with someone else's property prepares him to be faithful over that which is his own.[1]

The teen years are a time of transition; many changes are taking place, physically and emotionally. Teens desperately need their parents to be a stabilizing factor in their lives.

It is important that youth, as well as adults, have a vision, a direction in which to go. The Bible says that where there is no vision, people perish.[2] Today we can see many youth running aimlessly, wasting precious preparation time, and perishing without a vision. God has a special calling and plan for everyone. Teenagers should seek God for His plan for their lives. Knowing God's plan and direction for them is a great motivator. When parents also know God's plan, they can encourage their teens in it.

In addition to a specific plan for each life, God has written in His Word, some general instructions to youth. One is to remember their Creator in the time of their youth.[3] Another is to set a good example as a believer, in word, in love, in spirit, in faith, and in purity.[4] Timothy, a young man in the New Testament was well reported of because of his good example.[5]

---

[1] Luke 16:10 He that is faithful in that which is least is faithful also in much: and he that is unjust in the least is unjust also in much.... 12 And if ye have not been faithful in that which is another man's, who shall give you that which is your own?

[2] Prov. 29:18 Where *there is* no vision, the people perish: but he that keepeth the law, happy *is* he.

[3] Eccl. 12:1 **Remember now thy Creator in the days of thy youth**, while the evil days come not, nor the years draw nigh, when thou shalt say, I have no pleasure in them;

[4] 1 Tim. 4:12 **Let no man despise thy youth; but be thou an example** of the believers, in word, in conversation, in charity, in spirit, in faith, in purity.
Titus 2:6 **Young men** likewise exhort to be sober minded. 7 **In all things shewing thyself a pattern of good works:** in doctrine *shewing* uncorruptness, gravity, sincerity, 8 Sound speech, that cannot be condemned; that he that is of the contrary part

God's Word also gives warnings to youth. It says that youth can rejoice and let their hearts cheer them as they walk in the way of their own hearts and their own eyes ("doing their own thing"). However, if they do these things, God will bring them into judgment. It would be much better to avoid the sorrow by putting evil away from themselves.[6]

One of the ways many youth waste their lives is by putting harmful substances into their bodies. The Bible warns against strong drink and gluttony.[7] These warnings can also apply to the use of drugs. Daniel is an Old Testament example of a young man who **purposed in his heart** that he would not defile himself. God upheld his commitment. You can read about this in the first chapter of Daniel.[8]

Parents should realize that teenagers who go after drugs, alcohol, and wrong relationships are actually crying out for help. Sometimes they have to "cry" **loudly** to get their parents' attention. They are seeking a means of escape or a way to fill an emptiness in their lives. This emptiness can only be filled by God. Even youths can become weary and faint. Instead of looking to the world for a means of escape, they can find renewal in the Lord.[9] As parents, we can encourage our children to come into a right relationship with Him.

Teenagers who do not feel accepted by their parents may seek acceptance from their peers by trying to be like them, doing the things that they do. We should show our children that we love and accept them for who they are. We should not base our love and acceptance of them on their performance.

---

may be ashamed, having no evil thing to say of you.... 11 For the grace of God that bringeth salvation hath appeared to all men, 12 Teaching us that, denying ungodliness and worldly lusts, we should live soberly, righteously, and godly, in this present world;

[5] Acts 16:1 Then came he to Derbe and Lystra: and, behold, **a certain disciple was there, named Timotheus**, the son of a certain woman, which was a Jewess, and believed; but his father *was* a Greek: 2 **Which was well reported of** by the brethren that were at Lystra and Iconium.

[6] Eccl. 11:9 Rejoice, O young man, in thy youth; and let thy heart cheer thee in the days of thy youth, and walk in the ways of thine heart, and in the sight of thine eyes: but know thou, that **for all these *things* God will bring thee into judgment**. 10 Therefore remove sorrow from thy heart, and put away evil from thy flesh: for childhood and youth *are* vanity.

[7] Prov. 20:1 Wine *is* a mocker, strong drink *is* raging: and whosoever is deceived thereby is not wise.
Prov. 23:19 Hear thou, my son, and be wise, and guide thine heart in the way. 20 Be not among winebibbers; among riotous eaters of flesh: 21 For the drunkard and the glutton shall come to poverty: and drowsiness shall clothe *a man* with rags.
Prov. 23:29 Who hath woe? who hath sorrow? who hath contentions? who hath babbling? who hath wounds without cause? who hath redness of eyes? 30 They that tarry long at the wine; they that go to seek mixed wine. 31 Look not thou upon the wine when it is red, when it giveth his colour in the cup, *when* it moveth itself aright. 32 At the last it biteth like a serpent, and stingeth like an adder. 33 Thine eyes shall behold strange women, and thine heart shall utter perverse things. 34 Yea, thou shalt be as he that lieth down in the midst of the sea, or as he that lieth upon the top of a mast. 35 They have stricken me, *shalt thou say, and* I was not sick; they have beaten me, *and* I felt *it* not: when shall I awake? I will seek it yet again.

[8] Dan. 1:8 But Daniel **purposed in his heart that he would not defile himself** with the portion of the king's meat, nor with the wine which he drank: therefore he requested of the prince of the eunuchs that he might not defile himself.... 12 Prove thy servants, I beseech thee, ten days; and let them give us pulse to eat, and water to drink.... 15 And at the end of ten days their countenances appeared fairer and fatter in flesh than all the children which did eat the portion of the king's meat.

[9] Isa. 40:28 Hast thou not known? hast thou not heard, *that* the everlasting God, the LORD, the Creator of the ends of the earth, fainteth not, neither is weary? *there is* no searching of his understanding. 29 He giveth power to the faint; and to *them that have* no might he increaseth strength. 30 **Even the youths shall faint and be weary**, and the young men shall utterly fall: 31 **But they that wait upon the LORD shall renew *their* strength**; they shall mount up with wings as eagles; they shall run, and not be weary; *and* they shall walk, and not faint.

First Kings 12 and 1 Chronicles 10 tell that when King Solomon's son Rehoboam became king, he sought counsel from the old men who had counseled his father. However, instead of taking their advice, he followed the advice of his peers, the young men who had grown up with him.[10] Many of the people rebelled when the king followed the wrong advice. The result was that Israel became a divided kingdom. Only two tribes followed Rehoboam as king; the other ten tribes separated from them.

The same type of thing happens in our day when teenagers seek advice from their peers who are not yet equipped to give wise counsel. I believe this is partly due to the age segregation in our society. This separation has spilled over into many church bodies. (More about this in Part Nine). We can encourage our youth to seek counsel from those who are older and wiser by providing more opportunities for fellowship with them. The Bible says that the younger ones should submit unto the elder ones. Those who are humble, God will exalt in due time.[11]

In Paul's letter to Timothy, he described the relationships that a young man should have with others. He should treat older men as fathers, older women as mothers, younger men as brothers, and younger women as sisters, "with all purity."[12] It is good for young people to fellowship with all ages, both male and female. However, all relationships should be pure. The Bible says to flee youthful lusts.[13] Young people should consider one another so that they will not provoke lust in the way they dress, talk, and act.

Many Bible references were given in Chapter 5 "Fornication and Adultery" which apply to youth as well as adults. Proverbs 2, 5, and 7 are especially directed to sons to encourage them to seek wisdom so they can avoid being seduced. In addition to the Scriptures in Chapter 5, we will look at some others that may apply to young people.

The Bible says that if a man lies with a maid who is not engaged to someone else, he must marry her. If her father forbids the marriage, the man must pay a required amount of money.[14]

2 Samuel 13 tells the story of David's son Amnon who lusted after Tamar. He pretended to be sick and had her bring some food into his room. Then he raped her. Afterward he hated her.[15] Many young men

---

[10] 1 Kings 12:6 And king Rehoboam consulted with the old men, that stood before Solomon his father while he yet lived, and said, How do ye advise that I may answer this people?... 8 But he forsook the counsel of the old men, which they had given him, and consulted with the young men that were grown up with him, *and* which stood before him:

[11] 1 Peter 5:5 Likewise, **ye younger, submit yourselves unto the elder**. Yea, all *of you* be subject one to another, and be clothed with humility: for God resisteth the proud, and giveth grace to the humble. 6 Humble yourselves therefore under the mighty hand of God, **that he may exalt you in due time**: 7 Casting all your care upon him; for he careth for you.

[12] 1 Tim. 5:1 Rebuke not an elder, but intreat *him* as a father; *and* the younger men as brethren; 2 The elder women as mothers; the younger as sisters, **with all purity**.

[13] 2 Tim. 2:22 **Flee also youthful lusts**: but follow righteousness, faith, charity, peace, with them that call on the Lord out of a **pure** heart.

[14] Exod. 22:16 And if a man entice a maid that is not betrothed, and lie with her, he shall surely endow her to be his wife. 17 If her father utterly refuse to give her unto him, he shall pay money according to the dowry of virgins.

[15] 2 Sam. 13:14 Howbeit he would not hearken unto her voice: but, being stronger than she, forced her, and lay with her. 15 Then Amnon hated her exceedingly; so that the hatred wherewith he hated her *was* greater than the love wherewith he had loved her. And Amnon said unto her, Arise, be gone. 16 And she said unto him, *There is* no cause: this evil in sending me away *is* greater than the other that thou didst unto me. But he would not hearken unto her. 17 Then he called his servant that ministered unto him, and said, Put now this *woman* out from me, and bolt the door after her.

today are like Amnon. The young man who seems to be so "in love" with a girl when he tries to seduce her, will suddenly "drop" her for someone else once he has had his way with her. His motivation is to fulfill his own lust; he has no love for her. Young women, do not be deceived by this kind of persuasion. It is only within the lifelong covenant and commitment of marriage that love and intimacy can grow best.

In the Bible, Joseph literally **fled** from adultery. In Genesis 39 it tells how Joseph was made overseer in Potiphar's house. Potiphar's wife tried to seduce Joseph. She caught him by his clothes, but he fled from her leaving his garment in her hand.[16]

As Paul desired to present the people as a chaste virgin (in a spiritual sense) to Christ,[17] so we parents should desire to present each of our grown-up children as a chaste virgin (in a natural sense) to his (or her) future spouse.

Choosing a spouse should not be taken lightly. The custom of "dating" is not the Scriptural way to choose a spouse. Parents and their youth should realize the seriousness of not only the marriage covenant, but also the betrothal commitment (the engagement). Genesis 24 tells the beautiful story of when Abraham's servant went to get a wife for Isaac. He sought God's direction, and God gave it to him clearly. Isaac married the young woman that was brought to him. This shows me that the success of the marriage is based more on the couple's commitment to the marriage covenant than on how much they like about each other or how long they have known each other.

In the Old Testament, parents were involved in choosing a spouse for their son or daughter. I believe parents today should be involved also. Parents should be praying for each child's future spouse even before they know who he (or she) is. Both the parents and their offspring should be seeking the Lord for His choice of a spouse. Neither parents nor their adult children are wise enough on their own to make the right choice. Just as God gave clear direction to Abraham's servant, He will give it to us when we seek him. The Scripture is clear that Christians should not be yoked with unbelievers, so there is no question there. If parents do not believe their son or daughter is making a right choice for a possible spouse, they should say so early on in the relationship. Parents should encourage them to seek God more diligently for His direction. If parents just wait to see how things will turn out, that could cost too much heartache. Marriage is a lifetime commitment, and there should be God-given peace for all those involved in the covenant, including the parents of the covenant-partners.

Young adults should be prepared to leave their parents and begin their own family and home when the time is right for that.[18] The world's idea is for youth to spend their time "partying" and enjoying

---

[16] Gen. 39:7 And it came to pass after these things, that his master's wife cast her eyes upon Joseph; and she said, Lie with me. 8 But he refused, and said unto his master's wife, Behold, my master wotteth not what *is* with me in the house, and he hath committed all that he hath to my hand; 9 *There is* none greater in this house than I; neither hath he kept back any thing from me but thee, because thou *art* his wife: how then can I do this great wickedness, and sin against God? 10 And it came to pass, as she spake to Joseph day by day, that he hearkened not unto her, to lie by her, *or* to be with her. 11 And it came to pass about this time, that *Joseph* went into the house to do his business; and *there was* none of the men of the house there within. 12 And she caught him by his garment, saying, Lie with me: and he left his garment in her hand, and fled, and got him out.

[17] 2 Cor. 11:2 For I am jealous over you with godly jealousy: for I have espoused you to one husband, **that I may present** *you as* **a chaste virgin** to Christ.

[18] Eph. 5:31 **For this cause** shall a man leave his father and mother, and shall be joined unto his wife, and they two shall be one flesh.

themselves. This can result in starting their own households in debt because they have spent their time and money on temporary pleasures and have not prepared for the next season of life. The Bible says that it is good to bear the yoke in youth.[19] It is important that young people not waste their season of training.[20] If they do, they will enter the next season of their lives unprepared.

Before we send our youth out from us, we should make sure they are trained to take care of themselves. This includes our sons, as well as our daughters. They should be able to prepare meals, do laundry, clean house, operate a car (including basic maintenance), handle finances, and do other basic life skills. This training can contribute to a healthier life for them. Also, if they are able to care for themselves, they will not be so dependent on someone else. (Some young people get into wrong relationships just so they can have someone to do these things for them.)

Your child's future spouse will appreciate how you have trained him (or her) in life skills and establishing good habits. Consider the good things you or your spouse brought into your marriage and train your children in those things. If either of you were lacking in any areas, train your children in those so they will not be lacking in them.

In the Old Testament, those who had bondservants were instructed to send them out furnished when they let them go free.[21] I believe parents should send their offspring out furnished when it is time for them to leave home. This furnishing would not be just "giving them the fish," but should also include the training for them "to fish" for themselves. If grown children have been trained properly and have prepared themselves, they should be ready for their next season of life.

---

[19] Lam. 3:25 The LORD *is* good unto them that wait for him, to the soul *that* seeketh him. 26 *It is* good that *a man* should both hope and quietly wait for the salvation of the LORD. 27 *It is* good for a man that he **bear the yoke in his youth.**

[20] Prov. 10:5 He that gathereth in summer *is* a wise son: *but* he that sleepeth in harvest *is* a son that causeth shame.
Prov. 29:3 Whoso loveth wisdom rejoiceth his father: but **he that keepeth company with harlots spendeth** *his* **substance.**

[21] Deut. 15:12 *And* if thy brother, an Hebrew man, or an Hebrew woman, be sold unto thee, and serve thee six years; then in the seventh year thou shalt let him go free from thee. 13 And **when thou sendest him out free from thee, thou shalt not let him go away empty:** 14 Thou shalt **furnish him liberally** out of thy flock, and out of thy floor, and out of thy winepress: *of that* wherewith the LORD thy God hath blessed thee thou shalt give unto him. 15 And thou shalt remember that thou wast a bondman in the land of Egypt, and the LORD thy God redeemed thee: therefore I command thee this thing to day.

Part Seven

Father God's Relationship with His Children

Chapter 19

Father God as Example of Parent

Our relationship with our children should compare to God's relationship with His children. In our efforts to understand God better, we often compare Him to our earthly fathers. Yet in order to learn how to be good earthly parents, we should look to God, our Father, as our ultimate example to follow (imitate).[1] In this chapter, we will look at some examples of God as Father. So much of the Bible speaks about God as Father that I have been selective of the verses I have chosen to show as examples. Yet I have included many Scriptures in this chapter. I encourage you to read them; they can help you to know God's heart. As we learn God's heart for His children and experience His love and care for us, we are better able to receive His heart attitude toward our children.

God the Father and Jesus the Son are the perfect example of a parent-child relationship. God loves His son and is with Him. He teaches and shows Him what to do and is pleased with Him. Jesus does and says what He sees and hears of His Father. He always pleases His Father.[2]

God's Heart and Care for His Children

God is the source of our lives. It is in Him that we live and move and have our being.[3] Parents are the channels through which a child's life is brought forth.

God makes and molds us as a potter molds clay. If the clay gets marred, God can remold us.[4] Parents also help to shape their children's lives. When our children make mistakes, we should not give up on them, but help to reshape them for a better life.

---

[1] Eph. 5:1 Be ye therefore **followers of God**, as dear children:

[2] Luke 3:22 And the Holy Ghost descended in a bodily shape like a dove upon him, and a voice came from heaven, which said, **Thou art my beloved Son; in thee I am well pleased.**
John 5:19 Then answered Jesus and said unto them, Verily, verily, I say unto you, The Son can do nothing of himself, but **what he seeth the Father do**: for what things soever he doeth, these also doeth the Son likewise. 20 For the **Father loveth the Son, and sheweth him all things that himself doeth**: and he will shew him greater works than these, that ye may marvel.
John 8:28 Then said Jesus unto them, When ye have lifted up the Son of man, then shall ye know that I am *he*, and *that* I **do nothing of myself; but as my Father hath taught me, I speak** these things. 29 And **he** that sent me **is with me**: the **Father hath not left me alone**; for I do always those things that **please him.**

[3] Acts 17:28 For **in him we live, and move, and have our being**; as certain also of your own poets have said, For we are also his offspring.

[4] Jer. 18:3 Then I went down to the potter's house, and, behold, he wrought a work on the wheels. 4 And the vessel that he made of **clay was marred in the hand of the potter: so he made it again another vessel**, as seemed good to the potter to make *it*. 5 Then the word of the LORD came to me, saying, 6 O house of Israel, cannot I do with you as this potter? saith the LORD. Behold, **as the clay** *is* **in the potter's hand, so** *are* **ye in mine hand**, O house of Israel.

God is faithful and unchanging.[5] Parents should also be faithful and consistent with their children. Children should be able to depend on their parents and trust their word.

God is in covenant with His children. The new covenant has replaced the old one.[6] The old and new covenants can be compared to the training stages in a child's life.[7] In the Old Testament, God gave the children of Israel laws to obey, and disobedience brought punishment. Earthly parents set rules for their children to obey, and disobedience brings punishment. When Jesus was on earth, He explained the intent of the law and the heart attitude for obeying it. He gave us His example to follow. As children mature and are able to understand, earthly parents explain the intents of the rules they set. They encourage their children to desire to obey from the heart, not just to avoid punishment.

Under the new covenant, Jesus set us free from the law of sin and death[8] and gave us the commandment of love. He put this in our hearts and gave us the Holy Spirit and His Word to guide us. As our children get our words into their hearts and are motivated from within, they are less dependent on outside rules to govern them.

God our Father is just and is not a respecter of persons.[9] Neither should parents show favoritism among their children.

God thinks more of us than we can imagine. His thoughts toward us are precious; they are of peace and not of evil.[10] God is love, and He loves us enough to call us His children. He loves us as He loves His Son Jesus. His love is everlasting, and nothing can separate us from His love.[11]

---

[5] Lam. 3:22 *It is of* the LORD'S mercies that we are not consumed, because his compassions fail not. 23 *They are* new every morning: **great *is* thy faithfulness**.
Mal. 3:6 For I *am* the LORD, **I change not**; therefore ye sons of Jacob are not consumed.
Heb. 13:8 Jesus Christ **the same** yesterday, and to day, and for ever.

[6] Heb. 8:6 But now hath he obtained a more excellent ministry, by how much also he is the mediator of a **better covenant**, which was established upon **better promises**. 7 For if that first *covenant* had been faultless, then should no place have been sought for the second. 8 For finding fault with them, he saith, Behold, the days come, saith the Lord, when I will make a new covenant with the house of Israel and with the house of Judah: 9 Not according to the covenant that I made with their fathers in the day when I took them by the hand to lead them out of the land of Egypt; because they continued not in my covenant, and I regarded them not, saith the Lord. 10 For this *is* the covenant that I will make with the house of Israel after those days, saith the Lord; **I will put my laws into their mind, and write them in their hearts**: and I will be to them a God, and they shall be to me a people: 11 And they shall not teach every man his neighbour, and every man his brother, saying, Know the Lord: for **all shall know me, from the least to the greatest**. 12 For I will be merciful to their unrighteousness, and their sins and their iniquities will I remember no more. 13 In that he saith, A **new *covenant*,** he hath made the first old. Now that which decayeth and waxeth old *is* ready to vanish away.

[7] Gal. 4:1 Now I say, *That* the heir, as long as he is a child, differeth nothing from a servant, though he be lord of all; 2 But is under tutors and governors until the time appointed of the father. 3 Even so we, when we were children, were in bondage under the elements of the world: 4 But when the fulness of the time was come, God sent forth his Son, made of a woman, made under the law, 5 To redeem them that were under the law, that we might receive the adoption of sons. 6 And because ye are sons, God hath sent forth the Spirit of his Son into your hearts, crying, Abba, Father. 7 Wherefore thou art no more a servant, but a son; and if a son, then an heir of God through Christ.

[8] Rom. 8:2 For the law of the Spirit of life in Christ Jesus hath made me free from the law of sin and death.

[9] 1 Peter 1:17 And if ye call on the Father, who **without respect of persons** judgeth according to every man's work, pass the time of your sojourning *here* in fear:

God makes a distinction between His children and the children of the world. This was made clear during the plagues in Egypt when He protected His children in Goshen.[12] God keeps His children as "the apple of His eye."[13] In the New Testament, Jesus said that the children should be filled first; it is not right for the children's bread to be taken from them and given to outsiders.[14]

God cares for His children. It is not His will for any to perish.[15] God carries us from birth to old age. Throughout our lives, He goes before us, fights for us, and cares for us as a father does for his son.[16] He does

---

[10] Psalm 139:17 How precious also are thy thoughts unto me, O God! how great is the sum of them! 18 *If* I should count them, they are more in number than the sand: when I awake, I am still with thee.
Jer. 29:11 For I know the thoughts that I think toward you, saith the LORD, thoughts of peace, and not of evil, to give you an expected end.

[11] 1 John 4:16 And we have known and believed the **love that God hath to us. God is love**; and he that dwelleth in love dwelleth in God, and God in him. 17 Herein is our love made perfect, that we may have boldness in the day of judgment: because as he is, so are we in this world. 18 There is no fear in love; but perfect love casteth out fear: because fear hath torment. He that feareth is not made perfect in love. 19 We love him, because **he first loved us**.
1 John 3:1 Behold, **what manner of love the Father hath bestowed upon us, that we should be called the sons of God**: therefore the world knoweth us not, because it knew him not.
John 17:23 I in them, and thou in me, that they may be made perfect in one; and that the world may know that thou hast sent me, and **hast loved them, as thou hast loved me**.
Jer. 31:3 The LORD hath appeared of old unto me, *saying*, Yea, **I have loved thee with an everlasting love**: therefore with lovingkindness have I drawn thee.
Rom. 8:35 Who shall separate us from the love of Christ? *shall* tribulation, or distress, or persecution, or famine, or nakedness, or peril, or sword?...38 For I am persuaded, that neither death, nor life, nor angels, nor principalities, nor powers, nor things present, nor things to come, 39 Nor height, nor depth, nor any other creature, shall be able to separate us from the love of God, which is in Christ Jesus our Lord.

[12] Exod. 8:22 And I will sever in that day the land of Goshen, in which **my people** dwell, that no swarms *of flies* shall be there; to the end thou mayest know that I *am* the LORD in the midst of the earth. 23 And **I will put a division between my people and thy people**: to morrow shall this sign be.
Exod. 9:4 And the LORD shall sever between the cattle of Israel and the cattle of Egypt: and there shall nothing die of all *that is* the children's of Israel. 5 And the LORD appointed a set time, saying, To morrow the LORD shall do this thing in the land. 6 And the LORD did that thing on the morrow, and all the cattle of Egypt died: but of the cattle of the children of Israel died not one. 7 And Pharaoh sent, and, behold, there was not one of the cattle of the Israelites dead. And the heart of Pharaoh was hardened, and he did not let the people go.... 26 Only in the land of Goshen, where the children of Israel *were*, was there no hail.
Exod. 10:23 They saw not one another, neither rose any from his place for three days: but all the children of Israel had light in their dwellings.
Exod. 11:7 But against any of the children of Israel shall not a dog move his tongue, against man or beast: that ye may know how that the **LORD doth put a difference between the Egyptians and Israel.**

[13] Deut. 32:10 He found him in a desert land, and in the waste howling wilderness; he led him about, he instructed him, **he kept him as the apple of his eye.**
Psalm 17:8 **Keep me as the apple of the eye**, hide me under the shadow of thy wings,
Zech. 2:8 For thus saith the LORD of hosts; After the glory hath he sent me unto the nations which spoiled you: for he that toucheth you toucheth **the apple of his eye.**

[14] Mark 7:27 But Jesus said unto her, Let the **children first be filled**: for it is not meet to take the children's bread, and to cast *it* unto the dogs.

[15] Matt. 18:14 Even so it is **not the will of your Father** which is in heaven, **that one of these little ones should perish.**
2 Peter 3:9 The LORD is not slack concerning his promise, as some men count slackness; but is longsuffering to us-ward, **not willing that any should perish**, but that all should come to repentance.

not forget us; we are engraved on the palms of His hands.[17] He does not even forget a sparrow, and He considers us of much more value than they are. He even knows the number of hairs on our heads.[18] God's care of His children is compared to an eagle's care for her young and a hen's care for her chicks.[19] Psalm 23 compares God's care for us to a shepherd's care for his sheep. Jesus describes the Good Shepherd in John 10. He calls His sheep by name and leads them out. He goes before Him, and they follow Him because they know His voice. He gives His life for His sheep so they can have abundant and eternal life.[20] The Lord's prayer also speaks of our heavenly Father's care. He provides for us, forgives us, and protects us from evil.[21]

God protects His children. Sometimes He keeps us in a special place of protection as calves growing up in a stall[22] (or as plants in a greenhouse). However, God's protection is with us even when we go out into dangerous places. God is our helper; we should not fear. He will never leave us nor forsake us.[23] Psalm 91

---

[16] Isa. 46:3 Hearken unto me, O house of Jacob, and all the remnant of the house of Israel, which are borne *by me* from the belly, which are **carried from the womb**: 4 **And *even* to *your* old age** I *am* he; and *even* to hoar hairs will **I carry *you*: I have made, and I will bear; even I will carry**, and will deliver *you*.
Deut. 1:30 The LORD your God which goeth before you, he shall fight for you, according to all that he did for you in Egypt before your eyes; 31 And in the wilderness, where thou hast seen how that the LORD thy **God bare thee**, as a man doth bear his son, in all the way that ye went, until ye came into this place.

[17] Isa. 49:15 Can a woman forget her sucking child, that she should not have compassion on the son of her womb? yea, they may forget, **yet will I not forget thee**. 16 Behold, **I have graven thee upon the palms of** *my* **hands**; thy walls *are* continually before me.

[18] Luke 12:6 Are not five sparrows sold for two farthings, and **not one of them is forgotten** before God? 7 But even the **very hairs of your head are all numbered**. Fear not therefore: **ye are of more value than many sparrows**.

[19] Deut. 32:6 Do ye thus requite the LORD, O foolish people and unwise? *is* not he thy father *that* hath bought thee? hath he not made thee, and established thee?...11 **As an eagle** stirreth up her nest, fluttereth **over her young**, spreadeth abroad her wings, taketh them, **beareth them on her wings**: 12 *So* the LORD alone did lead him, and *there was* no strange god with him. 13 He made him ride on the high places of the earth, that he might eat the increase of the fields; and he made him to suck honey out of the rock, and oil out of the flinty rock; 14 Butter of kine, and milk of sheep, with fat of lambs, and rams of the breed of Bashan, and goats, with the fat of kidneys of wheat; and thou didst drink the pure blood of the grape.
Matt. 23:37 O Jerusalem, Jerusalem, *thou* that killest the prophets, and stonest them which are sent unto thee, **how often would I have gathered thy children together, even as a hen gathereth her chickens** under *her* wings, and ye would not!

[20] John 10:2 But he that entereth in by the door is the shepherd of the sheep. 3 To him the porter openeth; and the sheep hear his voice: and he calleth his own sheep by name, and leadeth them out. 4 And when he putteth forth his own sheep, he goeth before them, and the sheep follow him: for they know his voice.... 10 The thief cometh not, but for to steal, and to kill, and to destroy: I am come that they might have life, and that they might have *it* more abundantly. 11 **I am the good shepherd**: the good shepherd giveth his life for the sheep.... 14 I am the good shepherd, and know my *sheep*, and am known of mine. 15 As the Father knoweth me, even so know I the Father: and I lay down my life for the sheep.... 27 My sheep hear my voice, and I know them, and they follow me: 28 And I give unto them eternal life; and they shall never perish, neither shall any *man* pluck them out of my hand. 29 My Father, which gave *them* me, is greater than all; and no *man* is able to pluck *them* out of my Father's hand. 30 I and *my* Father are one.

[21] Matt. 6:9 After this manner therefore pray ye: **Our Father which art in heaven**, Hallowed be thy name. 10 Thy kingdom come. Thy will be done in earth, as *it is* in heaven. 11 Give us this day our daily bread. 12 And forgive us our debts, as we forgive our debtors. 13 And lead us not into temptation, but deliver us from evil: For thine is the kingdom, and the power, and the glory, for ever. Amen.

[22] Mal. 4:2 But unto you that fear my name shall the Sun of righteousness arise with healing in his wings; and ye shall go forth, and **grow up as calves of the stall**.

[23] Isa. 43:1 But now thus saith the LORD that created thee, O Jacob, and he that formed thee, O Israel, Fear not: for I have redeemed thee, I have called *thee* by thy name; thou *art* mine. 2 When thou passest through the waters, **I *will be* with thee**; and through the rivers, they shall not overflow thee: when thou walkest through the fire, thou shalt not be burned; neither shall the

describes God's protection and lists categories or examples of dangers from which we are protected. These include traps, pestilence, terror, weapons, destruction, evil, plagues, wild and poisonous beasts, and all kinds of trouble. He will deliver us from all of these when we love Him and call upon Him.[24]

God provides for us; it is His will for His children to prosper and be in health. He does not withhold good from those who walk uprightly. He fills us with the finest of wheat. When we seek Him first, all our needs will be provided. It pleases Him to give us of His kingdom.[25] He gives us power to get wealth, so that He may establish His covenant. He has abundant blessings and benefits for His children. These include forgiveness of sin, healing of diseases, and deliverance from destruction. God treats us with lovingkindness and tender mercy. He satisfies our mouths and renews our youth. He makes His ways and acts known to us.[26] He gives good gifts to His children.[27] Whatever we ask in His name and according to His will, He will give us.[28]

---

flame kindle upon thee. 3 For I *am* the LORD thy God, the Holy One of Israel, thy Saviour: I gave Egypt *for* thy ransom, Ethiopia and Seba for thee. 4 Since thou wast **precious in my sight**, thou hast been honourable, and **I have loved thee**: therefore will I give men for thee, and people for thy life.
    Heb. 13:6 So that we may boldly say, **The Lord *is* my helper**, and I will **not fear** what man shall do unto me.
    John 14:18 **I will not leave you comfortless**: I will come to you.
    Heb. 13:5b … for he hath said, **I will never leave thee**, nor forsake thee.

[24] Psalm 91:1 He that dwelleth in the secret place of the most High shall abide under the shadow of the Almighty. 2 I will say of the LORD, *He is* my refuge and my fortress: my God; in him will I trust. 3 Surely he shall deliver thee from the snare of the fowler, *and* from the noisome pestilence. 4 He shall cover thee with his feathers, and under his wings shalt thou trust: his truth *shall be thy* shield and buckler. 5 Thou shalt not be afraid for the terror by night; *nor* for the arrow *that* flieth by day; 6 *Nor* for the pestilence *that* walketh in darkness; *nor* for the destruction *that* wasteth at noonday. 7 A thousand shall fall at thy side, and ten thousand at thy right hand; *but* it shall not come nigh thee. 8 Only with thine eyes shalt thou behold and see the reward of the wicked. 9 Because thou hast made the LORD, *which is* my refuge, *even* the most High, thy habitation; 10 There shall no evil befall thee, neither shall any plague come nigh thy dwelling. 11 For he shall give his angels charge over thee, to keep thee in all thy ways. 12 They shall bear thee up in *their* hands, lest thou dash thy foot against a stone. 13 Thou shalt tread upon the lion and adder: the young lion and the dragon shalt thou trample under feet. 14 Because he hath set his love upon me, therefore will I deliver him: I will set him on high, because he hath known my name. 15 He shall call upon me, and I will answer him: I *will be* with him in trouble; I will deliver him, and honour him. 16 With long life will I satisfy him, and shew him my salvation.

[25] 3 John 2 Beloved, I wish above all things that **thou mayest prosper and be in health**, even as thy soul prospereth.
    Psalm 84:11 For the LORD God *is* a sun and shield: the LORD will give grace and glory: **no good *thing* will He withhold** from them that walk uprightly.
    Psalm 147:14 He maketh peace *in* thy borders, *and* **filleth thee with the finest of the wheat**.
    Luke 12:22 And he said unto his disciples, Therefore I say unto you, Take no thought for your life, what ye shall eat; neither for the body, what ye shall put on. 23 The life is more than meat, and the body *is more* than raiment. 24 Consider the ravens: for they neither sow nor reap; which neither have storehouse nor barn; and God feedeth them: how much more are ye better than the fowls? 25 And which of you with taking thought can add to his stature one cubit? 26 If ye then be not able to do that thing which is least, why take ye thought for the rest? 27 Consider the lilies how they grow: they toil not, they spin not; and yet I say unto you, that Solomon in all his glory was not arrayed like one of these. 28 If then God so clothe the grass, which is to day in the field, and to morrow is cast into the oven; how much more *will he clothe* you, O ye of little faith? 29 And seek not ye what ye shall eat, or what ye shall drink, neither be ye of doubtful mind. 30 For all these things do the nations of the world seek after: and your Father knoweth that ye have need of these things. 31 But rather **seek ye the kingdom of God; and all these things shall be added unto you**. 32 Fear not, little flock; for **it is your Father's good pleasure to give you the kingdom**.

[26] Deut. 8:18 But thou shalt remember the LORD thy God: for *it is* he that giveth thee power to get wealth, that he may establish his covenant which he sware unto thy fathers, as *it is* this day.
    Psalm 103:2 Bless the LORD, O my soul, and forget not **all his benefits**: 3 Who forgiveth all thine iniquities; who healeth all thy diseases; 4 Who redeemeth thy life from destruction; who crowneth thee with lovingkindness and tender mercies; 5 Who satisfieth thy mouth with good *things; so that* thy youth is renewed like the eagle's. 6 The LORD executeth righteousness and judgment for all that are oppressed. 7 He made known his ways unto Moses, his acts unto the children of Israel. 8 The LORD *is* merciful and gracious, slow to anger, and plenteous in mercy. 9 He will not always chide: neither will he keep *his anger* for ever. 10 He hath not dealt with us after our sins; nor rewarded us according to our iniquities. 11 For as the heaven is high

God teaches His children.[29] He desires that we go to Him for instruction instead of to the world system. (I imagine that when His children go to the world for instruction, that makes Him feel as I did when I first sent my kindergarten-aged son on the school bus to be instructed by the public school system. I felt very sad then, but now I am glad God has provided for us to give our children a God-centered education.) God teaches us by His Word, through His teachers and others in the Body of Christ, and by the anointing of the Holy Spirit.

Just as God requires children to honor and obey their parents, so He requires His children to honor and obey Him. This is for our own benefit; it keeps us **out** of the devil's snares and **in** God's love. When we honor and obey God, it will go well with us.[30]

---

above the earth, *so* great is his mercy toward them that fear him. 12 As far as the east is from the west, *so* far hath he removed our transgressions from us. 13 Like as a father pitieth *his* children, *so* the LORD pitieth them that fear him.

[27] James 1:17 Every **good gift** and every perfect gift is **from above**, and cometh down **from the Father** of lights, with whom is no variableness, neither shadow of turning.
Matt. 7:9 Or what man is there of you, whom if his son ask bread, will he give him a stone? 10 Or if he ask a fish, will he give him a serpent? 11 If ye then, being evil, know how to give good gifts unto your children, **how much more shall your Father which is in heaven give good things** to them that ask him?

[28] Luke 11:9 And I say unto you, **Ask, and it shall be given you**; seek, and ye shall find; knock, and it shall be opened unto you. 10 For **every one that asketh receiveth**; and he that seeketh findeth; and to him that knocketh it shall be opened. 11 If a son shall ask bread of any of you that is a father, will he give him a stone? or if *he ask* a fish, will he for a fish give him a serpent? 12 Or if he shall ask an egg, will he offer him a scorpion? 13 If ye then, being evil, know how to give good gifts unto your children: how much more shall *your* heavenly Father give the Holy Spirit to them that ask him?
John 14:13 And whatsoever ye shall **ask in my name, that will I do**, that the Father may be glorified in the Son. 14 If ye shall **ask any thing in my name, I will do** *it*.
1 John 3:22 And **whatsoever we ask, we receive of him**, because we keep his commandments, and do those things that are pleasing in his sight.

[29] Deut. 4:36a Out of heaven he made thee to hear his voice, that he might **instruct** thee....
Neh. 9:20a Thou gavest also thy good spirit to **instruct** them....
Psalm 25:12 What man *is* he that **feareth the LORD**? him shall he **teach** in the way *that* he shall choose.
Psalm 32:8 I will **instruct** thee and **teach** thee in the way which thou shalt go: I will **guide** thee with mine eye.
Isa. 2:3 And many people shall go and say, Come ye, and let us go up to the mountain of the LORD, to the house of the God of Jacob; and he will **teach** us of his ways, and we will walk in his paths: for out of Zion shall go forth the law, and the word of the LORD from Jerusalem.
Isa. 48:17 Thus saith the LORD, thy Redeemer, the Holy One of Israel; I *am* the LORD thy God which **teacheth thee to profit**, which **leadeth thee by the way** *that* **thou shouldest go**.
John 6:45 It is written in the prophets, And **they shall be all taught of God**. Every man therefore that hath heard, and hath learned of the Father, cometh unto me.
Isa. 54:13 And all thy children *shall be* **taught of the LORD**; and great *shall be* the peace of thy children.
John 14: But the Comforter, *which is* the Holy Ghost, whom the Father will send in my name, he shall **teach** you all things, and bring all things to your remembrance, whatsoever I have said unto you.
1 John 2:27 But the anointing which ye have received of him abideth in you, and ye need not that any man teach you: but as the same **anointing teacheth** you of all things, and is truth, and is no lie, and even as it hath **taught** you, ye shall abide in him.

[30] Mal. 1:6a A **son honoureth** *his* **father**, and a servant his master: **if then I be a father, where is mine honour?** and if I *be* a master, where *is* my fear? saith the LORD of hosts....
Prov 7:2 **Keep my commandments**, and live; and my law as the apple of thine eye.
Isa. 1:19 If ye be **willing and obedient**, ye shall eat the good of the land: 20 But if ye refuse and rebel, ye shall be devoured with the sword: for the mouth of the LORD hath spoken *it*.
John 14:15 If ye **love me, keep my commandments**.
John 15:10 If ye **keep my commandments**, ye shall abide in my love; even as I have kept my Father's commandments, and abide in his love.

God's Correction and Mercy

God is the perfect example of a Father, but even He has children who rebel against Him.[31] He has made us with an ability to choose. When people allow influences that are not from God to dominate their lives, they tend to rebel against God and follow the wrong way. That is why it is so important for parents to protect their children from ungodly influences. Even so, there can be times when parents feel they have done all they know to do in training their children, yet they still rebel.

God compares His children to the planting of a choice vine with much care given. Yet the vine turned out to produce wild fruit.[32] Thank God, there is hope, even for the rebellious! God gives opportunity for repentance and restoration.[33] When a rebellious child returns to the Lord, he finds God's mercy extended to him. When he acknowledges his sin and turns from it, God will heal his backslidings.[34]

God makes it clear in His Word that it is normal and proper for a father to chasten his son. It is an expression of love.[35] Chastening includes instruction and training and implies disciplinary correction. It is

---

[31] Deut. 9:24 Ye have been **rebellious against the LORD** from the day that I {Moses} knew you.
Jer. 22:21 I spake unto thee in thy prosperity; *but* thou saidst, I will not hear. This *hath been* **thy manner from thy youth**, that thou **obeyedst not** my voice.
Jer. 32:33 And they have turned unto me the back, and not the face: though I **taught them, rising up early** and teaching *them*, yet **they have not hearkened to receive instruction**.

[32] Isa. 5:1 Now will I sing to my wellbeloved a song of my beloved touching his vineyard. My wellbeloved hath a vineyard in a very fruitful hill: 2 And he fenced it, and gathered out the stones thereof, and planted it with the choicest vine, and built a tower in the midst of it, and also made a winepress therein: and he looked that it should bring forth grapes, and it brought forth wild grapes. 3 And now, O inhabitants of Jerusalem, and men of Judah, judge, I pray you, betwixt me and my vineyard. 4 What could have been done more to my vineyard, that I have not done in it? wherefore, when I looked that it should bring forth grapes, brought it forth wild grapes?
Jer. 2:21 Yet I had **planted thee a noble vine**, wholly a right seed: how then art thou turned into the degenerate plant of **a strange vine unto me**?

[33] Isa. 1:1 The vision of Isaiah the son of Amoz, which he saw concerning Judah and Jerusalem in the days of Uzziah, Jotham, Ahaz, *and* Hezekiah, kings of Judah. 2 Hear, O heavens, and give ear, O earth: for the LORD hath spoken, **I have nourished and brought up children, and they have rebelled against me.** 3 The ox knoweth his owner, and the ass his master's crib: *but* Israel doth not know, my people doth not consider.... 18 Come now, and let us reason together, saith the LORD: **though your sins be as scarlet, they shall be as white as snow**; though they be red like crimson, they shall be as wool.

[34] Jer. 3:12 Go and proclaim these words toward the north, and say, **Return, thou backsliding** Israel, saith the LORD; *and* I will not cause mine anger to fall upon you: for **I am merciful**, saith the LORD, *and* I will not keep *anger* for ever. 13 Only **acknowledge thine iniquity**, that thou hast transgressed against the LORD thy God, and hast scattered thy ways to the strangers under every green tree, and ye have not obeyed my voice, saith the LORD.... 21 A voice was heard upon the high places, weeping *and* supplications of the children of Israel: for they have perverted their way, *and* they have forgotten the LORD their God. 22 **Return, ye backsliding children,** *and* I will **heal your backslidings**. Behold, we come unto thee; for thou *art* the LORD our God.

[35] Deut. 8:5 Thou shalt also consider in thine heart, that, **as a man chasteneth his son,** *so* the **LORD thy God chasteneth thee.** 6 Therefore thou shalt keep the commandments of the LORD thy God, to walk in his ways, and to fear him.
Prov. 3:11 My son, **despise not the chastening of the LORD**; neither be weary of his **correction**: 12 For whom the LORD loveth he **correcteth**; even **as a father** the son *in whom* he delighteth.
Heb. 12:5 And ye have forgotten the exhortation which speaketh unto you as unto children, My son, **despise not thou the chastening of the Lord,** nor faint when thou art rebuked of him: 6 For whom the Lord loveth he chasteneth, and scourgeth every son whom he receiveth. 7 **If ye endure chastening, God dealeth with you as with sons**; for what son is he whom the father chasteneth not? 8 But if ye be without chastisement, whereof all are partakers, then are ye bastards, and not sons. 9 Furthermore we have had fathers of our flesh which corrected *us*, and we gave *them* reverence: shall we not much rather be in subjection unto

far better to run to a father (especially our heavenly Father) for correction than to run away from correction.[36] Sin brings bondage and death. When God exposes our sin, it is so that it can be dealt with, and we can be forgiven and set free from it. The sooner the wrong is dealt with, the quicker the restoration of fellowship.

When children are so rebellious that they will not come for correction, they still cannot hide from God. He will chastise them.[37] Correction can come in different forms. God's Word is used to teach, reprove, and correct.[38] Consequences of wickedness can cause a turn-around.[39] This is why parents should **not** always shield their children from the consequences of their actions. Consequences can cause a change of heart. When children find that they cannot keep getting by with disobedience and rebellion, they will begin to realize that they must take responsibility for their own actions. The rod and stripes may be required to change the behavior. God has authorized parents to use the rod on their children (as was mentioned in Chapter 17). He has also ordained law enforcement ministers to punish evildoers.[40]

---

the Father of spirits, and live? 10 For they verily for a few days chastened *us* after their own pleasure; but he for *our* profit, that *we* might be partakers of his holiness. 11 Now no **chastening** for the present seemeth to be joyous, but grievous: nevertheless **afterward it yieldeth the peaceable fruit of righteousness** unto them which are exercised thereby.

[36] Job 5:17 Behold, **happy** *is* **the man whom God correcteth**: therefore despise not thou the **chastening** of the Almighty:
  1 Cor. 11:31 For if we would judge ourselves, we should not be judged. 32 But when we are judged, we are **chastened of the Lord**, that we should **not be condemned with the world**.
  Jer. 10:23 O LORD, I know that the **way of man *is* not in himself**: *it is* not in man that walketh to direct his steps. 24 **O LORD, correct me**, but with judgment; not in thine anger, lest thou bring me to nothing.
  Prov. 1:23 Turn you at my **reproof**: behold, I will pour out my spirit unto you, I will make known my words unto you.
  Jer. 30:11 For **I *am* with thee, saith the LORD, to save thee**: though I make a full end of all nations whither I have scattered thee, yet will I not make a full end of thee: but I will **correct thee in measure**, and will not leave thee altogether unpunished.
  Hosea 14:4 I will **heal their backsliding, I will love them freely**: for mine anger is turned away from him.
  Rev. 3:19 **As many as I love, I rebuke and chasten**: be zealous therefore, and repent. 20 Behold, I stand at the door, and knock: if any man hear my voice, and open the door, I will come in to him, and will sup with him, and he with me. 21 To him that overcometh will I grant to sit with me in my throne, even as I also overcame, and am set down with my Father in his throne. 22 He that hath an ear, let him hear what the Spirit saith unto the churches.

[37] Psalm 94:10 He that **chastiseth** the heathen, shall not he **correct**? he that **teacheth** man **knowledge**, *shall not he know*? 11 The LORD knoweth the thoughts of man, that they *are* vanity. 12 Blessed *is* the man whom thou **chastenest**, O LORD, and **teachest** him out of thy law; 13 That thou mayest give him rest from the days of adversity, until the pit be digged for the wicked. 14 For the LORD will not cast off his people, **neither will he forsake his inheritance**.

[38] 2 Tim. 3:16 All scripture *is* given by inspiration of God, and *is* profitable **for doctrine, for reproof, for correction, for instruction** in righteousness:

[39] Jer. 2:19 Thine **own wickedness shall correct thee**, and thy **backslidings shall reprove thee**: know therefore and see that *it is* an evil *thing* and bitter, that thou hast forsaken the LORD thy God, and that my fear *is* not in thee, saith the Lord GOD of hosts.

[40] Psalm 89:31 If they break my statutes, and keep not my commandments; 32 Then will I visit their transgression with the **rod**, and their iniquity with **stripes**. 33 Nevertheless my lovingkindness will I not utterly take from him, nor suffer my faithfulness to fail. 34 My covenant will I not break, nor alter the thing that is gone out of my lips.
  2 Sam. 7:14 I will be his father, and he shall be my son. If he commit **iniquity**, I will **chasten** him with the **rod of men**, and with the **stripes of the children of men**:
  Rom. 13:4 For he is the minister of God to thee for good. But if thou do that which is evil, be afraid; for he beareth not the sword in vain: for he is the minister of God, a revenger to *execute* wrath upon him that doeth evil.

Our heavenly Father is full of compassion and mercy toward His children. He is slow to anger and ready to forgive.[41] The story of the prodigal son in Luke 15 is a beautiful illustration of God's love for his children.[42] He is willing to forgive and restore fellowship even when the children have turned away from Him and gone their own way. As parents, we should have the same attitude and heart of love and forgiveness as the father in the story.

---

[41] Psalm 86:5 For thou, Lord, *art* good, and **ready to forgive**; and **plenteous in mercy** unto all them that call upon thee.
Dan. 9:9 To the Lord our God *belong* **mercies** and **forgivenesses**, though we have rebelled against him;
Psalm 78:37 For their heart was not right with him, neither were they stedfast in his covenant. 38 But he, *being* full of **compassion, forgave *their* iniquity**, and destroyed *them* not: yea, many a time turned he his anger away, and did not stir up all his wrath. 39 For he remembered that they *were but* flesh; a wind that passeth away, and cometh not again.
Psalm 145:8 The LORD is gracious, and **full of compassion; slow to anger, and of great mercy**. 9 The LORD is good to all: and his **tender mercies** *are* over all his works.
Lam. 3:31 For the Lord will not cast off for ever: 32 But though he cause grief, yet will he have **compassion** according to the multitude of his **mercies**. 33 For **he doth not afflict willingly nor grieve the children of men**.
Micah 7:18 Who *is* a God like unto thee, that **pardoneth iniquity**, and passeth by the transgression of the remnant of his heritage? he **retaineth not his anger for ever**, because he **delighteth *in*** mercy. 19 He will turn again, he will have **compassion** upon us; he will subdue our iniquities; and **thou wilt cast all their sins into the depths of the sea**.

[42] Luke 15:11 And he said, A certain man had two sons: 12 And the younger of them said to *his* father, Father, give me the portion of goods that falleth *to me*. And he divided unto them *his* living. 13 And not many days after the **younger son** gathered all together, and took his journey into a far country, and there **wasted his substance with riotous living**. 14 And when he had spent all, there arose a mighty famine in that land; and **he began to be in want**. 15 And he went and joined himself to a citizen of that country; and he sent him into his fields to feed swine. 16 And he would fain have filled his belly with the husks that the swine did eat: and no man gave unto him. 17 And **when he came to himself**, he said, How many hired servants of my father's have bread enough and to spare, and I perish with hunger! 18 I will arise and go to my father, and will say unto him, Father, I have sinned against heaven, and before thee, 19 And am no more worthy to be called thy son: make me as one of thy hired servants. 20 And he arose, and came to his father. But when he was yet a great way off, **his father saw him, and had compassion, and ran, and fell on his neck, and kissed him**. 21 And the son said unto him, Father, I have sinned against heaven, and in thy sight, and am no more worthy to be called thy son. 22 But the father said to his servants, **Bring forth the best robe, and put *it* on him**; and **put a ring on his hand, and shoes on *his* feet**: 23 And **bring hither the fatted calf, and kill *it*; and let us eat, and be merry**: 24 For this **my son was dead, and is alive again; he was lost, and is found**. And they began to be merry.

Part Eight

Improving Family Relationships

Chapter 20

Overcoming Division

The rules given in the Bible for relationships with others **also apply** to family relationships. Although our tendency may be to treat those outside our family better than those within it, that is not the way it should be. Instead, we should see each member of our family as a person that God loves and for whom Jesus died. If family members are born again, they have become members of God's family and should be treated with honor and respect. If any are not yet born again, then we should have the same compassion for them that Jesus has for the lost.

As mentioned in Chapter 10, here we will deal with getting **bad seed out** and sowing **good seed into** our families. Examples of bad seed (seeds of death) are strife, hatred, envy, pride, evil speaking, and selfishness. Good seeds (seeds of life) include love, forgiveness, peace, and blessing.

Strife

Strife is one of the major problems in family relationships. Proverbs speaks of the difficulties of living in the same house with a contentious woman.[1] However, that can apply to any contentious family member. Strife is one of Satan's big weapons used to cause division in families. Jesus said that division keeps a house from standing.[2] We must remember that our fight is not with one another, but against Satan.[3] We should not be wrestling with our own flesh and blood, but we should stand together with them against the attacks of the enemy. We should not allow the devil a foothold in our families.[4]

Strife is stirred up by hatred, anger, and wrath.[5] It is also associated with envy. James 3:16 says that where there is envy and strife, there **is** confusion and every evil work.[6] I remember when I first started taking

---

[1] Prov. 19:13b ... the **contentions** of a wife *are* a continual dropping.
Prov. 21:9 *It is* better to dwell in a corner of the housetop, than with a **brawling** woman in a wide house.
Prov. 21:19 *It is* better to dwell in the wilderness, than with a **contentious** and an **angry** woman.
Prov. 25:24 *It is* better to dwell in the corner of the housetop, than with a **brawling** woman and in a wide house.
Prov. 27:15 A continual dropping in a very rainy day and a **contentious** woman are alike. 16 Whosoever hideth her hideth the wind, and the ointment of his right hand, *which* bewrayeth *itself*.

[2] Mark 3:25 And if a house be **divided** against itself, that house cannot stand.

[3] Eph. 6:12 For **we wrestle not against flesh and blood**, but against principalities, against powers, against the rulers of the darkness of this world, against spiritual wickedness in high *places*.

[4] Eph. 4:27 Neither give place to the devil.

[5] Prov. 10:12 **Hatred** stirreth up **strifes**: but love covereth all sins.
Prov. 15:18 A **wrathful** man stirreth up **strife**: but *he that is* slow to anger appeaseth strife.
Prov. 29:22 An **angry** man stirreth up **strife**, and a furious man aboundeth in transgression.
Prov. 30:33 Surely the churning of milk bringeth forth butter, and the wringing of the nose bringeth forth blood: so the forcing of **wrath** bringeth forth **strife**.

that verse seriously. I had been a Christian for many years, but I was still worldly in my thinking. I knew the Bible spoke against strife, but I figured strife was in all families. I could not imagine it possible to live without strife. Then I got a revelation of that verse. **The Bible really means what it says!** I realized that if I did not take a stand against strife in our home, then I was allowing an open door for Satan to bring in confusion and every evil work. If I allowed strife, I also allowed confusion and every evil work. In order to keep out confusion and every evil work, I would have to keep out strife. So I decided that strife must go. A few weeks later, I noticed I was not screaming at the children, and our home was much more peaceful. I do not remember trying to make that happen; I had only made a decision. I believe that once I took God's Word seriously in that area of my life, He honored that and did a supernatural work in our family. Since then, whenever confusion or evil work shows up, I know the first place to check is to see if we have allowed strife to come into our home.

Strife is not new to our generation. The Bible gives examples of family members who got into strife through hatred, envy, and anger. Cain killed his brother Abel because of wrath and envy.[7] Another example is of Joseph and his brothers. Joseph's father showed favoritism toward him, and gave him a coat of many colors.[8] His brothers were envious and hated him. Joseph told his brothers about two dreams he had that indicated that they would some day bow down to him.[9] This caused his brothers to hate him even more, and they sold him as a slave.[10]

Another example is that of David and his brothers. David was the youngest of eight brothers. In their presence, he was anointed to be king.[11] David was chosen to play music for King Saul and became his armorbearer.[12] When the Philistines gathered to battle against Israel, King Saul went to battle; and David

---

[6] James 3:14 But if ye have bitter **envying** and **strife** in your hearts, glory not, and lie not against the truth. 15 This wisdom descendeth not from above, but *is* earthly, sensual, devilish. 16 For where **envying** and **strife** *is*, there *is* confusion and every evil work.

[7] Gen. 4:3 And in process of time it came to pass, that Cain brought of the fruit of the ground an offering unto the LORD. 4 And Abel, he also brought of the firstlings of his flock and of the fat thereof. And the LORD had respect unto Abel and to his offering: 5 But unto Cain and to his offering he had not respect. And Cain was very wroth, and his countenance fell.... 8 And Cain talked with Abel his brother: and it came to pass, when they were in the field, that Cain rose up against Abel his brother, and slew him.
Heb. 11:4 By faith Abel offered unto God a more excellent sacrifice than Cain, by which he obtained witness that he was righteous, God testifying of his gifts: and by it he being dead yet speaketh.
1 John 3:12 Not as Cain, *who* was of that wicked one, and slew his brother. And wherefore slew he him? Because his own works were evil, and his brother's righteous.

[8] Gen. 37:3 Now Israel loved Joseph more than all his children, because he *was* the son of his old age: and he made him a coat of *many* colours. 4 And when his brethren saw that their father loved him more than all his brethren, they **hated** him, and could not speak peaceably unto him.

[9] Gen. 37:5 And Joseph dreamed a dream, and he told *it* his brethren: and they **hated** him yet the more.... 8 And his brethren said to him, Shalt thou indeed reign over us? or shalt thou indeed have dominion over us? And they **hated** him yet the more for his dreams, and for his words.

[10] Acts 7:9 And the patriarchs, moved with **envy**, sold Joseph into Egypt: but God was with him,

[11] 1 Sam. 16:13 Then Samuel took the horn of oil, and anointed him **in the midst of his brethren**: and the Spirit of the LORD came upon David from that day forward. So Samuel rose up, and went to Ramah.

[12] 1 Sam. 16:21 And David came to Saul, and stood before him: and he loved him greatly; and he **became his armourbearer**. 22 And Saul sent to Jesse, saying, Let David, I pray thee, stand before me; for he hath found favour in my sight.

returned from Saul to feed his father's sheep. His three eldest brothers followed Saul to the battle. David's father Jesse sent him to take food and to check on his brothers. David's oldest brother was angry toward him for coming and began to falsely accuse him.[13]

Those who love strife love sin.[14] Strife comes through those who are foolish and carnal, those who are led by their own human nature rather than by the Spirit of God.[15]

How should we deal with strife? As with all other sins, prevention is best. Realize the seriousness of strife. It is a work of the flesh, and they that do such things shall not inherit the kingdom of God.[16] Do not hate your brother; hate blinds you.[17] Do not envy others.[18] Remember that love is not envious.[19] Stop strife before it starts;[20] do not feed it or keep it going.[21] Respond to another's wrath with a soft answer, not with

---

23 And it came to pass, when the *evil* spirit from God was upon Saul, that **David took an harp, and played with his hand: so Saul was refreshed**, and was well, and the evil spirit departed from him.

[13] 1 Sam. 17:13 And the three eldest sons of Jesse went *and* followed Saul to the battle: and the names of his three sons that went to the battle *were* Eliab the firstborn, and next unto him Abinadab, and the third Shammah. 14 And David *was* the youngest: and the three eldest followed Saul. 15 But David went and returned from Saul to feed his father's sheep at Bethlehem. 16 And the Philistine drew near morning and evening, and presented himself forty days. 17 And Jesse said unto David his son, Take now for thy brethren an ephah of this parched *corn*, and these ten loaves, and run to the camp to thy brethren; 18 And carry these ten cheeses unto the captain of *their* thousand, and look how thy brethren fare, and take their pledge.... 20 And David rose up early in the morning, and left the sheep with a keeper, and took, and went, as Jesse had commanded him; and he came to the trench, as the host was going forth to the fight, and shouted for the battle.... 28 And Eliab **his eldest brother** heard when he spake unto the men; and Eliab's **anger** was kindled against David, and he said, Why camest thou down hither? and with whom hast thou left those few sheep in the wilderness? I know thy pride, and the naughtiness of thine heart; for thou art come down that thou mightest see the battle.

[14] Prov. 17:19a He loveth transgression that loveth strife....

[15] Prov. 18:6 A **fool's** lips enter into **contention**, and his mouth calleth for strokes.
Titus 3:3 For we ourselves also were sometimes **foolish**, disobedient, deceived, serving divers lusts and pleasures, living in malice and **envy, hateful,** *and* **hating** one another.
1Cor. 3:3 For ye are yet **carnal**: for whereas *there is* among you **envying**, and **strife**, and **divisions**, are ye not carnal, and walk as men?

[16] Gal. 5:19 Now the **works of the flesh** are manifest, which are *these*; Adultery, fornication, uncleanness, lasciviousness, 20 Idolatry, witchcraft, **hatred**, variance, emulations, **wrath, strife**, seditions, heresies, 21 **Envyings**, murders, drunkenness, revellings, and such like: of the which I tell you before, as I have also told *you* in time past, that **they which do such things shall not inherit the kingdom of God**.

[17] Lev. 19:17a Thou shalt **not hate thy brother** in thine heart....
1 John 2:9 He that saith he is in the light, and **hateth** his brother, is in darkness even until now. 10 He that **loveth** his brother abideth in the light, and there is none occasion of stumbling in him. 11 But he that **hateth** his brother is in darkness, and walketh in darkness, and knoweth not whither he goeth, because **that darkness hath blinded his eyes**.
1 John 3:15 Whosoever **hateth** his brother is a murderer: and ye know that no murderer hath eternal life abiding in him.

[18] Gal. 5:26 **Let us not be** desirous of vain glory, provoking one another, **envying** one another.

[19] 1Cor. 13:4 Charity suffereth long, *and* is kind; **charity envieth not**; charity vaunteth not itself, is not puffed up,

[20] Prov. 17:14 The beginning of **strife** *is as* when one letteth out water: therefore leave off **contention**, before it be meddled with.

[21] Prov. 26:20 Where no wood is, *there* the fire goeth out: so where *there is* no talebearer, the strife ceaseth. 21 *As* coals *are* to burning coals, and wood to fire; so *is* a **contentious** man to kindle **strife**.

grievous words.[22] It is honorable to stop being in strife. It is foolish and dangerous to meddle in someone else's strife. It is like grabbing an angry dog by the ears;[23] it is hard to let go without getting bit.

What if strife is already going on? Then what should you do about it? As soon as you recognize strife, stop and take a stand against it. Pray for God's wisdom in the situation at hand. The book of Proverbs gives wisdom for dealing with strife. If your children are arguing about who will go first or who will get to do what, casting lots (drawing straws, flipping a coin, etc.) can settle that argument.[24] Another solution to strife given in Proverbs is to separate the one causing the strife.[25]

A friend recommended using Psalm 133:1 for dealing with strife between children. It says, "Behold, how good and how pleasant it is for brethren to dwell together in unity!"[26] When our children got in strife with one another, they had to say this verse, putting their names in the place of "brethren." They were speaking the Word of God over the situation, and strife could not stay around. (This would be good for husbands and wives also!)

The New Testament agrees that unity is the way to stay out of strife. It says we should all speak the same thing, that there be no divisions among us, but that we be perfectly joined together in the same mind and same judgment.[27]

Pride

The root of strife is pride. In the book of Proverbs, we read that contention comes only by pride,[28] and that strife is stirred up by those of a proud heart.[29] It is sobering to realize that strife is a symptom of pride. When we get into strife, it shows that there is underlying pride that needs to be rooted out. Pride is not of God, but of the world.[30]

---

[22] Prov. 15:1 A soft answer turneth away wrath: but grievous words stir up anger.

[23] Prov. 20:3 *It is* an honour for a man to cease from **strife**: but every fool will be meddling.
Prov. 26:17 He that passeth by, *and* meddleth with **strife** *belonging* not to him, *is* like one that taketh a dog by the ears.

[24] Prov. 18:18 The lot causeth **contentions** to cease, and parteth between the mighty. 19 A brother offended *is harder to be won* than a strong city: and *their* **contentions** *are* like the bars of a castle.

[25] Prov. 22:10 Cast out the scorner, and **contention** shall go out; yea, **strife** and reproach shall cease.

[26] Psalm 133:1 Behold, **how good and how pleasant** *it is* **for brethren to dwell together in unity!** 2 *It is* like the precious ointment upon the head, that ran down upon the beard, *even* Aaron's beard: that went down to the skirts of his garments; 3 As the dew of Hermon, *and as the dew* that descended upon the mountains of Zion: **for there the LORD commanded the blessing,** *even* life for evermore.

[27] 1 Cor. 1:10 Now I beseech you, brethren, by the name of our Lord Jesus Christ, that ye all speak the same thing, and *that* there be **no divisions** among you; but *that* ye **be perfectly joined together** in the same mind and in the same judgment.

[28] Prov. 13:10 **Only by pride cometh contention**: but with the well advised *is* wisdom.

[29] Prov. 28:25 He that is of a **proud heart stirreth up strife**: but he that putteth his trust in the LORD shall be made fat.

[30] 1 John 2:16 For all that *is* in the world, the lust of the flesh, and the lust of the eyes, and the **pride** of life, is not of the Father, but is of the world.

Proverbs has more to say about pride. Pride is sin, and the Lord hates it.[31] It is an abomination to Him. Those who are proud will be punished.[32] Those who fear the Lord will also hate pride,[33] but the foolish and the scorner are full of pride.[34] Pride brings a person low and brings forth shame. Pride precedes destruction and a fall. On the other hand, those who are wise are humble. Humility precedes honor.[35]

The Lord says do not be proud.[36] He brings down high looks and scatters the proud.[37] God respects the lowly, but knows the proud afar off.[38] He resists the proud, but gives grace to the humble.[39] Those who fear Him, He protects from the pride of man and from the strife of tongues.[40]

Considering others first will help us to stay out of pride. We should be subject to one another and be clothed with humility. Nothing should be done through strife or conceit, but we should regard others as better than ourselves. We should not just consider our own things, but also have consideration for others.[41]

If we must boast, then let our boast be in the Lord! Let us glory in Him! We can boast of Him all day long and praise Him forever![42]

---

[31] Prov. 21:4 An high look, and **a proud heart**, *and* the plowing of the wicked, *is* sin.
Prov. 6:16 These six *things* doth the **LORD hate**: yea, seven *are* an abomination unto him: 17 **A proud look**, a lying tongue, and hands that shed innocent blood, 18 An heart that deviseth wicked imaginations, feet that be swift in running to mischief, 19 A false witness *that* speaketh lies, and **he that soweth discord among brethren**.

[32] Prov. 16:5 Every one *that is* **proud in heart** *is* an abomination to the LORD: *though* hand *join* in hand, he shall not be unpunished.
Prov. 15:25a The LORD will destroy the house of the **proud**....

[33] Prov. 8:13 The fear of the LORD *is* to hate evil: **pride**, and **arrogancy**, and the evil way, and the froward mouth, do I hate.

[34] Prov. 14:3 In the mouth of the foolish *is* a rod of **pride**: but the lips of the wise shall preserve them.
Prov. 21:24 **Proud** *and* **haughty scorner** *is* his name, who dealeth in **proud wrath**.

[35] Prov. 29:23 A man's **pride** shall bring him low: but honour shall uphold the **humble** in spirit.
Prov. 11:2 *When* **pride** cometh, then cometh shame: but with the lowly *is* wisdom.
Prov. 18:12 Before destruction the heart of man is **haughty**, and before honour *is* **humility**.
Prov. 16:18 **Pride** *goeth* before destruction, and an **haughty** spirit before a fall. 19 Better *it is to be* of an **humble** spirit with the lowly, than to divide the spoil with the **proud**.

[36] Jer. 13:15 Hear ye, and give ear; **be not proud**: for the LORD hath spoken.

[37] Psalm 18:27 For thou wilt save the afflicted people; but wilt bring down **high looks**.
Luke 1:51 He hath shewed strength with his arm; he hath **scattered the proud** in the imagination of their hearts.

[38] Psalm 138:6 Though the LORD *be* high, yet hath he respect unto the lowly: but the **proud** he knoweth afar off.

[39] James 4:6 But he giveth more grace. Wherefore he saith, **God resisteth the proud**, but **giveth grace unto the humble**.

[40] Psalm 31:20 Thou shalt hide them in the secret of thy presence from the **pride** of man: thou shalt keep them secretly in a pavilion from the **strife** of tongues.

[41] 1 Peter 5:5 Likewise, ye younger, submit yourselves unto the elder. Yea, all *of you* be subject one to another, and be clothed with humility for **God resisteth the proud, and giveth grace to the humble**.
Phil. 2:3 *Let* nothing *be done* through **strife** or **vainglory**; but in lowliness of mind let each **esteem other better** than themselves. 4 Look not every man on his own things, but every man also on the things of others.

[42] Psalm 34:2 My soul shall make her **boast in the LORD**: the **humble** shall hear *thereof*, and be glad.

Selfishness

The root of pride is selfishness. Satan first brought pride into the world. He started out as a special angel named Lucifer, who was created by God. Later **he** decided to exalt **himself** above God and was cast out of heaven. Notice what he said in his heart: "**I** will ascend into heaven, **I** will exalt my throne above the stars of God: **I** will sit also upon the mount of the congregation, in the sides of the north: **I** will ascend above the heights of the clouds; **I** will be like the most High."[43] See how many times he said, "I." "I" is selfish.

If we are to live in victory, selfishness must go from our lives. Beware of those "self" words, like "**self**-conscious," "**self**-esteem," "**self**-pity." I used to be very shy and self-conscious. I thought I was being humble to not think I was good enough or important enough or talented enough or looked good enough to say or do certain things. In reality **I** was more concerned about **myself** and what others thought of **me** than I was about saying or doing something that would benefit others.

Today we hear much about building self-esteem. This is the world's answer for those who feel inferior and inadequate. But self-esteem borders on pride; it is not God's answer. God's answer to our unworthiness is to make us worthy through Jesus. Without Him we can do nothing.[44] Through Him we can do all things.[45]

Self-pity is feeling sorry for oneself. It is that attitude of "why-is-everybody-always-picking-on-me?" Some people seem to get picked on continually. Self-pity draws that kind of response. When I was a child, if I complained to my mother that people were picking on me; she would tell me to ignore them. When I refused to be annoyed by their "picking," they lost interest. I think the devil is the same way in that he will keep attacking you as long as he is getting his desired response from you. When you stand up to him and refuse to let him steal your joy, he loses his control over you.

We may think we have a "right" to be depressed and feel sorry for ourselves. After all, "look at all we have been through." The truth is that we do not have a right to self-pity. We have been bought with a price and are no longer our own; we belong to God.[46] Self-pity would only pull us deeper into depression, but Jesus paid the price for us to be delivered from self-pity and depression.

Selfishness can express itself through a family member who is controlling, critical, and demanding. It seems impossible to please such a person no matter how hard you may try. On the other hand, selfishness also shows up in the person who is easily offended. No matter what is said or done, that person can find

---

2 Cor. 10:17 But he that glorieth, let him **glory in the Lord**.
Psalm 44:8 **In God we boast** all the day long, and praise thy name for ever. Selah.

[43] Isa. 14:12 How art thou fallen from heaven, O Lucifer, son of the morning! *how* art thou cut down to the ground, which didst weaken the nations! 13 For **thou hast said in thine heart**, I will ascend into heaven, I will exalt my throne above the stars of God: I will sit also upon the mount of the congregation, in the sides of the north: 14 I will ascend above the heights of the clouds; I will be like the most High. 15 Yet thou shalt be brought down to hell, to the sides of the pit. 16 They that see thee shall narrowly look upon thee, *and* consider thee, *saying, Is* this the man that made the earth to tremble, that did shake kingdoms;

[44] John 15:5 I am the vine, ye *are* the branches: He that abideth in me, and I in him, the same bringeth forth much fruit: **for without me ye can do nothing**.

[45] Phil. 4:13 I can do all things through Christ which strengtheneth me.

[46] 1 Cor. 6:20 For ye are bought with a price: therefore glorify God in your body, and in your spirit, which are God's.

some way to be offended by it. It is an especially bad situation if both of these types are in the same family. The selfishness of one feeds on the selfishness of the other. Selfishness in any form is wrong. When we become Christians, we identify with Jesus in His crucifixion and should reckon ourselves as dead to sin.[47] Therefore, we should not be controlling, critical, demanding, or offended.

We must remind ourselves that our family members are not our enemies. Satan, the originator of selfishness and pride, is our enemy. He tries to set family members at odds with one another. He is the one who shoots the darts of depression, self-pity, criticism, and such things. When we yield ourselves to these things, we are yielding to him. That is why we must unite with our family to stand against the devil's attacks. When we submit to God and resist the devil, he must flee from us.[48]

When I was in the seventh grade in school, a Christian friend wrote in my autograph book:

Jesus
Others
Yourself

This is still the way to maintain your **joy**: Put Jesus first in your life, others next, and yourself last!

---

[47] Rom. 6:1 What shall we say then? Shall we continue in sin, that grace may abound? 2 God forbid. How shall we, that are **dead to sin**, live any longer therein?... 6 Knowing this, that **our old man is crucified with *him***, that the body of sin might be destroyed, that henceforth **we should not serve sin**. 7 For **he that is dead is freed from sin**.... 11 Likewise **reckon ye also yourselves to be dead indeed unto sin**, but alive unto God through Jesus Christ our Lord.
  Col. 3:1 If ye then be risen with Christ, seek those things which are above, where Christ sitteth on the right hand of God. 2 Set your affection on things above, not on things on the earth. 3 For **ye are dead**, and **your life is hid with Christ in God**.

[48] James 4:7 Submit yourselves therefore to God. Resist the devil, and he will flee from you.

Chapter 21

Love One Another

Love is without selfishness. When selfishness is gotten out of the way, love becomes easier. Love is not a feeling. It is a commandment. We have the choice of whether to obey it or not. The greatest commandment is to love God; the second is to love your neighbor.[1] These two commandments are related. You cannot love your brother unless you love God, and you cannot love God unless you love your brother.[2]

Love fulfills the law, which includes the Ten Commandments. If you are walking in love, you will love God above all else. If you love your neighbor, you will not do anything to harm him.[3]

The love God has for us and desires us to have for one another is described in 1 Corinthians 13.[4] This love is patient and kind. It does not envy and is neither proud nor puffed up. It behaves properly; it is not selfish or easily provoked or offended. It does not think evil or rejoice in sin, but it rejoices in truth. It bears, believes, hopes, and endures all things. Love is the answer to family problems because love never fails.

Love includes the fruit of the Spirit: love, joy, peace, patience, gentleness, goodness, faith, meekness, and self-control.[5] These fruit are all expressions of love.

All things should be done with love.[6] When you operate in love among one another, that love will cover a multitude of sins.[7] Love must be shown in action, not just in word. We must have kind affection for

---

[1] Mark 12:30 And thou shalt **love the Lord thy God** with all thy heart, and with all thy soul, and with all thy mind, and with all thy strength: this *is* the **first** commandment. 31 And the **second** *is* like, *namely* this, Thou shalt **love thy neighbour** as thyself. There is none other commandment greater than these.

[2] 1 John 4:7 Beloved, let us **love one another**: for **love** is of God; and every one that **loveth** is born of God, and knoweth God. 8 He that **loveth not** knoweth not God; for **God is love**.... 11 Beloved, if God so **loved** us, we ought also to **love one another**. 12 No man hath seen God at any time. If we **love one another**, God dwelleth in us, and **his love** is perfected in us.... 20 If a man say, **I love** God, and hateth his brother, he is a liar: for he that **loveth not** his brother whom he hath seen, how can he **love** God whom he hath not seen? 21 And this commandment have we from him, That he who **loveth** God **love** his brother also.
1 John 3:14 We know that we have passed from death unto life, because we **love** the brethren. He that **loveth not** *his* brother abideth in death.

[3] Rom. 13:8 Owe no man any thing, but to **love** one another: for he that **loveth** another hath fulfilled the law. 9 For this, Thou shalt not commit adultery, Thou shalt not kill, Thou shalt not steal, Thou shalt not bear false witness, Thou shalt not covet; and if *there be* any other commandment, it is briefly comprehended in this saying, namely, Thou shalt **love** thy neighbour as thyself. 10 **Love** worketh no ill to his neighbour: therefore **love** *is* the fulfilling of the law.

[4] 1 Cor. 13:4 **Charity** suffereth long, *and* is kind; **charity** envieth not; **charity** vaunteth not itself, is not puffed up, 5 Doth not behave itself unseemly, seeketh not her own, is not easily provoked, thinketh no evil; 6 Rejoiceth not in iniquity, but rejoiceth in the truth; 7 Beareth all things, believeth all things, hopeth all things, endureth all things. 8a **Charity** never faileth....

[5] Gal. 5:22 But the fruit of the Spirit is love, joy, peace, longsuffering, gentleness, goodness, faith, 23 Meekness, temperance: against such there is no law.

[6] 1 Cor .16:14 Let all your things be done with **charity**.

one another, holding each other in honor above ourselves.[8] The greatest act of love is to lay down your life for others.[9] This may not require dying for them, but it does require living for them. In other words, you lay aside your own needs and desires so that you can fulfill theirs.

Our love must continue and increase.[10] When others see our family operating in God's kind of love, they will know that we are His disciples and His children.[11]

God's love for us is unconditional. Even while we were sinners, He loved us enough to send His Son to die for us.[12] Our love for others should also be unconditional. When our love is unconditional, it is not based on our feelings toward others or on their performance. It is based on our obedience to God's command to love. Because of this, we can love our enemies, which God also commands.

Sometimes we may feel like members of our own family are our enemies. It may be because they are not in agreement with us on a certain issue, or even because they have not yet been born again. Even if a family member seems like an enemy to us, we still are commanded to love him.[13] When you are pleasing the Lord, He makes your enemies to be at peace with you[14] (even if they are in your own household).

---

[7] 1 Peter 4:8 And above all things have **fervent charity** among yourselves: for **charity shall cover the multitude of sins.**

[8] Rom. 12:10 *Be* kindly affectioned one to another with **brotherly love**; in honour preferring one another;

[9] John 15:13 Greater **love** hath no man than this, that a man lay down his life for his friends.
1 John 3:16 Hereby perceive we the love *of God*, because he laid down his life for us: and we ought to lay down *our* lives for the brethren. 17 But whoso hath this world's good, and seeth his brother have need, and shutteth up his bowels *of compassion* from him, how dwelleth the love of God in him? 18 My little children, let us **not love in word**, neither in tongue; **but in deed and in truth**.

[10] Heb. 13:1 Let **brotherly love** continue.
1 Thess. 4:9 But as touching **brotherly love** ye need not that I write unto you: for ye yourselves are taught of God to **love one another.** 10 And indeed ye do it toward all the brethren which are in all Macedonia: but we beseech you, brethren, that ye **increase more and more**;

[11] John 13:34 A new commandment I give unto you, That ye **love one another**; as I have loved you, that ye also **love one another.** 35 **By this** shall all *men* know that ye are my disciples, if ye have **love one to another.**
1 John 3:10 In this the children of God are manifest, and the children of the devil: whosoever doeth not righteousness is not of God, neither he that **loveth not** his brother. 11 For this is the message that ye heard from the beginning, that we should **love one another.**

[12] John 3:16 For God so **loved** the world, that he gave his only begotten Son, that whosoever believeth in him should not perish, but have everlasting life.
Rom. 5:8 But God commendeth his **love** toward us, in that, **while we were yet sinners**, Christ died for us. 9 Much more then, being now justified by his blood, we shall be saved from wrath through him. 10 For if, when we were enemies, we were reconciled to God by the death of his Son, much more, being reconciled, we shall be saved by his life.

[13] Matt. 5:43 Ye have heard that it hath been said, Thou shalt love thy neighbour, and hate thine enemy. 44 But I say unto you, **Love your enemies**, bless them that curse you, do good to them that hate you, and pray for them which despitefully use you, and persecute you 45 That ye may be the children of your Father which is in heaven: for he maketh his sun to rise on the evil and on the good, and sendeth rain on the just and on the unjust. 46 For if ye love them which love you, what reward have ye? do not even the publicans the same?
Rom. 12:14 Bless them which persecute you: bless, and curse not.

[14] Prov. 16:7 When a man's ways please the LORD, he maketh even his **enemies** to be at peace with him.

Love begins with a choice that affects our attitudes and thoughts. It shows up in our words and actions. We must walk it out in daily life. Every day there are opportunities to show love in a practical way to our families.

In our attitudes and thoughts, we must consider one another.[15] It is not wise to compare ourselves with one another.[16] We should show mercy and compassion for one another. We should not imagine evil against one another.[17] The devil will try to tempt us with evil thoughts against one another. If we entertain those thoughts, they will continue to build until they explode into negative words or actions. It is up to us to cast down those imaginations before they get a foothold in our thinking.

We should not be prejudiced toward others nor show partiality.[18] Being judgmental of others can be a major temptation for some Christians. We think we know the members of our own family, yet only God can justly judge their hearts. If we would do what the Bible says and get the board out of our own eye before we try to pull the speck out of our brother's eye,[19] that would keep many of us busy. We would have to leave it to God to straighten out our brother's faults. Jesus said that we would be judged according to the same measure that we judge others.[20] To that I must say, "Lord, forgive me and have mercy on me."

Love can be shown in our conversations. We must remember that conversation includes both listening and speaking. Listening is a very important part. We should be swift to hear and slow to speak.[21] Answering too quickly is foolish and can make us ashamed.[22] When it is time to speak, we should speak only truth.[23] We should not murmur about one another or with one another.[24] We should not speak evil of

---

[15] 1 Cor. 10:24 Let no man seek his own, but every man another's *wealth*.
Heb. 10: 24 And let us **consider one another** to provoke unto love and to good works:

[16] 2 Cor. 10:12 For we dare not make ourselves of the number, or compare ourselves with some that commend themselves: but they measuring themselves by themselves, and **comparing themselves among themselves, are not wise**.

[17] Zech. 7:9 Thus speaketh the LORD of hosts, saying, Execute true judgment, and **shew mercy and compassions** every man to his brother: 10 And oppress not the widow, nor the fatherless, the stranger, nor the poor; and **let none of you imagine evil against his brother in your heart**.

[18] 1 Tim. 5:21 I charge *thee* before God, and the Lord Jesus Christ, and the elect angels, that thou observe these things **without preferring one before another, doing nothing by partiality**.
James 2:8 If ye fulfil the royal law according to the scripture, Thou shalt love thy neighbour as thyself, ye do well: 9 But if ye have **respect to persons**, ye commit sin, and are convinced of the law as transgressors.

[19] Luke 6:41 And why beholdest thou the mote that is in thy brother's eye, but perceivest not the beam that is in thine own eye? 42 Either how canst thou say to thy brother, Brother, let me pull out the mote that is in thine eye, when thou thyself beholdest not the beam that is in thine own eye? Thou hypocrite, cast out first the beam out of thine own eye, and then shalt thou see clearly to pull out the mote that is in thy brother's eye.

[20] Matt. 7:1 **Judge not,** that ye be not judged. 2 For with what judgment ye judge, ye shall be judged: and with what measure ye mete, it shall be measured to you again.

[21] James 1:19 Wherefore, my beloved brethren, let every man be **swift to hear**, slow to speak, slow to wrath: 20 For the wrath of man worketh not the righteousness of God.

[22] Prov. 18:13 He that answereth a matter before he heareth *it*, it *is* folly and shame unto him.

[23] Eph. 4:25 Wherefore putting away lying, **speak** every man **truth** with his neighbour: for we are members one of another.

[24] Phil. 2:14 Do all things without murmurings and disputings:

one another.[25] All corrupt communication grieves the Holy Spirit. We should speak only that which is good to build up others and minister grace to them.[26]

In our actions, we should show care for one another. We should suffer with the one who is suffering and rejoice with the one who is honored.[27] We should encourage and edify (build up) one another.[28] We should serve one another.[29] That may even include washing another's feet as Jesus did.[30]

We must learn to share with one another. This may mean bearing one another's burdens.[31] It includes fellowship[32] and giving.[33] We should not withhold good from them to whom it is due when it is in our power to do it.[34] Sometimes our children ask us for something, and we say "maybe tomorrow" or next week or some other time that seems like "never" to them. We should not put them off when we are able to

---

[25] Psalm 50:19 Thou givest thy mouth to evil, and thy tongue frameth deceit. 20 Thou sittest *and* **speakest against thy brother**; thou slanderest thine own mother's son.
James 4:10 Humble yourselves in the sight of the Lord, and he shall lift you up. 11 **Speak not evil** one of another, brethren. He that speaketh evil of *his* brother, and judgeth his brother, speaketh evil of the law, and judgeth the law: but if thou judge the law, thou art not a doer of the law, but a judge.

[26] Eph. 4:29 Let **no corrupt communication** proceed out of your mouth, but that which is good to the use of edifying, that it may minister grace unto the hearers. 30 And **grieve not the holy Spirit of God**, whereby ye are sealed unto the day of redemption. 31 Let all bitterness, and wrath, and anger, and clamour, and **evil speaking**, be put away from you, with all malice:

[27] 1 Cor. 12:25 That there should be no schism in the body; but *that* the members should have the same **care one for another**. 26 And whether one member suffer, all the members suffer with it; or one member be honoured, all the members rejoice with it.
Rom. 12:15 Rejoice with them that do rejoice, and weep with them that weep.

[28] Rom. 15:1 We then that are strong ought to bear the infirmities of the weak, and not to please ourselves. 2 Let every one of us **please *his* neighbour for *his* good to edification**. 3a For even Christ pleased not himself....
1 Thess. 5:11 Wherefore comfort yourselves together, and **edify one another**, even as also ye do.

[29] Gal. 5:13 For, brethren, ye have been called unto liberty; only *use* not liberty for an occasion to the flesh, but **by love serve one another**.

[30] John 13:4 He {Jesus} riseth from supper, and laid aside his garments; and took a towel, and girded himself. 5 After that he poureth water into a bason, and began to wash the disciples' feet, and to wipe *them* with the towel wherewith he was girded. ... 12 So after he had washed their feet, and had taken his garments, and was set down again, he said unto them, Know ye what I have done to you? 13 Ye call me Master and Lord: and ye say well; for *so* I am. 14 If I then, *your* Lord and Master, have washed your feet; ye also ought to **wash one another's feet**. 15 For I have given you an example, that ye should do as I have done to you. 16 Verily, verily, I say unto you, The servant is not greater than his lord; neither he that is sent greater than he that sent him. 17 If ye know these things, happy are ye if ye do them.

[31] Gal. 6:2 Bear ye one another's burdens, and so fulfil the law of Christ.

[32] 1 John 1:3 That which we have seen and heard declare we unto you, that ye also may have fellowship with us: and truly our fellowship *is* with the Father, and with his Son Jesus Christ.... 7 But if we walk in the light, as he is in the light, **we have fellowship one with another**, and the blood of Jesus Christ his Son cleanseth us from all sin.

[33] Luke 6:38 **Give**, and it shall be given unto you; good measure, pressed down, and shaken together, and running over, shall men give into your bosom. For with the same measure that ye mete withal it shall be measured to you again.

[34] Prov. 3:27 Withhold not good from them to whom it is due, when it is in the power of thine hand to do *it*. 28 Say not unto thy neighbor, Go, and come again, and to morrow I will give; when thou hast it by thee.

give it now. The Bible says we should not charge interest when we lend to our brother so that God can bless us in all we set our hands to.[35]

We must not deal treacherously against one another,[36] but be a peacemaker.[37] We should do all we can to follow after things that make for peace.[38] As we live in peace, the God of love and peace will be with us.[39] When we do wrong, we must be willing to admit our faults to one another and pray for one another.[40]

The "Golden Rule" sums up how to walk in right relationship with one another. We are not to say, "I'll treat him like he treats me,"[41] but instead we should treat him like we would like to be treated.[42] Peter also gives a good summary of right relationships with one another:

> "**Finally**, *be ye* **all of one mind**, having **compassion one of another**, love as brethren, *be* pitiful, *be* **courteous**: Not rendering evil for evil, or railing for railing: but contrariwise **blessing**; knowing that ye are thereunto called, that ye should inherit a blessing. For he that will love life, and see good days, let him refrain his tongue from evil, and his lips that they speak no guile: Let him eschew evil, and do good; let him **seek peace**, and ensue it. For the eyes of the Lord *are* over the righteous, and his ears *are open* unto their prayers: but the face of the Lord *is* against them that do evil." (1 Peter 3: 8-12)

Now that we know it, it's time to **do it!**[43]

---

[35] Deut. 23:19 Thou shalt **not lend upon usury to thy brother**; usury of money, usury of victuals, usury of any thing that is lent upon usury: 20 Unto a stranger thou mayest lend upon usury; but unto thy brother thou shalt not lend upon usury: **that the LORD thy God may bless thee** in all that thou settest thine hand to in the land whither thou goest to possess it.

[36] Mal. 2:10 Have we not all one father? hath not one God created us? **why do we deal treacherously every man against his brother**, by profaning the covenant of our fathers?

[37] Matt. 5:9 Blessed *are* the peacemakers: for they shall be called the children of God.

[38] Rom. 12:17 Recompense to no man evil for evil. Provide things honest in the sight of all men. 18 If it be possible, as much as lieth in you, **live peaceably with all men**. 19 Dearly beloved, avenge not yourselves, but *rather* give place unto wrath: for it is written, Vengeance *is* mine; I will repay, saith the Lord.
Rom. 14:19 Let us therefore **follow after the things which make for peace**, and things wherewith one may edify another.

[39] 2 Cor. 13:11 Finally, brethren, farewell. Be perfect, be of good comfort, be of one mind, **live in peace**; and the God of love and peace shall be with you.

[40] James 5:16 **Confess your faults one to another**, and **pray one for another**, that ye may be healed. The effectual fervent prayer of a righteous man availeth much.

[41] Prov. 24:29 Say not, I will do so to him as he hath done to me: I will render to the man according to his work.

[42] Luke 6:31 And as ye would that men should do to you, do ye also to them likewise.

[43] James 4:17 Therefore to him that knoweth to **do good**, and doeth *it* not, to him it is sin.

Chapter 22

Forgiveness

Forgiveness is letting go of resentment against someone who has wronged us. It is a decision not to hold a person's sin against him. When we have let go of pride and selfishness, forgiveness becomes easier. As with love, God commands us to forgive, and we have the choice to obey Him or not. Forgiveness is not based on feelings or on the actions of others, but on our making a decision. When we make the decision to forgive, God has a channel in which to get involved. Then He can do the work in our hearts and emotions to restore peace.

I remember getting very upset with someone because of something she had done. The situation kept running over and over through my mind. I could not think about this person without thinking about what she had done, but I finally made a decision to forgive her. The ill feelings toward her did not disappear immediately, but God was at work in my heart. A short time later, she and I spent most of the day at a school event. It was not until the day was over that I realized I had not once thought about what she had done. God had taken all the bitterness away, and had reconciled our relationship.

God reconciled us to Himself by Jesus and has given to us the ministry of reconciliation (restoring to favor).[1] Reconciliation involves forgiveness. We are to forgive others as God has forgiven us.

If our brother has something against us, we are responsible to go to him and be reconciled with him. (Jesus even said to be reconciled with an offended brother **before** we offer a gift to God.[2] If we are at odds with our brother, it affects our fellowship with God.) If we have something against someone else, we are also responsible to forgive him.[3] So it makes no difference whether we offended someone else, or someone offended us. Either way, we must take the initiative to either ask him to forgive us or to forgive him. If **any** one has **any** complaint against **any**, there must be forgiveness.[4]

---

[1] 2 Cor. 5:17 Therefore if any man *be* in Christ, *he is* a new creature: old things are passed away; behold, all things are become new. 18 And all things *are* of God, who hath reconciled us to himself by Jesus Christ, and **hath given to us the ministry of reconciliation**; 19 To wit, that God was in Christ, reconciling the world unto himself, not imputing their trespasses unto them; and **hath committed unto us the word of reconciliation**.
Eph. 4:32 And be ye kind one to another, tenderhearted, **forgiving one another, even as God for Christ's sake hath forgiven you**.

[2] Matt. 5:21 Ye have heard that it was said by them of old time, Thou shalt not kill; and whosoever shall kill shall be in danger of the judgment: 22 But I say unto you, That whosoever is angry with his brother without a cause shall be in danger of the judgment: and whosoever shall say to his brother, Raca, shall be in danger of the council: but whosoever shall say, Thou fool, shall be in danger of hell fire. 23 Therefore if thou bring thy gift to the altar, and there rememberest that **thy brother hath ought against thee**; 24 Leave there thy gift before the altar, and go thy way; **first be reconciled to thy brother**, and then come and offer thy gift.

[3] Mark 11:25 And when ye stand praying, **forgive, if ye have ought against any**: that your Father also which is in heaven may forgive you your trespasses. 26 But if ye do not forgive, neither will your Father which is in heaven forgive your trespasses.

[4] Col. 3:13 Forbearing one another, and forgiving one another, **if any man have a quarrel against any**: even as Christ forgave you, so also *do* ye.

When we forgive, then we will be forgiven.[5] In the Lord's Prayer, Jesus taught us to pray for our debts to be forgiven **as** we forgive our debtors. After teaching the prayer, He explained that if we do not forgive, neither would God forgive us.[6]

Jesus told a story that explained how forgiveness works in the kingdom of heaven. He told of a servant who owed the king a large amount, but could not pay the debt. The king had mercy on him and forgave the debt. Then that same servant found one of his fellowservants who owed him a much smaller amount and demanded that he pay it. The fellowservant was not able to pay it, so the first servant had him thrown into prison until it was paid. Other servants saw what had been done and told the king. The king called the first servant in and told him he should have had compassion and forgiven the debt as the king had forgiven his. The king then delivered the servant to the tormentors until his debt was paid. Jesus said that our heavenly Father would do to us as the king did if we do not from our hearts forgive our brothers' trespasses.[7]

It is necessary for us to forgive others, for we will need forgiveness ourselves. Refusing to forgive is, in itself, a sin that needs forgiveness.

People have offered all kinds of excuses for not forgiving others. One is, "If I forgive them, they will just do it again." Jesus blows away that excuse. When Peter asked how often he must forgive his brother; Jesus said not seven times (as Peter suggested), but seventy times seven.[8] No matter how many times someone offends you, you must forgive every time. However, Jesus did say that those who are forgiven more would love more.[9] If you have much to forgive someone in your family, you can expect much love from him.

---

[5] Luke 6:37 Judge not, and ye shall not be judged: condemn not, and ye shall not be condemned: **forgive**, and ye shall be forgiven:

[6] Matt. 6:12 And forgive us our debts, as we forgive our debtors.... 14 For if ye forgive men their trespasses, your heavenly Father will also forgive you: 15 But if ye forgive not men their trespasses, neither will your Father forgive your trespasses.

[7] Matt. 18:23 Therefore is the **kingdom of heaven likened unto a certain king, which would take account of his servants**. 24 And when he had begun to reckon, one was brought unto him, which **owed him ten thousand talents**. 25 But forasmuch as he had not to pay, his lord commanded him to be sold, and his wife, and children, and all that he had, and payment to be made. 26 The servant therefore fell down, and worshipped him, saying, **Lord, have patience with me**, and I will pay thee all. 27 Then the lord of that servant was **moved with compassion, and loosed him, and forgave him the debt**. 28 But the **same servant** went out, and **found one of his fellowservants, which owed him an hundred pence**: and he laid hands on him, and took *him* by the throat, saying, Pay me that thou owest. 29 And his fellowservant fell down at his feet, and besought him, saying, Have patience with me, and I will pay thee all. 30 And he would not: but went and **cast him into prison, till he should pay the debt**. 31 So when his fellowservants saw what was done, they were very sorry, and came and told unto their lord all that was done. 32 Then **his lord**, after that he had called him, **said unto him, O thou wicked servant, I forgave thee all that debt**, because thou desiredst me: 33 **Shouldest not thou also have had compassion on thy fellowservant, even as I had pity on thee?** 34 And his lord was wroth, and **delivered him to the tormentors, till he should pay all that was due unto him**. 35 **So likewise shall my heavenly Father do also unto you, if ye from your hearts forgive not every one his brother their trespasses.**

[8] Matt. 18:21 Then came Peter to him, and said, Lord, **how oft** shall my brother sin against me, and **I forgive him**? till seven times? 22 Jesus saith unto him, I say not unto thee, Until seven times: but, **Until seventy times seven.**

[9] Luke 7:40 And Jesus answering said unto him, Simon, I have somewhat to say unto thee. And he saith, Master, say on. 41 There was a certain creditor which had two debtors: the one owed five hundred pence, and the other fifty. 42 And when they had nothing to pay, he frankly forgave them both. Tell me therefore, which of them will love him most? 43 Simon answered and said, I suppose that *he*, to whom he forgave most. And he said unto him, Thou hast rightly judged.... 47 Wherefore I say unto thee, Her sins, which are many, are forgiven; for she loved much: but to whom little is forgiven, *the same* loveth little.

Another excuse people may use for not forgiving is that the offender has not repented or asked forgiveness. They could look at Luke 17:3 and point out that it says, "**if** he repent, forgive him."[10] It does say that, but it does **not** say do not forgive him if he does not repent. If you had to wait for someone to repent before you could forgive him, then that person could keep you from obeying God because God says to forgive. It is possible **and** necessary to forgive even if the offender does not repent or ask for forgiveness. Jesus forgave his killers, and so did Stephen.[11] The killers had not repented or asked for forgiveness.

Some people refuse to forgive because "they treated me so badly, I just cannot forgive them." Well, no one reading this book has been crucified or stoned to death.

One more excuse that I will mention here is the one that says, "If I forgave them, I would be condoning their wrongdoing." This is not a valid reason, and it does not even make sense. Forgiveness is only needed for wrongdoing. There is nothing to forgive unless someone has done something wrong.

There is no valid excuse for unforgiveness; we should not carry grudges.[12] Unforgiveness can block the flow of God's power in your life. It can hinder your ability to receive healing and provision from God. It can make it harder for you to hear His guidance. Unforgiveness leads to bitterness; it can "eat you alive" and poison those around you.[13] If you always forgive before sundown, bitterness will not have time to take root.[14]

Situations can occur that just do not seem fair: here we are, minding our own business, when all of a sudden someone comes on the scene and does us wrong. We are the "innocent," and we have been greatly wronged by someone. Then we have to deal with the offense. Once we have been offended, it becomes our problem. We must make the decision to forgive. Satan uses this trap often. Have you noticed that He does not play fair? He could ruin a life by setting up an offense. The offense itself is not what would ruin the life, but unforgiveness could.

Jesus said He would give the church the keys of the kingdom of heaven and whatever we bind on earth would be bound in heaven; whatever we loose on earth would be loosed in heaven.[15] I believe forgiveness is one of those keys. God has shown me that forgiveness is a key to victory. Forgiveness releases the forgiver and the forgiven. It releases the forgiver to be healed of the offense; it releases the forgiven from the bondage of our unforgiveness. If we refuse to forgive someone, we could be holding him

---

[10] Luke 17:3 Take heed to yourselves: If thy brother trespass against thee, rebuke him; and if he repent, **forgive** him. 4 And if he trespass against thee seven times in a day, and seven times in a day turn again to thee, saying, I repent; **thou shalt forgive him.**

[11] Luke 23:34a Then **said Jesus, Father, forgive them**; for they know not what they do....
Acts 7:59 And they stoned **Stephen**, calling upon *God*, and saying, Lord Jesus, receive my spirit. 60 And he kneeled down, and cried with a loud voice, **Lord, lay not this sin to their charge.** And when he had said this, he fell asleep.

[12] James 5:9 **Grudge not one against another**, brethren, lest ye be condemned: behold, the judge standeth before the door.

[13] Heb. 12:15 Looking diligently lest any man fail of the grace of God; lest any **root of bitterness** springing up trouble *you*, and **thereby many be defiled**;

[14] Eph. 4:26 Be ye angry, and sin not: **let not the sun go down upon your wrath**:

[15] Matt. 16:19 And I will give unto thee the keys of the kingdom of heaven: and whatsoever thou shalt bind on earth shall be bound in heaven: and whatsoever thou shalt loose on earth shall be loosed in heaven.

in bondage to that sin. If we forgive him, that could release him to repentance.[16] When an offender does repent and ask forgiveness, then he can **receive** the forgiveness that has already been given.

When Stephen was stoned, Saul consented to and witnessed his death.[17] When Stephen forgave those who were involved in putting him to death, Saul was included. Soon after that, Saul turned **from** persecuting Christians to becoming one of them. He became Paul the apostle who worked **for** Jesus instead of **against** Him. Later Paul forgave those who did him wrong.[18]

It is our responsibility to forgive, love, bless, do good to, and pray for those who come against us.[19] It is God's responsibility to judge and deal with them.[20] He will judge righteously and reward accordingly.[21] We must leave that to Him.

After a person is confronted with his sin and has been forgiven, it is important to comfort him and show him love. We must confirm our love toward him that he not be swallowed up in sorrow. This is a matter of obedience. It will keep Satan from getting an advantage over us.[22] (Unforgiveness is one of his devices he uses against us.)

In Chapter 20, we noted how Joseph's brothers hated him and because of envy, sold him as a slave. In the following passages, Joseph not only forgave his brothers, but also comforted them and confirmed his love toward them:

"And Joseph said unto his brethren, Come near to me, I pray you. And they came near. And he said, I *am* Joseph your brother, whom ye sold into Egypt. Now therefore be not grieved, nor angry with yourselves, that ye sold me hither: for God did send me before you to preserve life. For these two years *hath* the famine *been* in the land: and yet *there are* five years, in the

---

[16] John 20:23 Whose soever sins ye remit, they are remitted unto them; *and* whose soever *sins* ye retain, they are retained.

[17] Acts 7:58 And cast *him* {Stephen} out of the city, and stoned *him*: and **the witnesses laid down their clothes at a young man's feet, whose name was Saul.** 8:1 **And Saul was consenting unto his death.** And at that time there was a great persecution against the church which was at Jerusalem; and they were all scattered abroad throughout the regions of Judaea and Samaria, except the apostles. 2 And devout men carried Stephen *to his burial*, and made great lamentation over him. 3 **As for Saul, he made havock of the church**, entering into every house, and haling men and women committed *them* to prison.

[18] 2 Tim. 4:16 At my first answer no man stood with me {Paul}, but all *men* forsook me: *I pray God* that it may not be laid to their charge.

[19] Matt. 5:44 But I say unto you, Love your enemies, bless them that curse you, do good to them that hate you, and pray for them which despitefully use you, and persecute you;

[20] Heb. 10:30 For we know him that hath said, Vengeance *belongeth* unto me, I will recompense, saith the Lord. And again, The Lord shall judge his people.

[21] 2 Tim. 4:14 {Paul said} Alexander the coppersmith did me much evil: the **Lord reward him according to his works:**

[22] 2 Cor. 2:6 Sufficient to such a man *is* this punishment, which *was inflicted* of many. 7 So that contrariwise ye *ought* rather to **forgive** *him*, and **comfort** *him*, lest perhaps such a one should be swallowed up with overmuch sorrow. 8 Wherefore I beseech you that ye would **confirm** *your* **love toward him.** 9 For to this end also did I write, that I might know the proof of you, whether ye be obedient in all things. 10 To whom ye forgive any thing, I *forgive* also: for if I forgave any thing, to whom I forgave *it*, for your sakes *forgave I it* in the person of Christ; 11 Lest Satan should get an advantage of us: for we are not ignorant of his devices.

which *there shall* neither *be* earing nor harvest. And God sent me before you to preserve you a posterity in the earth, and to save your lives by a great deliverance. So now *it was* not you *that* sent me hither, but God: and he hath made me a father to Pharaoh, and lord of all his house, and a ruler throughout all the land of Egypt…. Moreover **he kissed all his brethren, and wept upon them**: and after that his brethren talked with him." (Genesis 45:4-8, 15)

"And when Joseph's brethren saw that their father was dead, they said, Joseph will peradventure hate us, and will certainly requite us all the evil which we did unto him. And they sent a messenger unto Joseph, saying, Thy father did command before he died, saying, So shall ye say unto Joseph, **Forgive**, I pray thee now, the trespass of thy brethren, and their sin; for they did unto thee evil: and now, we pray thee, **forgive** the trespass of the servants of the God of thy father. And Joseph wept when they spake unto him. And his brethren also went and fell down before his face; and they said, Behold, we *be* thy servants. And Joseph said unto them, Fear not: for *am* I in the place of God? But as for you, ye thought evil against me; *but* God meant it unto good, to bring to pass, as *it is* this day, to save much people alive. Now therefore fear ye not: I will nourish you, and your little ones. And he **comforted** them, and **spake kindly** unto them." (Genesis 50:15-21)

Forgiveness is truly a blessing![23]

---

[23] Psalm 32:1 Blessed *is he whose* transgression *is* **forgiven**, *whose* sin *is* covered.

Part Nine

Family and Church Relationships

Chapter 23

Congregation or Segregation?

The Bible compares Jesus to a shepherd and Christians to sheep. The word we use today to describe a church body is "congregation." Originally, congregate meant to gather into a flock. On the other hand, segregate literally means to separate from the flock or the main group. Separate means to divide into groups or disunite. It implies that what was once together, such as a family, is being divided. What happens to families in churches today? Do we find congregation or segregation? Churches can either support the family unit or cause division. Likewise, families can either support the church or cause division. The rest of this book is intended to encourage churches and families to support one another and to cooperate in building the kingdom of God on earth.

One of the specific areas that I felt God led me to share with the body of Christ concerns the treatment of their children in church settings. God is grieved when children are pushed aside and separated from their parents. This has been going on in the world system for a long time, but now is rampant in many churches. There is a two-fold cause: parents who do not take responsibility for their own children and churches that usurp parents' authority over their children.

The Scriptural principles for parent and child relationships already presented in this book apply in church settings, as well as in the home. Family relationships and responsibilities do not temporarily cease when the church gathers together. Parents are still responsible for the training of their own children. Teaching of God's Word in church settings does not relieve parents of God's command to teach their children His Word in their daily lives.

Worldly Influence

I searched through the Bible for Scriptures relating to family and church, but I found no mention of nurseries, age-segregated Sunday schools, children's church, youth groups, and the like. God never says in the Bible to separate children from their parents to be taught by someone else in a tabernacle, temple, synagogue, or church setting. Age segregation in the church is not rooted in God's Word. If not, then where is it rooted? It has to be rooted in something contrary to His Word. Jesus said that whoever is not with Him is against Him.[1]

Separating children from parents for teaching is based on the world's system. It is the system used in public schools. It groups the children by ages and puts an adult with them to teach them. If the group is large, more adults are added to help keep order. This system provides a way to deal with a large number of children. It makes administration easier and frees up more space for adults. But it is not the best arrangement for the children, and it is not God's way. He says we should not be conformed to this world.[2]

---

[1] Matt. 12:30 He that is not with me is against me; and he that gathereth not with me scattereth abroad.

[2] Rom. 12:2 And **be not conformed to this world**: but be ye transformed by the renewing of your mind, that ye may prove what is that good, and acceptable, and perfect, will of God.

Many parents have become accustomed to sending their children to school to be taught by someone else during the week. Now some of them expect the church to teach their children in separate classes during church meetings. They seem quite willing to drop their children off in any nursery or children's ministry available at any meeting. These parents seem to trust their children with anyone, whether or not they know anything about who will be with them or what they will be doing.

Many churches have responded to those parents' demands by setting up separate children's ministries. This became a comfortable arrangement for many parents and church leaders. The parents could listen, and the preachers could preach without any distractions from the children. After a while, in some churches, children were not even welcome any more in the main meetings. Children from babies to teens had their own separate services. It seemed no one thought they were capable of receiving any benefit from the main services. Even parents who recognized their responsibility for their own children were discouraged from keeping their children with them in the adult services. Their children were encouraged by others to enjoy the fun and games of children's church. A pattern of separating children from their parents was established, and many churches have followed this pattern.

Once the church has copied the world's way of separating children from parents; it follows that it would look to the world system to find out what to do with the separated children, especially since there are no Biblical examples. Some ministries are in such competition with the world for the attention of the children that it seems like they are trying to make church acceptable to the world. No longer are the Word of God and the use of modern parables and object lessons enough for them. Instead they try to appeal to the carnal nature. Now artificial environments are set up in children's church. Things the world uses to entertain children are now being used by the church. Churches offer "Christian" alternatives to what the world offers, but "Christian alternatives" are compromises. Why is all this fantasy used to teach the truth? How does a child tell the difference when it is all mixed together?

I asked the Lord about this because it did not seem right to me. The answer I got is that mixing in the world's way is like eating food offered to idols: it offends the weak conscience. If a person sees a ministry presenting something that looks "worldly" to him, he may think it is all right for him to do worldly things. In 1 Corinthians 8, it says that we should take heed that our liberty does not become a stumblingblock to those who are weak. If we sin against a weak brother in wounding his conscience, we sin against Christ.[3]

Whatever a ministry advertises to attract people to its meetings; that is what they will come for, whether it be food, games, prizes, fun, or whatever. Even though people can be brought to a meeting through wrong motives, they may not be interested in the Gospel that is offered. The church can try to duplicate the world, but why should they? The church has something genuine to offer: a personal relationship with Jesus

---

[3] 1 Cor. 8:1 Now as touching things offered unto idols, we know that we all have knowledge. Knowledge puffeth up, but charity edifieth. 2 And if any man think that he knoweth any thing, he knoweth nothing yet as he ought to know. 3 But if any man love God, the same is known of him. 4 As concerning therefore the eating of those things that are offered in sacrifice unto idols, we know that an idol *is* nothing in the world, and that *there is* none other God but one. 5 For though there be that are called gods, whether in heaven or in earth, (as there be gods many, and lords many,) 6 But to us *there is but* one God, the Father, of whom *are* all things, and we in him; and one Lord Jesus Christ, by whom *are* all things, and we by him. 7 Howbeit *there is* not in every man that knowledge: for some with conscience of the idol unto this hour eat *it* as a thing offered unto an idol; and their conscience being weak is defiled. 8 But meat commendeth us not to God: for neither, if we eat, are we the better; neither, if we eat not, are we the worse. 9 **But take heed lest by any means this liberty of yours become a stumblingblock to them that are weak.** 10 For if any man see thee which hast knowledge sit at meat in the idol's temple, shall not the conscience of him which is weak be emboldened to eat those things which are offered to idols; 11 And through thy knowledge shall the weak brother perish, for whom Christ died? 12 **But when ye sin so against the brethren, and wound their weak conscience, ye sin against Christ.** 13 Wherefore, if meat make my brother to offend, I will eat no flesh while the world standeth, lest I make my brother to offend.

Christ. Church can offer relief **from** the world's ways, so why copy them? The church is supposed to imitate Christ, not imitate the world.

Biblical Examples

As I stated earlier in this chapter, I did not find anywhere in the Bible that God said to separate children from parents for teaching in church.

I did find one example of a woman who took her son to the house of the Lord and left him there because of a vow she had made unto the Lord. This woman was Hannah, the mother of Samuel. She vowed that if God would give her a son, she would give him to the Lord all the days of his life. **She** made this vow in bitterness of soul because she had no children;[4] the Bible does not say that God required it of her. However, Hannah was faithful to keep her vow. After she had weaned Samuel, she and her husband Elkanah took him to the house of the Lord and left him with Eli the priest.[5] The Bible indicates that Samuel saw his parents once a year when they came to offer the yearly sacrifice.[6] Even though Samuel became great in the Lord, his sons did not walk in his ways.[7] Eli had not been a good father to his own sons, and Samuel seems to have followed his poor example. Samuel did not pass on to his own sons the good character that he had.

In contrast to separating families in church, I found many Scriptures showing that all ages worshiped together. There are passages in the Old Testament that mention assemblies of the people. Some included feasting, bringing of tithes, entering into covenant with God, reading of God's Word, and praying. Others included dedications, offering of sacrifices, praising, rejoicing, and fasting.

---

[4] 1 Sam. 1:10 And **she *was* in bitterness of soul**, and prayed unto the LORD, and wept sore. 11 And **she vowed a vow**, and said, O LORD of hosts, if thou wilt indeed look on the affliction of thine handmaid, and remember me, and not forget thine handmaid, but wilt give unto thine handmaid a man child, then **I will give him unto the LORD all the days of his life**, and there shall no razor come upon his head.

[5] 1 Sam. 1:24 And **when she had weaned him**, she took him up with her, with three bullocks, and one ephah of flour, and a bottle of wine, and **brought him unto the house of the LORD** in Shiloh: and the **child *was* young**. 25 And they slew a bullock, and brought the child to Eli. 26 And she said, Oh my lord, *as* thy soul liveth, my lord, I *am* the woman that stood by thee here, praying unto the LORD. 27 **For this child I prayed**; and the **LORD hath given me my petition** which I asked of him: 28 **Therefore also I have lent him to the LORD; as long as he liveth** he shall be lent to the LORD. And he worshipped the LORD there.

[6] 1 Sam. 2:18 But Samuel ministered before the LORD, *being* a **child**, girded with a linen ephod. 19 Moreover his mother made him a little coat, and brought *it* to him **from year to year**, when she came up with her husband to offer the **yearly sacrifice**.

[7] 1 Sam. 8:1 And it came to pass, when **Samuel** was old, that he made his sons judges over Israel. 2 Now the name of his firstborn was Joel; and the name of his second, Abiah: *they were* judges in Beersheba. 3 And **his sons walked not in his ways**, but turned aside after lucre, and took bribes, and perverted judgment. 4 Then all the elders of Israel gathered themselves together, and came to Samuel unto Ramah, 5 And said unto him, Behold, thou art old, and **thy sons walk not in thy ways**: now make us a king to judge us like all the nations.

When Moses asked Pharaoh to let the people go so that they could serve the Lord, Pharaoh asked who would go. Moses replied that they would go with their young and their old and with their sons and their daughters to hold a feast unto the Lord.[8]

After the Israelites were delivered from Egypt, the Lord told them that He would choose a sanctuary where His name would dwell. They were commanded to bring to that place their offerings, sacrifices, and tithes. There they were to rejoice with their sons and their daughters.[9] In this place, they were also to keep the "feast of tabernacles" for seven days with their sons and daughters.[10] When the Israelites entered into covenant with the Lord, they gathered together with their little ones and their wives.[11] Every seven years during the "feast of tabernacles," the law was to be read to all Israel. They, including the children, were to listen and learn to fear the Lord and do His Word.[12] After Moses was gone, Joshua took his place and read all the words of the law that Moses had commanded. He read to all the congregation of Israel, including the women and little ones.[13]

---

[8] Exod. 10:8 And Moses and Aaron were brought again unto Pharaoh: and he said unto them, Go, serve the LORD your God: *but* who *are* they that shall go? 9 And Moses said, We will go **with our young and with our old, with our sons and with our daughters**, with our flocks and with our herds will we go; for we *must hold* a **feast** unto the LORD.

[9] Deut. 12:11 Then there shall be a place which the LORD your God shall choose to cause his name to dwell there; thither shall ye **bring** all that I command you; your **burnt offerings**, and your **sacrifices**, your **tithes**, and the **heave offering** of your hand, and all your **choice vows** which ye vow unto the LORD: 12 And ye shall **rejoice before the LORD** your God, **ye, and your sons, and your daughters**, and your menservants, and your maidservants, and the Levite that *is* within your gates; forasmuch as he hath no part nor inheritance with you.... 17 Thou mayest not eat within thy gates the tithe of thy corn, or of thy wine, or of thy oil, or the firstlings of thy herds or of thy flock, nor any of thy vows which thou vowest, nor thy freewill offerings, or heave offering of thine hand: 18 But thou must eat them before the LORD thy God in the place which the LORD thy God shall choose, **thou, and thy son, and thy daughter**, and thy manservant, and thy maidservant, and the Levite that *is* within thy gates: and thou shalt **rejoice** before the LORD thy God in all that thou puttest thine hands unto.

[10] Deut. 16:11 And thou shalt **rejoice** before the LORD thy God, **thou, and thy son, and thy daughter**, and thy manservant, and thy maidservant, and the Levite that *is* within thy gates, and the stranger, and the fatherless, and the widow, that *are* among you, in the place which the LORD thy God hath chosen to place his name there. 12 And thou shalt remember that thou wast a bondman in Egypt: and thou shalt observe and do these statutes. 13 Thou shalt observe the **feast** of tabernacles seven days, after that thou hast gathered in thy corn and thy wine: 14 And thou shalt **rejoice in thy feast, thou, and thy son, and thy daughter**, and thy manservant, and thy maidservant, and the Levite, the stranger, and the fatherless, and the widow, that *are* within thy gates.

[11] Deut. 29:10 **Ye stand this day all of you before the LORD your God**; your captains of your tribes, your elders, and your officers, *with* all the men of Israel, 11 **Your little ones, your wives**, and thy stranger that *is* in thy camp, from the hewer of thy wood unto the drawer of thy water: 12 That thou shouldest **enter into covenant with the LORD thy God**, and into his oath, which the LORD thy God maketh with thee this day: 13 That he may establish thee to day for a people unto himself, and *that* he may be unto thee a God, as he hath said unto thee, and as he hath sworn unto thy fathers, to Abraham, to Isaac, and to Jacob.... 29 The secret *things belong* unto the LORD our God: but those *things which are* revealed *belong* unto **us and to our children** for ever, that *we* may do all the words of this law.

[12] Deut. 31:10 And Moses commanded them, saying, At the end of *every* seven years, in the solemnity of the year of release, in the **feast** of tabernacles, 11 When all Israel is come to appear before the LORD thy God in the place which he shall choose, thou shalt **read this law** before all Israel in their hearing. 12 **Gather the people together, men, and women, and children**, and thy stranger that *is* within thy gates, **that they may hear, and that they may learn, and fear the LORD your God, and observe to do all the words of this law:** 13 **And** *that* **their children**, which have not known *any thing*, **may hear, and learn to fear the LORD your God**, as long as ye live in the land whither ye go over Jordan to possess it.

[13] Josh. 8:35 There was not a word of all that Moses commanded, which Joshua read not before **all the congregation of Israel, with the women, and the little ones**, and the strangers that were conversant among them.

While the house of the Lord was being repaired under the direction of King Josiah, the high priest found the book of the law. The king gathered all the people, both great and small, to the house of the Lord to hear the reading of all the words of the book of the covenant that had been found.[14] When enemies came against Judah to do battle, King Jehoshaphat set himself to seek the Lord. He proclaimed a fast and gathered all the people, including wives, little ones, and children, to stand before the Lord and seek His direction.[15]

After some of the exiles returned from Babylon to Jerusalem, Ezra the priest gathered the people, men, women, and all that could hear with understanding, to hear the reading of the law from morning until midday. He had other men there to help the people to understand what was read. The people listened attentively and worshipped the Lord there.[16] At the dedication of the wall of Jerusalem, the people gathered to offer sacrifices and rejoice. The wives and children also rejoiced, and their sounds of joy were heard afar off.[17] In the book of Psalms, it says that young men and maidens, old men and children should praise the name of the Lord.[18]

Jeremiah prophesied the return of the captives and the restoration of Israel. He said that God would bring together a great company, including the woman with child and the travailing woman. The virgins would rejoice in the dance, both young men and old ones, because God would turn their mourning into joy.[19]

---

[14] 2 Kings 23:1 And the king sent, and they gathered unto him all the elders of Judah and of Jerusalem. 2 And the king went up into the **house of the LORD**, and all the men of Judah and all the inhabitants of Jerusalem with him, and the priests, and the prophets, and **all the people, both small and great**: and **he read in their ears all the words of the book of the covenant** which was found in the house of the LORD.
 2 Chron. 34:29 Then the king sent and gathered together all the elders of Judah and Jerusalem. 30 And the king went up into the house of the LORD, and all the men of Judah, and the inhabitants of Jerusalem, and the priests, and the Levites, and **all the people, great and small**: and **he read in their ears all the words of the book of the covenant** that was found in the house of the LORD.

[15] 2 Chron. 20:12 O our God, wilt thou not judge them? for we have no might against this great company that cometh against us; neither know we what to do: but our eyes *are* upon thee. 13 And **all Judah stood before the LORD, with their little ones, their wives, and their children**.

[16] Neh. 8:2 And **Ezra the priest brought the law before the congregation both of men and women, and all that could hear with understanding**, upon the first day of the seventh month. 3 And he read therein before the street that *was* before the water gate **from the morning until midday, before the men and the women, and those that could understand; and the ears of all the people *were attentive*** unto the book of the law. 4 And Ezra the scribe stood upon a pulpit of wood, which they had made for the purpose; and beside him stood Mattithiah, and Shema, and Anaiah, and Urijah, and Hilkiah, and Maaseiah, on his right hand; and on his left hand, Pedaiah, and Mishael, and Malchiah, and Hashum, and Hashbadana, Zechariah, *and* Meshullam. 5 And Ezra opened the book in the sight of all the people; (for he was above all the people;) and when he opened it, all the people stood up: 6 And Ezra blessed the LORD, the great God. And all the people answered, Amen, Amen, with lifting up their hands: and they bowed their heads, and worshipped the LORD with *their* faces to the ground. 7 Also Jeshua, and Bani, and Sherebiah, Jamin, Akkub, Shabbethai, Hodijah, Maaseiah, Kelita, Azariah, Jozabad, Hanan, Pelaiah, and the Levites, **caused the people to understand the law**: and the people *stood* in their place. 8 So they **read in the book in the law of God distinctly, and gave the sense, and caused *them* to understand the reading**.

[17] Neh. 12:43 Also that day **they offered great sacrifices, and rejoiced**: for God had made them rejoice with great joy: **the wives also and the children rejoiced**: so that the joy of Jerusalem was heard even afar off.

[18] Psalm 148:12 **Both young men, and maidens; old men, and children**: 13 **Let them praise the name of the LORD**: for his name alone is excellent; his glory *is* above the earth and heaven.

[19] Jer. 31:8 Behold, **I will bring them** from the north country, and gather them from the coasts of the earth, *and* with them the blind and the lame, **the woman with child and her that travaileth with child together**: a great company shall return thither. 9 They shall come with weeping, and with supplications will I lead them: I will cause them to walk by the rivers of

Through the prophet Joel, God called the people to a solemn assembly to fast and pray. This assembly included elders, children, nursing infants, brides and bridegrooms.[20]

The New Testament also gives several examples of assemblies that indicate children were included in the meetings with the adults. Three different Gospels tell the story of Jesus setting a child in their midst and teaching a lesson. He used the child as an example to the adults. Jesus called a little child unto him. (If Jesus were in some churches today, He would not be able to find a child in the meeting. He would have to send an usher to a different room, floor, or building to bring a child into the meeting.) Jesus said that to receive a little child is to receive Him. He also said not to offend little ones.[21] The Gospel of Mark adds that Jesus took the child in His arms, which indicates that the child was a small one.[22] The Luke version adds that the least among you shall be great.[23]

The same three Gospels tell about the children being brought to Jesus. Matthew calls them "little children," Mark calls them "young children," and Luke calls them "infants". The disciples rebuked those who brought the children. (Some ushers today are like those disciples.) Jesus was much displeased. He said to "suffer" the little children to come to Him, and not to forbid them. The word "suffer" in the King James Version often means to permit or allow, but the way it is used here is stronger. It indicates that we should not **just** permit our children to go to Jesus, but we must make sure they go to Him. Jesus took some special time with the children to hold them, to put His hands upon them and to bless them.[24]

---

waters in a straight way, wherein they shall not stumble: for I am a father to Israel, and Ephraim *is* my firstborn. 10 Hear the word of the LORD, O ye nations, and declare *it* in the isles afar off, and say, He that scattered Israel will gather him, and keep him, as a shepherd *doth* his flock. 11 For the LORD hath redeemed Jacob, and ransomed him from the hand of *him that was* stronger than he. 12 Therefore they shall come and sing in the height of Zion, and shall flow together to the goodness of the LORD, for wheat, and for wine, and for oil, and for the young of the flock and of the herd: and their soul shall be as a watered garden; and they shall not sorrow any more at all. 13 **Then shall the virgin rejoice in the dance, both young men and old together**: for I will turn their mourning into joy, and will comfort them, and make them rejoice from their sorrow. 14 And I will satiate the soul of the priests with fatness, and my people shall be satisfied with my goodness, saith the LORD.

[20] Joel 2:15 Blow the trumpet in Zion, sanctify a **fast**, call a **solemn assembly**: 16 **Gather the people, sanctify the congregation, assemble the elders, gather the children, and those that suck the breasts**: let the bridegroom go forth of his chamber, and the bride out of her closet. 17 Let the priests, the ministers of the LORD, weep between the porch and the altar, and let them say, Spare thy people, O LORD, and give not thine heritage to reproach, that the heathen should rule over them: wherefore should they say among the people, Where *is* their God?

[21] Matt. 18:1 At the same time came the disciples unto Jesus, saying, Who is the greatest in the kingdom of heaven? 2 And Jesus **called a little child unto him**, and **set him in the midst of them**, 3 And said, Verily I say unto you, Except ye be converted, and become as little children, ye shall not enter into the kingdom of heaven. 4 Whosoever therefore shall humble himself as this little child, the same is greatest in the kingdom of heaven. 5 And **whoso shall receive one such little child in my name receiveth me**. 6 But **whoso shall offend one of these little ones** which believe in me, it were **better for him that a millstone were hanged about his neck, and** *that* **he were drowned in the depth of the sea**.... 10 **Take heed that ye despise not one of these little ones**; for I say unto you, That in heaven their angels do always behold the face of my Father which is in heaven. 11 For the Son of man is come to save that which was lost.

[22] Mark 9:36 And he took a child, and set him in the midst of them: and when **he had taken him in his arms**, he said unto them,

[23] Luke 9:48 And said unto them, Whosoever shall receive this child in my name receiveth me: and whosoever shall receive me receiveth him that sent me: for **he that is least among you all, the same shall be great**.

[24] Mark 10:13 And **they brought young children to him, that he should touch them: and** *his* **disciples rebuked those that brought** *them*. 14 But when **Jesus saw** *it*, **he was much displeased**, and said unto them, **Suffer the little children to come unto me, and forbid them not: for of such is the kingdom of God**. 15 Verily I say unto you, Whosoever shall not receive the

Another example is the time Jesus fed the five thousand **men, plus women and children**, with a **little boy's** lunch. The little boy had to be present in the meeting to be able to share his lunch. This story is told in all four Gospels.[25] People today may wonder if it is possible to have all the children attend the main church service in a large church meeting. But in this crowd, there were over five thousand people gathered. Jesus had ministered to them for hours and without our modern sound systems. I believe the difference in then and now has to do with how the children were trained.

Paul was holding a meeting just before he was to leave on the next day. He preached until midnight, and a **young** man in the meeting fell asleep. He fell from the third loft. After Paul went to him, and the young man was alive, Paul continued talking till break of day.[26] Another time when Paul was leaving, the people (including wives and children) followed him out of the city and prayed with him before he left.[27]

The prophetic book of Revelation tells of a voice that came out of the throne room. The voice says for all God's servants, both small and great, to praise Him.[28]

In the book of Hebrews, we are told not to forsake the **assembling** of ourselves **together**.[29] I noticed that it does not just say assemble, but it says assemble together. In other words, we are to "gather **together**" (not gather separately). The family unit has been weakened because of so much separation of its members. Sad to say, many churches have contributed to the breakdown of the family rather than strengthening its unity.

---

kingdom of God as a little child, he shall not enter therein. 16 And **he took them up in his arms, put** *his* **hands upon them**, and **blessed them**.
(See also Matt. 19:13-15 and Luke 18:15-17.)

[25] John 6:5 When Jesus then lifted up *his* eyes, and saw a great company come unto him, he saith unto Philip, Whence shall we buy bread, that these may eat? 6 And this he said to prove him: for he himself knew what he would do. Philip answered him, Two hundred pennyworth of bread is not sufficient for them, that every one of them may take a little. 8 One of his disciples, Andrew, Simon Peter's brother, saith unto him, 9 **There is a lad here, which hath five barley loaves, and two small fishes**: but what are they among so many? 10 And Jesus said, Make the men sit down. Now there was much grass in the place. So the men sat down, in number about five thousand. 11 And Jesus took the loaves; and when he had given thanks, he distributed to the disciples, and the disciples to them that were set down; and likewise of the fishes as much as they would.
Matt. 14:21 And they that had eaten were about five thousand men, **beside women and children**.
(See also Matt. 14:15-21; Mark 6:34-44; Luke 9:10-17; and John 6:1-13.)

[26] Acts 20:7 And upon the first *day* of the week, when the disciples came together to break bread, Paul preached unto them, ready to depart on the morrow; and continued his speech until midnight. 8 And there were many lights in the upper chamber, where **they were gathered together**. 9 And there sat in a window a certain **young man** named Eutychus, being fallen into a deep sleep: and as Paul was long preaching, he sunk down with sleep, and fell down from the third loft, and was taken up dead. 10 And Paul went down, and fell on him, and embracing *him* said, Trouble not yourselves; for his life is in him. 11 When he therefore was come up again, and had broken bread, and eaten, and talked a long while, even till break of day, so he departed. 12 And they brought the young man alive, and were not a little comforted.

[27] Acts 21:5 And when we had accomplished those days, we departed and went our way; and **they all** brought us on our way, **with wives and children**, till *we were* out of the city: and we kneeled down on the shore, and prayed.

[28] Rev. 19:5 And a voice came out of the throne, saying, Praise our God, all ye his servants, and ye that fear him, **both small and great**.

[29] Heb. 10:25 Not forsaking the **assembling** of ourselves **together**, as the manner of some *is*; but exhorting *one another*: and so much the more, as ye see the day approaching.

Jesus said that a house divided cannot stand.[30] Churches should not separate the body of Christ based on race, economic status, cultural background, denomination, sex, age, or other such differences. The Bible says there is no difference between Jew and Greek, bond or free, male or female in their relationship with Christ.[31] This also applies to age; God's kingdom is for all ages and all generations.[32]

---

[30] Mark 3:25 And if a house be divided against itself, that house cannot stand.

[31] Rom. 10:12 For there is **no difference** between the Jew and the Greek: for the same Lord over all is rich unto all that call upon him.
    Gal. 3:28 There is neither Jew nor Greek, there is neither bond nor free, there is neither male nor female: for **ye are all one in Christ Jesus**. 29 And if ye *be* Christ's, then are ye Abraham's seed, and heirs according to the promise.

[32] Psalm 145:13 Thy kingdom *is* an everlasting kingdom {a kingdom of all ages}, and thy dominion *endureth* throughout all generations.
    Psalm 100:5 For the LORD *is* good; his mercy *is* everlasting; and his truth *endureth* to all generations.

Chapter 24

Family and Church Ministry

God began families in the Garden of Eden. His church is made up of members of families. As the body of Christ on the earth, we are to do what Jesus, who is the Head of the church, directs us to do. Building the kingdom of God is the end goal for us individually, as a family, and as a church. We have different spheres of opportunity for ministry. There are some situations in which an individual or a family has opportunity to minister. Other situations may require the involvement of the church body to meet certain needs. We help each other in fulfilling God's plan.

Many churches today are organized like a business with separate departments of ministry. However, the different needs people have are often related. I believe it is better to get to know the whole family and deal with the root of the problems rather than only minister to separate symptoms. Some church leaders do not think in terms of family, but God does. He has set up His kingdom as a family with Him as Father and us as His children. I believe the advice of Moses' father-in-law, Jethro, would be good for churches today. He advised Moses to provide able men to be heads over the people: over thousands, over hundreds, over fifties, and over tens.[1] Keeping up with all the people in a large church is too heavy a burden for one pastor to carry alone. Providing leaders over smaller groups of people would help to meet their needs and prevent many from falling away.

God has ordained certain areas of authority and responsibility to the family and certain areas to the church. The family has not been given authority to run the church, and the church has not been given authority to run the family. God designed the husband to be the head of the wife and parents to be in authority over the children. Jesus is the Head of the church, and He sets members in His Church as it pleases Him. Families and churches should not compete with one another, but should cooperate with what God is doing. The church should support the family, and the family should support the church. Each is ordained by God. Strong families make strong churches, and strong churches should strengthen families.

Families in Ministry

The home is a good training ground for the future. Adults who have a call to minister to others should begin in their own home. Children should also be trained for their future family and ministry. The Lord told Jeremiah that He had set him apart to be a prophet even before he was born.[2] What an awesome responsibility for parents to provide an environment and preparation for their children to fulfill God's call upon their lives.

---

[1] Exod. 18:21 Moreover thou shalt provide out of all the people able men, such as fear God, men of truth, hating covetousness; and place *such* over them, *to be* rulers of thousands, *and* rulers of hundreds, rulers of fifties, and rulers of tens:
(See verses 13-26 for more details.)

[2] Jer. 1:4 Then the word of the LORD came unto me, saying, 5 Before I formed thee in the belly I knew thee; and before thou camest forth out of the womb I sanctified thee, *and* I ordained thee a prophet unto the nations.

If God can trust you to be faithful over your own household, He can promote you to larger areas of responsibility.[3] Jesus told two similar parables about a man who left his goods with his servants. When he returned, he checked with them to see how they had handled his goods. Those who were faithful were rewarded with more.[4] God chose Abraham to be the father of many nations because God knew that he would command his children and his household to keep the way of the Lord.[5]

The list of qualifications for bishops (elders) and deacons includes being able to rule their own houses well and having faithful children.[6] A bishop is an overseer or superintendent who looks after, cares for and provides for those in his charge. If he does not know how to follow God in ruling and caring for his own household, how can he be trusted to follow God in ruling and caring for the church? A deacon is a minister or servant who carries out the orders of those in authority over him. By this definition, we all could be deacons, but do we meet the Biblical qualifications? Having rebellious children can disqualify a person for positions of church leadership. It is important that church leaders have proved faithful in taking care of their own households.

We must recognize what season of life we are in. Some may be in a season of preparation and are not yet ready to take on leadership responsibilities in a church body. Some may be involved in establishing their marriages. Some may be in the midst of a consuming task, as that of bringing up children. Others may have

---

[3] Matt. 24:45 Who then is a **faithful** and wise servant, whom his lord hath made **ruler over his household**, to give them meat in due season? 46 Blessed *is* that servant, whom his lord when he cometh shall find so doing. 47 Verily I say unto you, That **he shall make him ruler over all his goods**.

[4] Matt. 25:21 His lord said unto him, Well done, *thou* good and faithful servant: thou hast been faithful over a few things, I will make thee ruler over many things: enter thou into the joy of thy lord.
Luke 19:17 And he said unto him, Well, thou good servant: because thou hast been faithful in a very little, have thou authority over ten cities.

[5] Gen. 18:17 And the LORD said, Shall I hide from **Abraham** that thing which I do; 18 Seeing that **Abraham shall surely become a great and mighty nation**, and all the nations of the earth shall be blessed in him? 19 **For I know him, that he will command his children and his household after him**, and they shall keep the way of the LORD, to do justice and judgment; **that the LORD may bring upon Abraham that which he hath spoken of him**.

[6] 1 Tim. 3:1 This *is* a true saying, If a man desire the office of a bishop, he desireth a good work. 2 A **bishop** then must be blameless, the husband of one wife, vigilant, sober, of good behaviour, given to hospitality, apt to teach; 3 Not given to wine, no striker, not greedy of filthy lucre; but patient, not a brawler, not covetous; 4 **One that ruleth well his own house, having his children in subjection with all gravity;** 5 **(For if a man know not how to rule his own house, how shall he take care of the church of God?)** 6 **Not a novice**, lest being lifted up with pride he fall into the condemnation of the devil. 7 Moreover he must have a good report of them which are without; lest he fall into reproach and the snare of the devil. 8 Likewise *must* the **deacons** *be* grave, not doubletongued, not given to much wine, not greedy of filthy lucre; 9 Holding the mystery of the faith in a pure conscience. 10 And **let these also first be proved**; then let them use the office of a deacon, being *found* blameless. 11 Even so *must their* wives *be* grave, not slanderers, sober, faithful in all things. 12 Let the deacons be the husbands of one wife, **ruling their children and their own houses well**. 13 For they that have used the office of a deacon well purchase to themselves a good degree, and great boldness in the faith which is in Christ Jesus. 14 These things write I unto thee, hoping to come unto thee shortly: 15 But if I tarry long, that thou mayest **know how thou oughtest to behave thyself in the house of God**, which is the church of the living God, the pillar and ground of the truth.
Titus 1:4 To Titus, *mine* own son after the common faith: Grace, mercy, *and* peace, from God the Father and the Lord Jesus Christ our Saviour. 5 For this cause left I thee in Crete, that thou shouldest set in order the things that are wanting, and ordain **elders** in every city, as I had appointed thee: 6 If any be blameless, the husband of one wife, **having faithful children not accused of riot or unruly**. 7 For a **bishop** must be blameless, as the steward of God; not selfwilled, not soon angry, not given to wine, no striker, not given to filthy lucre; 8 But a **lover of hospitality**, a lover of good men, sober, just, holy, temperate; 9 Holding fast the faithful word as he hath been taught, that he may be able by sound doctrine both to exhort and to convince the gainsayers.

already proved that they are responsible enough to manage their own households well and are ready to handle leadership responsibilities in the church. Family members must make sure that their involvement in ministry does not overburden or cause division in the family. It is easy to justify neglecting our family if it is for "ministry." My husband and I have both been guilty of this at times. Whenever we volunteer for ministry, we are also volunteering our family because it will also increase their load. Any time we become so involved in a ministry that we neglect our families, we should take time out to set the family back in order.

Church leaders should know their congregation well enough to know which season of life they are in so that they do not overburden families with church work. The church should also recognize ministries that are carried out in homes as being part of God's work. Parents should be given time to care for and train their children. Later, not only will the parents be available to help in church work, but so will their children.

Jesus said that His yoke is easy and His burden is light.[7] When we get overburdened, it could be because we are doing something Jesus has not asked us to do or that we are not doing things His way. We may be trying to do them in our own strength.

There are many ways for families to minister from their homes as an extension of the church. Ministry is not all confined within the walls of the church nor is it always orchestrated by church leadership. Jesus expects us to minister in our daily lives as the Holy Spirit leads us. One way families can minister is by helping the poor and needy.[8] This includes people outside the church and also those within it so there will be none that lack.[9]

Another way for families to minister is through hospitality. (Being hospitable is also in the list of qualifications for elders.) There are many ways to show hospitality. You could invite someone to visit in your home or meet you at some other place for a planned activity. You might offer refreshment or a meal. Reaching out to someone who lives alone is a way to show hospitality. You can include them in some of

---

[7] Matt. 11:28 Come unto me, all *ye* that labour and are heavy laden, and I will give you rest. 29 Take my yoke upon you, and learn of me; for I am meek and lowly in heart: and ye shall find rest unto your souls. 30 For **my yoke *is* easy, and my burden is light.**

[8] Deut. 15:7 If there be among you a poor man of one of thy brethren within any of thy gates in thy land which the LORD thy God giveth thee, thou shalt not harden thine heart, nor shut thine hand from thy poor brother: 8 But thou shalt open thine hand wide unto him, and shalt surely lend him sufficient for his need, *in that* which he wanteth.... 10 Thou shalt surely give him, and thine heart shall not be grieved when thou givest unto him: because that for this thing the LORD thy God shall bless thee in all thy works, and in all that thou puttest thine hand unto. 11 For the poor shall never cease out of the land: therefore I command thee, saying, Thou shalt **open thine hand wide unto thy brother**, to thy **poor**, and to thy **needy**, in thy land.
Job 29:15 I was eyes to the blind, and feet *was* I to the lame. 16 I *was* a **father to the poor**: and the cause *which* I knew not I searched out.
Mark 14:7 For ye have the poor with you always, and whensoever ye will ye may do them good: but me ye have not always.
Gal. 2:10 Only *they would* that we should remember the poor; the same which I also was forward to do.

[9] Acts 4:32 And the multitude of them that believed were of one heart and of one soul: neither said any *of them* that ought of the things which he possessed was his own; but **they had all things common**. 33 And with great power gave the apostles witness of the resurrection of the Lord Jesus: and great grace was upon them all. 34 **Neither was there any among them that lacked**: for as many as were possessors of lands or houses sold them, and brought the prices of the things that were sold, 35 And laid *them* down at the apostles' feet: and **distribution was made unto every man according as he had need**.
2 Cor. 8:12 For if there be first a willing mind, *it is* accepted according to that a man hath, *and* not according to that he hath not. 13 **For *I mean* not that other men be eased, and ye burdened**: 14 But by an equality, *that* now at this time your abundance *may be a supply* for their want, that their abundance also may be *a supply* for your want: that there may be equality: 15 As it is written, He that *had gathered* much had nothing over; and he that *had gathered* little had no lack.

your family activities. Of course, those who live alone are not the only ones who could benefit from your hospitality. I fondly remember an older couple in our neighborhood that befriended me when I was a child. I grew up in a large family, so I certainly was not alone. However, this couple gave me attention that I would not have received otherwise. They often invited me to their home. They let me help gather the eggs and go with them to milk the cows. They took me to the store and bought me Popsicles and peanut butter log candy. They bought me dresses for Easter and always gave me gifts at Christmas. They made me feel like a princess.

The Bible gives numerous examples of hospitality. There was a woman who fed the prophet Elisha every time he passed by. She and her husband eventually made an addition to their house and furnished it for him to use when he passed by.[10] Job lodged travelers.[11] Simon Peter had people at his house after their meeting in the synagogue. His mother-in-law ministered to the guests after Jesus healed her.[12] Levi held large feasts at his house and invited Jesus. He provided a way for others to be in company with Jesus.[13] Jesus and his disciples depended on others' hospitality when they were traveling.[14]

The early church met in different houses.[15] Simon the tanner not only let Peter stay with him; but when three strangers came to visit Peter, he also let them stay overnight.[16] Homes were used for prayer meetings, such as the time that the church was praying for Peter when he was in jail.[17] Lydia offered her

---

[10] 2 Kings 4:8 And it fell on a day, that Elisha passed to Shunem, where *was* a great woman; and she constrained him to eat bread. And *so* it was, *that* as oft as he passed by, he turned in thither to eat bread. 9 And she said unto her husband, Behold now, I perceive that this *is* an holy man of God, which passeth by us continually. 10 Let us make a little chamber, I pray thee, on the wall; and let us set for him there a bed, and a table, and a stool, and a candlestick: and it shall be, when he cometh to us, that he shall turn in thither.

[11] Job 31:32 The stranger did not lodge in the street: *but* I opened my doors to the traveller.

[12] Luke 4:38 And he arose out of the synagogue, and entered into Simon's house. And Simon's wife's mother was taken with a great fever; and they besought him for her. 39 And he stood over her, and rebuked the fever; and it left her: and immediately **she arose and ministered unto them.**

[13] Luke 5:29 And Levi made him a great feast in his own house: and there was a great company of publicans and of others that sat down with them.

[14] Luke 10:5 And into whatsoever house ye enter, first say, Peace *be* to this house. 6 And if the son of peace be there, your peace shall rest upon it: if not, it shall turn to you again. 7 And in the same house remain, eating and drinking such things as they give: for the labourer is worthy of his hire. Go not from house to house. 8 And into whatsoever city ye enter, and they receive you, eat such things as are set before you: 9 And heal the sick that are therein, and say unto them, The kingdom of God is come nigh unto you.

[15] Acts 2:44 And all that believed were together, and had all things common; 45 And sold their possessions and goods, and parted them to all *men*, as every man had need. 46 And they, continuing daily with one accord in the temple, and **breaking bread from house to house**, did eat their meat with gladness and singleness of heart, 47 Praising God, and having favour with all the people. And the Lord added to the church daily such as should be saved.

[16] Acts 9:43 And it came to pass, that he tarried many days in Joppa with one Simon a tanner.
Acts 10:19 While Peter thought on the vision, the Spirit said unto him, Behold, three men seek thee.... 23 Then called he them in, and lodged *them*. And on the morrow Peter went away with them, and certain brethren from Joppa accompanied him.

[17] Acts 12:11 And when Peter was come to himself, he said, Now I know of a surety, that the Lord hath sent his angel, and hath delivered me out of the hand of Herod, and *from* all the expectation of the people of the Jews. 12 And when he had considered *the thing*, he came to the house of Mary the mother of John, whose surname was Mark; **where many were gathered together praying.**

home for Paul and Silas.[18] Paul stayed with Aquila and Priscilla for a while and worked with them making tents. Not only were they hospitable to Paul, but a church also met in their house.[19] Philemon had a church in his house, too, and provided lodging for Paul.[20] When Paul and those with him were shipwrecked, the people on the island gave them three days lodging and provisions when it was time for them to leave.[21] Paul taught the Word of God from his lodging from morning to evening.[22]

We can learn from these examples to open our homes to missionaries or others whom the Lord may send our way. It is important that we be given to hospitality and that we do it without reluctance.[23] We might even have the opportunity to entertain angels.[24] Jesus said that what we do for others, we are doing for Him.[25] As the world becomes darker, Christian families will shine brighter because of God's glory upon us. His light shining through us will draw others.[26] We must be prepared to minister to those who come to us.

---

[18] Acts 16:14 And a certain woman named Lydia, a seller of purple, of the city of Thyatira, which worshipped God, heard *us*: whose heart the Lord opened, that she attended unto the things which were spoken of Paul. 15 And when she was baptized, and her household, she besought *us*, saying, If ye have judged me to be faithful to the Lord, **come into my house, and abide** *there*. And she constrained us.... 40 And they went out of the prison, and entered into *the house of* Lydia: and when they had seen the brethren, they comforted them, and departed.

[19] Acts 18:1 After these things Paul departed from Athens, and came to Corinth; 2 And found a certain Jew named Aquila, born in Pontus, lately come from Italy, with his wife Priscilla; (because that Claudius had commanded all Jews to depart from Rome:) and came unto them. 3 And because he was of the same craft, **he abode with them**, and wrought: for by their occupation they were tentmakers.
1 Cor. 16:19 The churches of Asia salute you. Aquila and Priscilla salute you much in the Lord, with the **church that is in their house**.

[20] Philemon 2 And to *our* beloved Apphia, and Archippus our fellowsoldier, and to the **church in thy house**:... 22 But withal **prepare me also a lodging**: for I trust that through your prayers I shall be given unto you.

[21] Acts 28:7 In the same quarters were possessions of the chief man of the island, whose name was Publius; **who received us, and lodged us three days courteously**. 8 And it came to pass, that the father of Publius lay sick of a fever and of a bloody flux: to whom Paul entered in, and prayed, and laid his hands on him, and healed him. 9 So when this was done, others also, which had diseases in the island, came, and were healed: 10 Who also honoured us with many honours; and **when we departed, they laded** *us* **with such things as were necessary**.

[22] Acts 28:23 And when they had appointed him a day, **there came many to him into** *his* **lodging**; to whom **he expounded and testified the kingdom of God**, persuading them concerning Jesus, both out of the law of Moses, and *out of* the prophets, **from morning till evening**.

[23] Rom. 12:13 Distributing to the necessity of saints; **given to hospitality**.
1 Peter 4:9 Use **hospitality** one to another without grudging.

[24] Heb. 13:1 Let brotherly love continue. 2 **Be not forgetful to entertain strangers: for thereby some have entertained angels unawares**.

[25] Matt. 25:40 And the King shall answer and say unto them, Verily I say unto you, Inasmuch as ye have done *it* unto one of the least of these my brethren, ye have done *it* unto me.

[26] Isa. 60:1 Arise, shine; for thy light is come, and the **glory of the LORD is risen upon thee**. 2 For, behold, the darkness shall cover the earth, and gross darkness the people: but the LORD shall arise upon thee, and **his glory shall be seen upon thee**. 3 And the **Gentiles shall come to thy light**, and kings to the brightness of thy rising. 4 Lift up thine eyes round about, and see: all they gather themselves together, they come to thee: **thy sons** shall come from far, and **thy daughters** shall be nursed at *thy* side. 5 Then thou shalt see, and **flow together**, and thine heart shall fear, and be enlarged; because the abundance of the sea shall be converted unto thee, the forces of the Gentiles shall come unto thee.

In addition to ministering to others in homes, families can also find ministry opportunities in their local church. Specific ways depend somewhat on the vision of the church. Consult with church leadership to find out what is needed and seek the Lord for what He would have you do. There should be ministry opportunities in church that a family can do together instead of only those that require separation. Children like to minister to others. Ministering with their family provides the opportunity and the "watchful eye" that they should have. Children can help "usher" by handing out bulletins, offering envelopes, and visitor packets. If you have special "greeters" at church, why not have a **family** of greeters. Nothing puts a smile on someone's face like a little child, and people enjoy seeing family members working together.

The Bible gives some examples of family members working in ministry together. Moses and his brother Aaron ministered together; Aaron was Moses' spokesman.[27] Nehemiah put his brother in charge over Jerusalem because he knew he was faithful.[28] King David reigned over Israel and his sons were chief rulers.[29] Heman led his children in song and the playing of musical instruments in the house of the Lord.[30] (I especially like this example because my husband and our children sing together.) When Andrew found out about Jesus, he went **first** to tell his own brother.[31] Both became disciples of Jesus.

Whether at home or in church, God will give our families opportunities to minister. Let us be like the house of Stephanas: addicted to the ministry of the saints.[32] Let us always abound in the work of the Lord, for our labor is not in vain in the Lord.[33]

---

[27] Exod. 4:10 And Moses said unto the LORD, O my Lord, I *am* not eloquent, neither heretofore, nor since thou hast spoken unto thy servant: but I *am* slow of speech, and of a slow tongue.... 14 And the anger of the LORD was kindled against Moses, and he said, *Is* not Aaron the Levite thy brother? I know that he can speak well. And also, behold, he cometh forth to meet thee: and when he seeth thee, he will be glad in his heart. 15 And thou shalt speak unto him, and put words in his mouth: and I will be with thy mouth, and with his mouth, and will teach you what ye shall do. 16 And he shall be thy spokesman unto the people: and he shall be, *even* he shall be to thee instead of a mouth, and thou shalt be to him instead of God. 17 And thou shalt take this rod in thine hand, wherewith thou shalt do signs.

[28] Neh. 7:1 Now it came to pass, when the wall was built, and I had set up the doors, and the porters and the singers and the Levites were appointed, 2 That I gave my brother Hanani, and Hananiah the ruler of the palace, charge over Jerusalem: for he *was* a faithful man, and feared God above many.

[29] 2 Sam. 8:18 And Benaiah the son of Jehoiada *was over* both the Cherethites and the Pelethites; and David's sons were chief rulers.

[30] 1 Chron. 25:5 All these *were* the sons of Heman the king's seer in the words of God, to lift up the horn. And God gave to Heman **fourteen sons and three daughters. 6 All these** *were* **under the hands of their father for song** *in* **the house of the LORD**, with cymbals, psalteries, and harps, for the service of the house of God, according to the king's order to Asaph, Jeduthun, and Heman.

[31] John 1:40 One of the two which heard John *speak*, and followed him, was **Andrew, Simon Peter's brother.** 41 He **first findeth his own brother Simon,** and saith unto him, We have found the Messias, which is, being interpreted, the Christ. 42 And he brought him to Jesus. And when Jesus beheld him, he said, Thou art Simon the son of Jona: thou shalt be called Cephas, which is by interpretation, A stone.

[32] 1 Cor. 16:15 I beseech you, brethren, (ye know the house of Stephanas, that it is the firstfruits of Achaia, and *that* **they have addicted themselves to the ministry of the saints,**)

[33] 1 Cor. 15:58 Therefore, my beloved brethren, be ye stedfast, unmoveable, **always abounding in the work of the Lord,** forasmuch as ye know that your labour is not in vain in the Lord.

Ministry to Families

One of the basic principles of ministering to families is recognizing parental authority. Parents must recognize their responsibility for their own children. Church leaders must acknowledge parental authority.

God has given parents the responsibility and anointing for training their children. Christian parents should be working together at home to bring their family in order with the Word of God and not expect the church to fix all of their problems for them. If all Christian parents took the responsibility for their own children to make sure they were born again and nurtured in God's Word, think how much less work the church leadership would have to be doing in terms of evangelism and training! Then we could all put more focus on winning the world for Jesus and discipling those newly born again.

In addition to home training, church life is also an important part of child training. It is very difficult for parents to train their children in church if they are not even in the same room or building with them. When families are together in church, children can see the example their parents set as they worship God. Also parents can later answer any questions their children may have about the meeting or use the message that was preached to springboard into more teaching.

For some parents who work jobs outside their homes, Sundays may be the only full day of the week that they have free to spend with their children. Rather than turn them over for someone else to teach, this is a good opportunity to spend the time together. It contributes to family bonding. If any of you have been convicted about spending more time with your children, this is a good place to start. As parents, we have an awesome responsibility to prepare our children for the part God has for them in the mighty revival that will precede Jesus' coming back for His Church.

Churches should not usurp parents' authority, but rather support them in training their children. It is easier for parents to shirk their responsibility if someone else is willing to do their job for them. Instead of **standing in** for parents, churches should **stand with** parents. This allows the parents to fulfill their own responsibilities, yet have help and support as needed. Churches should do as Jesus did: when He ministered to children, He always did so under the authority of their parents, not separately. Bible examples include the times Jesus ministered to Jairus' daughter, the nobleman's son, the father with the lunatic son, and the Syrophenician woman's daughter. (We mentioned these in Chapter 15.)

There are many instances in which children come to church meetings without their parents. Some of these situations are the result of evangelism targeted at children and bus ministries in which children are picked up and brought to church without their parents. These methods do reach children with the Gospel. However, would it not be better to go through the chain of authority and work through parents instead of bypassing them? What if the Gospel were presented to the parents, as well as the children? Since children are under the authority of their parents, it is likely that the parents who become born again will share the Gospel with all their children. But if a child is saved first, there may be conflict with his unsaved parents. When that happens, the church should stand with the child in prayer and do all they can to reach the parents with the Gospel. In the meantime, the church should nurture the child in the Lord without usurping his parents' authority. I believe the very best ministry we can do for children is to get their parents saved and taught in God's Word (including how to be good parents). Then the parents will be in position to get their children saved and to provide an environment in the home for spiritual growth.

I personally do not think that pooling all the lone children together is the best way to minister to them. It is too easy for a child to miss the attention he needs. I believe these children should have personal attention, more of a one-on-one ministry. The whole point of bringing in children who have unsaved parents is to give them the love of Jesus that they are lacking in their home.

Scriptures were given in Chapter 9 that promise God's care for widows and the fatherless. He often works through His people to reach out and minister to them. One way He does this is by setting the solitary in families.[34] When children come to church meetings without their parents, or parents need help with their children, these are opportunities for stable families to "adopt" extra members during the church service. Or those needing help can "adopt" grandparents, young adults, or others to help them. A strong family can nurture a family who is just beginning in the things of God. They can sit together in meetings and reach out to them through the week. With one-on-one ministry, the family can have mature role models. They can get to know those helping them, and they do not have to turn their children over to strangers.

Teaching children separately in church meetings may solve some immediate problems, but what are the long-term results? Separate children's ministries are, at best, a temporary church. When children get too old for the nursery, they are "promoted" to the toddlers' class, then to the preschoolers' class, and then to children's church. After that, they move to the junior high class and then to youth group. They are allowed to stay in youth group only up to a certain age. Then where do they go? They are expected to attend all the "adult" church meetings. However, for eighteen or more years, they have been separated and have not built up relationships with the adults. Therefore, they do not feel like they fit in. Many drop out of church for a season or forever. Some come back after they have started families of their own, and the cycle repeats. Even some of those who do come back have had their lives devastated in the meantime.

I am not against ministry to children. I think most parents appreciate help in bringing up their children. However, I do not believe children's ministry should take the place of the main worship services of the church. I believe that any ministry to children should include their parents. Those who minister to children should meet with parents and find out how to help and support them. They should never usurp the parents' authority nor try to shut them out. Parents should always be welcome and encouraged to attend any meeting for their children. The goal of ministry to children and youth should **not** be to build a children's or youth ministry program, but to support and help parents in bringing their children up in the nurture and admonition of the Lord.

When parents keep their children with them in church meetings, it sets an example for other families. They get to see parents interacting with their children. Good role models will encourage other families to follow their example. People of different ages benefit one another when they are all living for Jesus. The elder ones guide and provide; the younger ones serve and support. The children grow in wisdom and grace and favor with God and man. Training in church can continue as the child grows so he will be ready to take on adult roles when the time is right.

There are two particular areas of ministry that need reviving in many churches today. One is in the area of "fathering," as Paul did with Timothy. He reached out to Timothy to nurture him in the Lord and to help prepare him for his call.[35] The other area is that of elder women teaching younger women. Such teaching would include how to love their families and be good ministers in their own homes.[36]

---

[34] Psalm 68:5 A father of the **fatherless**, and a judge of the **widows**, *is* God in his holy habitation. 6 **God setteth the solitary in families**: he bringeth out those which are bound with chains: but the rebellious dwell in a dry *land*.

[35] 1 Tim. 1:1 Paul, an apostle of Jesus Christ by the commandment of God our Saviour, and Lord Jesus Christ, *which is* our hope; 2 Unto Timothy, *my* **own son in the faith**: Grace, mercy, *and* peace, from God our Father and Jesus Christ our Lord.
Phil. 2:22 But ye know the proof of him, that, **as a son with the father**, he hath served with me in the gospel.

Some churches already encourage and support parents in taking responsibility for their children in the meetings. In others, there is a definite segregation of age groups. There are ways to adjust facilities and meetings to accommodate families **with** children. Churches must start where they are now and go forward. I will make some suggestions, but my advice may be limited to what God has shown me for a few situations. It is better to seek the Lord and follow His direction for your situation.

Facilities can be adapted to make it easier for families with children. A private place should be provided for nursing mothers. Another place should be provided to which either a woman or a man can take young children if they must leave the main service. Both these places should be equipped so that the minister's message can still be heard. Some churches are even equipped to provide video so the service can be heard and seen from another room. I have used a nursery monitor when we had meetings in our home, so that if a mother took her child to another room, she could still listen to the teaching that was given. I visited a large church a few years ago that had a loudspeaker outside of the meeting room. When I took my little ones to the bathroom, we could still hear the message being preached. It was such a blessing!

I have come to the conclusion that babies will be babies, and children will be children no matter where they are. They do require attention. Separating children from adults does not stop distractions; it simply pools all the distractions together out of the view and hearing of those in the main church service. When children are with their parents, they can be given the individual attention they need. However, parents should not allow their children to be too disruptive. If a child is making too much noise or moving around excessively, they should be taken out of the service. Churches should be willing to tolerate minor distractions caused by children or the adults who are training them. Parents should be considerate enough of the congregation to sit near an exit if they have a child who tends to be disruptive.

Adult meetings can be adjusted to accommodate children. If the current situation in your church is that the children are separated from their parents before the service begins, you could start changes by having them together for the singing part of the service. Include songs that are familiar to the children or ones that are easy for them to learn so they can enter in. We noticed that before our youngest child could read, she was not singing with us in church. When we asked her why, she said she was just listening to the words so she could learn them.

Another step toward bringing children back into church services with adults could be to have a "family" service once a month. Bring the children into the adult service, but not the paraphernalia from the children's ministry. God's Word and His presence in the meetings will keep the interest of both the young and the old better than any physical props could.

We should realize that children can receive from God. I believe that even a child in the womb can receive the Word of God in their spirits. This holds true after they are born: even if they are too young to understand with their minds, their spirits can receive what is being ministered by the Spirit of God. Young children hear what is being said even when we do not think they are listening. Their understanding is often purer because their minds are not as cluttered as adults' may be.

---

[36] Titus 2:3 The **aged women** likewise, that *they be* in behaviour as becometh holiness, not false accusers, not given to much wine, **teachers of good things;** 4 **That they may teach the young women** to be sober, to love their husbands, to love their children, 5 *To be* discreet, chaste, keepers at home, good, obedient to their own husbands, that the word of God be not blasphemed.

Whoever brings the message should remember that he is speaking to physical and spiritual children as well as to adults. He could include examples of children and situations that they deal with. This would be like a "cup of cold water" to the little ones. They would feel they were a part of what is going on in the service. The Gospel is simple and God's Word applies to all ages. When God's Word is preached, the Holy Spirit will apply it in the listener's life. Even while the speaker is giving examples to apply to a child's life, the Holy Spirit will show adults how it applies to their own lives. The Holy Spirit also knows the attention span of the congregation, so speakers should be sensitive to His timing.

I believe God is turning the hearts of Christian parents to their children and the children's to their parents in this generation. Many parents are already beginning to take back their responsibility for training their children. There are others who need more teaching, along with encouragement and support. As more families see examples of positive family interaction in their midst, I believe it will awaken their desire for family unity in church services.

Conclusion

Much has been brought forth to be considered by individuals, families, and churches. Some readers will be refreshed by this book because it confirms what has already been on their hearts. For others, this book may be difficult to accept because what has been presented is drastically different from that to which they have become accustomed. As for me, this study has pointed out many areas that must be corrected in my own personal life, in my family life, and in my church life. For all of us, the question now is: "Where do we go from here?"

We must seek the Lord for the answer to that question. In the past when we have sought for God's direction, we may have had our own ideas about what the answer would be. Our expectations may have been based on the circumstances we could see at that time or on our own presumptions and plans. It can be difficult to hear God's answer if we are limiting Him to our own choices. We may be asking God, "Should I go with Plan A or Plan B?" when His answer is Plan C, which is neither of the ones we mentioned.

We must be open to whatever direction God may give. If any parents are asking God which day care center to use for their children, they should be open to His telling them to care for their own children. If they are seeking Him about the education of their children, they should not limit Him to the choices of public school or private school. His answer may be for them to teach their own children at home. If a church leader is seeking God for direction for the children's ministry, he should be willing for God to tell him to refocus the goals of the children's ministry to concentrate on supporting parents in their role as the trainers of their own children. It may take a complete shift of thinking to get us on the right track with God.

Whatever God says to us, we should do. Let us not settle for less than His best! With His help, we can bring our relationships with Him, with our families, and with our churches up to a higher level. **Bring them up**; bring them all up to a higher level in God!

"Let us hear the conclusion of the whole matter: Fear God, and keep his commandments: for this is the whole *duty* of man. For God shall bring every work into judgment, with every secret thing, whether *it be* good, or whether *it be* evil." (Ecclesiastes 12:13-14)

"He that hath an ear, let him hear what the Spirit saith unto the churches."
(Revelation 2:29)